It's Not All in Your Head

Unearthing the Deep Roots of Depression

It's Not All in Your Head

Unearthing the Deep Roots of Depression

Tony Giordano

BOOKS

Winchester, UK
Washington, USA

First published by O-Books, 2010
O Books is an imprint of John Hunt Publishing Ltd., The Bothy, Deershot Lodge, Park Lane, Ropley,
Hants, SO24 0BE, UK
office1@o-books.net
www.o-books.com

For distributor details and how to order please visit the 'Ordering' section on our website.

Text copyright Tony Giordano 2009

ISBN: 978 1 84694 393 5

Design: Stuart Davies

Printed in the UK by CPI Antony Rowe
Printed in the USA by Offset Paperback Mfrs, Inc

We operate a distinctive and ethical publishing philosophy in all
areas of its business, from its global network of authors to
production and worldwide distribution.

CONTENTS

Tony Giordano writes with admirable clarity, has an important tale to tell, and makes persuasive arguments about the genesis of depression. I recognized parts of myself in Tony's story and I think this will be equally true for other readers. In the end, this will be a fundamental value of the book. It will provide a road map for others who are befuddled by their feelings of depression. The book does something distinctive – almost a new genre of writing – by shuttling between a personal story and analysis of the childhood-trauma roots of depression.
David A. Karp, Ph.D., Professor of Sociology at Boston College, author, and depression survivor.

It's Not All In Your Head is written by a depression sufferer who has personally experienced the propaganda of the pharmaceutical and insurance managed care industries as well as the impotence of simplistic cognitive behavioral therapies. I applaud Tony Giordano's insistence on the too often neglected significance of psychological trauma and his brave efforts to discover truths and heal.
Bruce E. Levine PhD, Clinical Psychologist and author of *Surviving America's Depression Epidemic.*

Dedicated to my children, Rob, Lauren and Steve,
who may now be able to understand why their father
has been a bit odd and moody at times.
Tony Giordano

Preface

Humankind has not woven the web of life. We are but one
thread within it.
Whatever we do to the web we do to ourselves.
All things are bound together — all things connect.
Chief Seattle

If you have ever suffered with depression, don't let anyone tell you that the condition is all in your head. And don't let them say it's your fault. And above all, don't let them say it's weakness of character. Let them try living a single day with the unbearable burden of this horrendous disorder.

The medical evidence is very slow to reach the general public, and even many caregivers, but the facts clearly show that depression is not in your head and it's not your fault. You have to be as strong or stronger than anyone else alive just to survive with this condition. Depression is as real and as destructive as any so-called *physical* disorder, with underlying physical and neuro-logical components. It is not simply *mental*. Its long roots go all the way back to childhood for many if not most sufferers. You could *not* have prevented it; but you can do something about it now. First, you need to understand what the hell happened to you.

If a family member or a friend of yours has ever suffered with depression, please cut through the stigma, the misinformation and the ignorance and make a genuine effort to understand what has happened. The forces that brought about the condition can be totally overpowering, particularly when they strike in childhood as they often do.

Figuring out what happened to me was a long, slow, and painful process. This is my story, the story of my search for the origin of a puzzling, stubborn and sometimes debilitating disorder. *It's Not All In Your Head* is a personal essay on the experience of depression, an all too common legacy of children of alcoholics and others with seriously dysfunctional histories. The book chronicles my journeys in and out of depression, what I have learned about the causes of disorders such as mine, and my experiences with the many treatments and techniques I tried on the bumpy road to recovery. In relating my experiences, the book attempts to identify universal truths about mood disorders that could be informative and supportive for other sufferers, their loved ones, or anyone interested in the ordeals a victim must endure in the fight to overcome these potentially life-threatening conditions.

A number of excellent books exist that describe the personal experiences of people who have struggled with depression, perhaps the most misunderstood disorder of our time, in spite of its exploding incidence. Most of these books are by or about the famous or near-famous—actors, authors, renowned doctors, activists, etc.—extraordinary people who, despite their difficulties, showed unusual energy, courage, and ability to endure and recover. Their stories are often heroic and inspiring.

My assumption is that many readers of this book will be people who have suffered with mood disorders such as depression and/or who are children of alcoholics or other substance abusers. The many people with loved ones who've fought these perplexing illnesses may also be interested in my story. I thought it might be of interest and comfort to describe the experience of someone perhaps more similar to the millions who battle these disorders; one of the many who might be without extraordinary talents or abilities or energy; who may not be highly successful professionally, but who just the same works hard to make a living or care for a family. This can be a formidable challenge for anyone suffering from an illness such as depression, which sucks the very life out of you.

My hope is that more people can identify with the experiences of a person closer to the 'average man on the street', who is not extraordinary or heroic. Many readers might therefore come away with a hope that healing does not require an extraordinary or heroic personality. Depression certainly does not often allow one the notion that you are heroic. On the contrary, depression typically brings feelings of weakness and futility. Nevertheless, everyone has the ability to recover. My hope is that readers who have suffered depression will see that by no means did they themselves do anything wrong that led to their problem. They are not weak or inferior, as some people mistakenly believe, or as they may often feel.

At one time I actually thought that *I* had unusual ability and potential to be highly successful. I was a top student all through school, graduated cum laude from a top college, and went on to graduate school at an Ivy League university. And I had a respectable if unremarkable 20 year career in consumer market research, rising to a management position that paid enough for my family to live fairly comfortably in a pleasant, upper-middle class community. This was before mental health issues interfered. Among other things, depression cost me two good jobs, put me on unemployment, ravaged my health, and almost destroyed my marriage.

But this book is more than a memoir of my journeys in and out of depression. It's a personal essay on my protracted search for the roots of a mysterious illness, and the lessons I learned along the way that aided my recovery. As my story unfolds, I relate my experiences to the observations and theories of leading experts in the fields of psychology, psychotherapy and medical science, whose books and articles have helped me enormously to understand the forces that drove my illness. As I learned about the devastating power of severe or repeated trauma occurring early in life, I began to put together the pieces of the puzzle of my illness. In my journeys through depression, I encountered many surprises, ordeals and setbacks. Only after several years of treatment was a complete, accurate diagnosis of my condition made, and this resulted more from my own knowledge than from any caregiver. It turned out there was more to my condition than depression, and my struggles exemplify the shamefully inadequate state of mental healthcare today. In many respects, mine is a universal story of victims of depression.

I believe the current explosion in the rate of depression is intimately linked to our culture and society, which is to say, our way of life. I also tie critical themes in the book not only to principles of psychotherapy, but to tidbits of wisdom found in philosophy, poetry, music, and literature, drawing in particular on humanistic philosophy. The surge of depression is linked to many of the broader challenges and conditions of our time. Depression is but one aspect, albeit an extreme one, of man's timeless fight to survive in a world he created but which is evolving to be incompatible with his basic nature and values. Ironically, as we 'progress' as a civilization, we find ourselves increasingly 'out of tune'. To fully understand depression, I think we have to place it in the broadest context—the struggle to be a whole, healthy being in an overwhelming technological, commercialized culture with an ever-accelerating and dehumanizing pace of life.

In my first episode of depression, I didn't want to talk about it, or read about it or even think about what might be wrong with me. It hurt too much. I was paralyzed by guilt and denial. But during my second episode, I developed a keen interest in learning more about the causes of depression and the conditions that often accompany it. I was inspired to write this book largely by two excellent books I read as I was struggling to understand what had hit me—*I Don't Want to Talk About It: Overcoming the Secret Legacy of Male Depression*, by Terrence Real, and *The Noonday Demon: An Atlas of Depression*, by Andrew Solomon. While I have come to disagree with some of Solomon's views, I applaud his resilience and his efforts to use his extraordinary writing skills to share deeply personal experiences that will inform and support so many. Terrence Real combines the expertise of a psychotherapist with the insight of a depression survivor to produce a most articulate and compelling book.

Two other books that helped me enormously to understand my illness were *Healing the Child Within: Discovery and Recovery for Adult Children of Dysfunctional Families*, and *The Truth about Depression: Choices for Healing*, both by Charles Whitfield, who is at the forefront of a revolution in thinking about depression and other mental disorders. While my wife Joanne warned that I was dwelling on too dismal a subject, I actually found it helpful and even therapeutic to read about depression and about children of alcoholics. I developed a compelling need to understand what had happened to me. This knowledge is vital for taking the necessary steps to identify the source and face our pain, resolve it, complete our grieving, and move on. According to best-selling author and renowned psychotherapist Alice Miller, the 'decisive factor' in therapy is 'recognition of the truth' about what happened to you. In this spirit, *It's Not All In Your Head* seeks to advance the ability to recognize the truth for the millions whose story is not unlike mine. I believe that 'deconstructing' the illness is key to defeating it. It was for me.

This book is intended to engage, inform, encourage and even inspire sufferers of mood and anxiety disorders or others who have been victimized by alcoholism or drug abuse in the family. I don't believe in patronizing victims or giving false hope. I've learned from painful personal experience that victims were virtually powerless to prevent their illness since the roots often reach back to early childhood. At the same time, they need to seize the many opportunities available to heal, and they invariably need a lift from others in this effort.

The other factor that led to my writing this book was simply that I had ample time on my hands. During this period of time I was unemployed and then employed part-time following my termination due to the symptoms of depression. You might think this is kicking a man when he's down, or even outright discrimination. Many of you may have experienced these kinds of injustices yourself. That's the way it seems to work, but you can do something about it.

1 The Legacy

Our behavior is a function of our experience. We act according
to the way we see things.
If our experience is destroyed, our behavior will be destructive.
If our experience is destroyed, we have lost our own selves.
R.D. Laing, *The Politics of Experience*

From the time I first read it as an undergraduate more than 30
years ago, I have remembered this passage from the contro-
versial book by psychiatrist and author R.D. Laing. It made an
immediate impact, but I wasn't sure why. I've had occasion to
think about it a number of times over the years. It's such a
succinct yet powerful statement of psychological damage and
'maladaptive behavior', as it's now known. Little did I know at
the time how well it would apply to me, although it appears I
had a suspicion it might. The words resonated in some
inexplicable way.

As I sat down to start writing this book and looked back at
how I arrived at this point in my life, the issue that most
commanded my attention was not depression, but how I've often
felt like an actor in a play. Thinking about this now, it seems so
strange. I've often felt like I was playing a part, only I didn't
exactly know the script or my precise role—what part I was
supposed to play. I was never sure about that. Everything has
seemed so unreal. Life didn't seem real, I didn't *feel real*. I asked
myself, was it actually happening? Is this real life? Or was it
some kind of school exercise or rehearsal or simulation? I
thought of games I had played as a child and asked, does this
count? Can I have another chance and do it differently? Why do
I feel separated from everything much of the time? Why am I
disconnected?

These were conversations routinely going on in my head as I

went about my business. I would actually debate different points of view about this to myself. I've done this kind of thing for so long that it was normal to me; I had no idea these were 'abnormal' thoughts that might be symptomatic of a potentially crippling disorder, or a complex of related disorders to be more precise. I surmise that I must have talked to myself many, many more times than I've talked to other people.

Even though there was a multitude of signs and clues throughout my early life, I never imagined that I would someday be personally afflicted by depression. This illness seemed totally foreign to me, irrelevant, something that maybe weak, delicate people have to worry about. Not someone like me. And certainly not a *man*! Of course, I knew virtually nothing about depression, nor about the warning signs. I did have an uncomfortable feeling that I was too often infected with unhealthy levels of apprehension and nervous distractions of various kinds. But I had no idea this was anything approaching abnormal, whatever that means. There's no way I could know as a youngster or adolescent what other people were feeling and what constitutes 'normal'.

When I was first told in middle age that I suffered from clinical depression, my analytical and investigative tendencies almost immediately had me searching for the roots of this strange, unexpected disorder. I say 'almost' immediately because my very first thought was the usual denial that it could happen to me. I thought about a lot of possible causes, but I had no idea what could have produced this cursed condition. It seemed to come out of nowhere. One thing did stand out, however, after some reflection, something that as an adult I could now see was clearly abnormal, dysfunctional and unhealthy. It was my father's drinking, which was often followed by uncontrollable rages that as a young boy I couldn't begin to understand or deal with. Is it possible that a father's habitual alcoholic rages could be related to a son's mood disorder in later life? Decades later?

I wondered, what could the connection be? How could the one

lead to the other?

It's widely known that alcoholic parents often have children who develop drinking problems or other addictions, which I could understand. But I wasn't aware of any connection with depression, nor could I begin to understand what connection there could be. When I thought about my unhealthy symptoms, I began to realize they've been with me most of my life—nervousness, uncertainty, continual mental distraction, a sense that everything was unreal, and of course, that dark cloud that I knew had to be just around the corner. Other than the latter symptom, how could these kinds of symptoms connect to depression? I thought that if I had been affected by my father's drinking, I would have become an alcoholic myself, and maybe would have even led a life of crime and drug addiction and all those other things you associate with alcoholism. But I was far from anything like that. No, I was a solid, sensible, strait-laced person who excelled as a student, enjoyed a respectable career, and had a wonderful home and family.

I think that one reason I wouldn't initially accept the possibility that my father's drinking could have caused some of my problems was because that would have let me off the hook. I mean, like many people in this situation, *I blamed myself* for my disorder. I couldn't so easily rid myself of the blame. Consideration of any causes outside of myself seemed like a rationalization, a cop-out. A dogged guilt turned out to be perhaps the most daunting challenge in my attempts to recover.

The number of people affected by alcoholism is mind-boggling. Some 30 million Americans grew up in families with an alcoholic. By no means are all children of alcoholics affected to the same degree—each situation is different—in the behavior of the alcoholic, the age and vulnerability of the child, how the family handles the problem—or *if* they handle it—and a host of other factors. Depending on how the various factors play out, for some people the effects can be ravaging. Literally millions of children of alcoholics suffer from depression, anxiety disorders, addictions, alcoholism, and other disorders.

The connection between family alcoholism and depression in their children is now indisputable. Recent studies are finding a substantially higher risk of depression in adult children of alcoholics (e.g. Anda et al, 2002). According to an increasing number of experts, the specific way in which children of alcoholics are adversely affected is by being exposed to severe or repeated *emotional trauma*. Being children of alcoholics, they are much more likely to be victims or witnesses of domestic violence or abuse. And the trauma need not be physical; fear alone, arising from unknown, threatening circumstances, can be extremely powerful and damaging. The resulting trauma impairs emotional development and is carried forth by the victim, actually encoded in the brain through conditioning, often leading to disorders such as depression years later. The effects of emotional trauma are especially severe for children, who are vulnerable and defenseless. They are still developing physiologically and have yet to form the personality and character that will enable them to cope with the world. Quite literally, a part of that child may be destroyed by major trauma.

The link has become clear: having an alcoholic parent often leads to emotional trauma in the child, which can create a vulnerability to disorders such as depression. The emotional trauma can be moderate or severe, and the depression can come sooner or it can come later. But its seeds are there, waiting for an opportune time to appear. And it is commonly accompanied by any number of other, often related disorders, ranging from substance abuse to eating disorders to severe mental illness. It sounds strange to say, but as horrible as depression is, you'd be fortunate if that was your only problem. It rarely strikes alone. More on this later.

Before we get too far along, it's important to note that depression and other types of mood disorders can often be traced back to many sources of severe, chronic emotional trauma, not just those produced by alcoholic families. Alcoholism just happens to be our most common source of major family dysfunction, abuse or even violence, which often leads to severe childhood trauma and subsequent disorder. Drug abuse in the family also commonly leads to the traumatizing of children. But the drug abuse or alcoholism per se is not the primary problem; its byproduct, *trauma*, is, particularly when it is a helpless, vulnerable child who is the unknown victim of that trauma. The child may carry around the damage of that trauma for the rest of his life; its effects are 'hard-wired' into the body.

It was barely more than 20 years ago that Dr. Janet Woititz wrote her path-blazing, best-selling book *Adult Children of Alcoholics*, which cast widespread attention on this previously neglected issue. When I first read the book's list of the telling characteristics of adult children of alcoholics, I was stunned at how much many of the characteristics applied to me. According to Dr. Woititz, adult children of alcoholics tend to, among other things, 'judge themselves without mercy', take things very seriously and 'have difficulty having fun', have difficulty with close relationships, continually seek approval, and over-react to things they can't control.

Ironically, I felt a kind of relief when I first read this. Because I saw myself in many of these characteristics, the information immediately began to *relieve my profound sense of guilt* — guilt that I was somehow completely to blame for these shortcomings. But how could I be to blame if these traits so commonly arise in children of alcoholics? There was an immediate therapeutic effect. Although it can take a very long time to alleviate all the guilt, this was at least a start for me. Many of these characteristics of children of alcoholics are also associated with depression or can contribute to the development of depression. Coincident with my relief at seeing that I wasn't entirely to blame for having these flaws, was a disappointment in myself that despite my education and belief that I was fairly knowledgeable and perceptive, I knew next to nothing about an issue that would prove to be so decisive for me—the life-changing consequences of being a child of an alcoholic.

As a young man looking back at my childhood and my father's history with alcohol, I thought it was nearly inevitable that I'd become an alcoholic too—like my father, and his father, and most of my uncles. It seemed to be my destiny; this was how men in the family coped with life's challenges and injustices. Drinking numbed the senses and relieved the pain. And it was one of the few pleasures for these hard-working men. They drank frequently and heavily, but never saw themselves as alcoholics. That was always the other guy, who couldn't stop, who couldn't control himself, who was hurting others around him. They were oblivious and they'd be very upset to be called alcoholics, which makes a part of me feel it's offensive to their memory to use this label. But it fits.

This is not to condemn the men in my family, not at all. These were all hard-working, dedicated, loving family men. They cherished their children, and I think their wives too, although it's hard to be sure about that. It was the marital relationship where the clashing values and viewpoints emerged. For each, this was the battleground, the relationship with his wife, who, as a woman in the 1950s and 60s, had much different wants and needs and personal history. This was typically where the primary clash occurred. The husband-wife relationship was a 'toxic' sort of legacy handed down from father to son to grandson, as with drinking. After all, consider the role models the children had. With my parents, as with several of my uncles and aunts, the marital relationship was often strained and distant.

Ambivalence—love-hate, or love-fear to be more precise—is a hallmark of the emotions and relationships that men such as my father generated, and it manifests itself in me too. At once I immensely respected and loved my father, my grandfather, and my uncles. They were giants to me as a boy—colorful, fiercely independent, spirited characters. But I was also left confused and terrified by some of the things they could do to their own families. No doubt they were unaware of the damaging effects of their actions. And I certainly understand that they were victims themselves, growing up in alcoholic families.

Despite their faults, I respected and envied these men in many ways, and I truly miss them. I also envied many things about the world they lived in. The direction in which our society is moving is not something I'm happy about. People today are much less friendly and trusting and few people have a genuine community spirit. Work environments are impersonal and isolated, if not downright cut-throat. Change is so rapid and disruptive that a person can no longer lead a secure, stable life. And everyone races around and around striving for the latest and greatest products that will make their meaningless lives marginally more comfortable. There is an overpowering commercialism and a stifling technology that blinds us to the things that could and should be more fulfilling and meaningful, among them community, relationships, and self-actualizing activity. It's become easy for people to lose sight of what's truly important.

My father used to remark, 'They don't make people like they used to.' 'The quality of people isn't the same anymore.' I couldn't agree more.

Clearly there were enormous challenges and obstacles to overcome when my parents were growing up and making their way in the world. Nevertheless, I'm led to believe they found their lives more fulfilling and enriching than most people do today. I would almost prefer an economic depression to today's decadence and arrogance. People back then were connected to each other and to the community. As a child, I remember the people my family dealt with for things like a major purchase, a home repair or home deliveries. All of them were people they had known for years, or they were a friend of a friend or relative.

They could count on these people to be fair and honest, and they had the kind of trusting, personal ties to people that you rarely see today. It wasn't unusual for my father to invite a repairman to have a cup of coffee, or a beer, and they'd talk like old friends. I envy that.

But, make no mistake, the hard times my parents' generation had to endure took a heavy toll, what with a brutal world war, severe Depression, ongoing economic hardship, and widespread racial and ethnic prejudice. My mother is of Polish descent while my father was Italian and in those days you were supposed to marry 'one of your own'. They were tough times. I think these conditions produced in that generation a kind of behavior that was terribly destructive to them and to their loved ones, a destructiveness they could hardly see or comprehend.

My father was truly a larger than life character, a rugged individualist and a maverick in every respect. He said and did what he pleased and there never was any pretension. When he walked into a room, everyone immediately felt his presence. No doubt sons say these kinds of things a lot about their fathers, but all my cousins and friends admired and commented on 'Uncle Sam's' strength of character and his refusal to concede or conform. Irrepressible and irreverent, he was his own man. Custom and convention were meaningless to him. Despite being comfortable financially as a result of his success in business, he dressed like a bum. Outward appearances mattered little to him.

I'll never forget the day my father and I went to the Willowbrook shopping mall to look at some tropical fish. This was one of the few activities we shared; we had more than a dozen fish tanks in the basement. This trip exemplified the unique, eccentric character that defined my father. Since I had just recently gotten a license, I elected to drive.

'I've never been to the mall,' my father said as we arrived.

Since the Willowbrook mall had been there at least ten years and was *the place* to shop in our area, I replied with surprise,

'What, you've *never* been here?'

'No, why do I need to go there? I can get most of the things I need from people down neck, and for a lot less.'

My father had no interest in shopping, certainly not for clothes, even though he always had more than enough cash in his pocket to treat himself. He seemed to enjoy making money, but not spending it, at least not on himself. He'd rather give it to his family. At first my mother bought all his clothes, and then my sisters took over this duty when my parents stopped talking to each other. My father didn't care about styles or fashion. If he wanted to go to a social occasion in an old shirt when everyone wore a jacket and tie, he didn't think twice about it. Nor was he concerned about covering his ample mid-section, which expanded dramatically when he quit smoking in his late 40s. He looked like Lou Costello, and couldn't care less.

One thing I admired about my father was that, unlike most everyone else, he never seemed too phased by other people's tastes or opinions. If he wanted to wear an old undershirt in public, so be it. He was what he was, take it or leave it. This isn't to say he was crude or undiscerning. He always knew exactly what was going on and was surprisingly adept at reading people. During the Depression, he had to drop out of school to work, but he became self-educated and a self-made success in business. I came to have enormous respect for my father and actually envy him, and part of me wants to say he was a great person, a giant among men. There was just that one fatal flaw. I don't know what happened or why, but there was some sort of demon inside him, a mysterious, unrelenting rage, and it nearly destroyed his life and many of those around him.

Sadly but not surprisingly, all the men in my family who drank heavily are now deceased, largely as a result of the destructive lifestyles they led—drinking, smoking, eating unwisely, and in some cases, working in a dangerous environment. They took many risks, not just for their own pleasure, but as a great sacrifice to make a living and support the family. They were heroes in many respects.

At the same time, when I was able to get more than a shallow glimpse into the character of these men, a terrible dark side was revealed. I once saw my grandfather take a live cigarette and burn our dog Lassie's nose so she would move away from him at a family party. She wasn't an aggressive or obnoxious dog, but I guess he just didn't want her around. And what I saw was barely the tip of the iceberg. My father relayed many a horror story about my grandfather's tyrannical actions toward others, including members of his immediate family. He was ultra patri-archal, to the point of being abusive. He was a Mussolini.

I'm struck by the enormous damage these men could do to their families, especially the young children. I may have sometimes suspected that I bore significant injury and trauma when I was younger, but it wasn't really until my *late 40s* that I fully realized the extent of the damage. This still astounds me. I thought I was a very astute, perceptive person with a great deal of self-knowledge. But I guess I missed this one, and for 40 years! I had pursued graduate study in sociology at Brown University in large part so I could better understand people—how social institutions, customs, and values shaped behavior, personality and beliefs. But this too was misguided I later realized. Sociology didn't adequately answer my core questions. It was too divorced from real people—theoretical, abstract and aloof. My apparent attempt to impress people—especially my parents, and *myself*—through attendance at an Ivy League school, diverted and distorted my thinking. Again, it was only much later that I realized this. Evidently I had a dire need to boost a sense of low self-esteem, which is a characteristic common among children of alcoholics.

Incidentally, the study of psychology would have been much more appropriate and instructive for my needs. By the time I learned *this* lesson I was in my 50s! So much for my smarts. I thought I was trying to understand people and society, but first and foremost, I was trying to understand *myself*—how and why I became the person I was.

Just for the record—and this may be my father's values of self-reliance and independence coming out here—I didn't rely on my family to pay for my graduate school education. I did this entirely through scholarships, teaching and research assistant-ships, and a frugal lifestyle. I waited a year after graduating college before going to graduate school, during which time I was married. In my two years in graduate school, my wife Joanne worked full-time as an assistant in a doctor's office, and I worked part-time as a research assistant and then as a teaching assistant. Having to skimp and sacrifice was actually an adventure and a challenge that made the accomplishment that much more meaningful.

Back in the 1950s and 60s it was extremely difficult for anyone to recognize the trauma and pain inflicted upon children by alcoholics like my father. The wounds persisted for decades, but few appreciated these vulnerabilities. No one could have antici-pated this in those days, at least not working class parents. The full, devastating effects of alcoholism on families were not widely known until much later. And the subtle psychological dynamics could not really be understood by lay people, not at this time anyway. Severely traumatized soldiers in bloody wars were not recognized by and large, so how could parents see serious trauma coming out of a loving family life? Certainly the men couldn't be expected to see it—hardened by a Great Depression and a World War, they exhibited the requisite mental toughness and machismo that precluded such insight. The typical man just moved ahead, day after day, trudging to an often dismal job to put bread on the table, and trying to somehow cope.

So, I'm not entirely blaming my father or the men in my family for what they did. They had no idea how they were harming their children. Sensitivity in men was not a widespread goal of upbringing until much later in the century. Still, as one who suffered at the hands of an alcoholic, it is understandable that I carry substantial resentment and bitterness, to say the least. I too felt the need to anesthetize, to numb the pain. Alcohol has always been an easy answer. I think there were just two things that prevented me from becoming an alcoholic also and 'fulfilling my destiny'—my three children, Rob, Lauren and Steve, who required from me a continual sense of fatherly duty and an obligation to be fully responsible—to support the family financially, and to maintain a household that was healthy—*psychologically and emotionally*, as well as physically. For, unlike my parents, I could see the silent but deadly effects of family dysfunction created by alcohol abuse.

The other thing that may have prevented me from becoming an alcoholic, oddly enough, was the fact that I often became physically ill if I drank too much. In the big picture, this seems trivial I know, but for me the resulting physical discomfort more than offset the positive effects, the wonderful high. Yes, I felt that high, like my predecessors. Oh, was it enticing, hypnotic, and addictive! I could certainly understand why the men in my family imbibed, just as men everywhere in all civilizations have sought out an escape from the tensions of life. If not for the nausea, the headaches, the flu-like aches following the extreme alcohol high, I have to believe that I could easily have developed this habit.

And without my beloved children, needing both unconditional love and proper nurturing to grow up healthy and whole, unlike me, I could also have more easily succumbed to the temptations of alcohol. For one, the times when Joanne and I were alone, without the children, it was an easy and pleasant habit to have a few and feel better.

In this sense, maybe it was just lucky that I too didn't get hooked on alcohol. For whatever reason, I don't feel that I can take too much credit for not becoming an alcoholic. It appears that I found other methods of anesthetizing, methods perhaps not as obvious or consuming as drinking. But they were probably just as harmful.

My story is about much more than the alcoholism in my family. As destructive as alcohol can be—and no one should ever underestimate the enormous potential for destructiveness—the trauma and dysfunction that millions of children have suffered and continue to suffer represent a much broader issue. For just as I found other means of coping with the pain and the ordeals, numerous people no doubt have found means other than alcohol. In a world without alcohol, I have to believe that people would have found other ways of accomplishing the same objectives, though possibly not as many people, and it's possible the damage wouldn't be as bad as with alcohol. Alcohol has always been readily available and it's been all too easy for people to self-medicate and drink away their problems.

Maybe a world without alcohol would have been much more likely to legalize and widely consume that other effective and abundant anesthetic, marijuana. I'm inclined to believe that when people feel there is an absolutely essential need, such as finding a means of coping with an often painful daily life, people will find a means, even if it is costly, dangerous, scarce or whatever. Consequently, my story—in many ways the story of millions of children of alcoholics—is about the trauma and wounds that children often suffer at the hands of parents and caregivers who are preoccupied with their own problems. There are many ways of producing dysfunction and trauma in families. Alcohol just happens to be the most common means in our society.

So, I never did develop a drinking problem, in spite of my fears and my family history. What I did develop was something I never imagined possible and something I couldn't begin to understand until I was completely enveloped by it. Depression is something I had mistakenly thought was simply a prolonged down mood associated with dwelling on one's problems, or just 'feeling sorry for yourself', something, by the way, that my father detested. I thought it was 'only mental'. I couldn't have been more wrong. It's likely that only those who get bowled over by it are ever able to comprehend its awesome power and the *physical* nature of the devastating symptoms. Depression may be as destructive as alcoholism, but the damage is primarily self-destructive. If you know someone who has been depressed, you can see damage done to others, but you can barely begin to imagine the terrible damage within the sufferer himself.

I've been very close to many of my cousins and have spent a lot of time with them and their families over the years. This has allowed me to see how my cousins as well as my sisters might have been affected by their fathers' drinking. Stark contrasts have been apparent to me for some time—I eventually came to realize I was different even though we all had fathers who were heavy drinkers. For me, it hit very hard. My cousins and sisters all seemed much better-adjusted. Ironically, among my cousins, I was generally viewed as the *most fortunate* one, because my family had a nice large home in the suburbs, new luxury cars, and enough money to buy color TVs, expensive furniture, and other things considered "luxuries" at the time. We were by no means wealthy, just reasonably well-off, especially in comparison to most of my extended family, many of whom lived essentially working-class lives in and around Newark, NJ. This kind of city was becoming less desirable in the explosive 1960s, and my family joined the thousands fleeing to the surrounding suburbs, mainly Belleville, Bloomfield and Nutley.

Oh, and the other reason I was viewed as the fortunate one was that I got to attend a private college, making others in my family and my town view me as virtual royalty. Although tuition at private colleges was a fraction of what it is today, it was nonetheless viewed as prohibitive in my day, and I did feel fortunate to be able to go to a prestigious, selective school like Lafayette College, where I transferred after a year at Rutgers.

Maybe due to the beliefs of others, I was made to actually *feel lucky* with my lot overall. This may have actually made it harder to deal with my growing sense of pain and turmoil inside, because I thought I *shouldn't* be feeling bad. After all, didn't I have it pretty good? Was I soft, or weak, or spoiled? As I grew older and became able to see stability and self-assurance in my cousins and in others, qualities that I lacked, I became increasingly aware that I was different, almost handicapped. For long periods of time, I was too busy with family and work to think about these things. But they don't just go away. I don't like to do what has become so commonplace these days and play the 'victim', but clearly there is a poisoned legacy handed down by alcoholics to their children. This can be overwhelming for some depending on their personal history and the situation they find themselves in.

The essential point I want to make in this book is, despite the terrible burden many of us have been given, *we can stop this toxic legacy, or at least begin to diminish it*. We have that ability. First we must learn from our fathers and mothers, be smarter than them, as they hoped that we'd be. And we must have the will to change. We need the help and support of our loved ones, who can be the benefactors of our success, rather than the victims of the rage and frustration from our festering wounds. And in most cases, we need professional help.

Success in this endeavor could be the most difficult thing any of us tries to do in his or her lifetime. And from what I understand from the experts, it doesn't mean that we simply have to 'suck it up', forget the past and move ahead as some seem to feel. Most people cannot begin to understand the incredibly complex, evil forces that are deeply entrenched within us, essentially running our lives. Whether you have encountered anxiety, depression, rage, addiction, or some other affliction as a result of the trauma from a parent's alcoholism or from some other family dysfunction, *you could not have stopped it as a child or adolescent. It's not your fault! It could never be your fault.* As a child, you could no more forestall the seeds of depression than you could avert diabetes or cancer.

Similarly, depression is not a result of weakness. This is an ignorant, archaic and thoughtless notion that does not warrant comment. We know, and the experts certainly know, that virtually *anyone* who had to endure severe trauma in childhood would have been seriously damaged, emotionally and otherwise; at least anyone who is *human,* who feels and loves. People who are free of such burdens as depression or anxiety are not stronger; they are simply more fortunate.

The fact of the matter is, 'sucking it up' is exactly the *wrong* approach. I tried that for a long time, and the end result was literally decades of denial and repression, while the pain and wounds slowly emerged from beneath the surface, to eventually explode and cripple me, nearly destroying my life as I knew it. Without a doubt, it will be necessary to suck it up many days and do your best to endure, but it is at best a short-term strategy that will not serve you well in the long run. I've learned the hard way what many experts are saying—we actually have to look at the pain and the wounds, relive the experience, fully feel it again, recognize what happened, then attempt to make resolution and complete the necessary grieving—if we are to have a chance of recovering. You need to understand and to forgive—*everyone,* including yourself; especially yourself.

Many sufferers seem to think they can stonewall the illness, believing that determination and willpower can prevail over it. Little chance. Willpower is no match for the years of conditioning from these experiences that dictate how the mind / body governs your emotions, thoughts and actions. Unfortunately, you cannot simply will away the damage from childhood trauma that has shaped you, not just emotionally, but physiologically and neurologically as well. Many have tried, and failed miserably.

Getting treatment is not wallowing in your misery; it's not feeling sorry for yourself, as people like my father would have said. It's doing what's necessary, taking risks, even if it initially produces yet more shame, or embarrassment or misunderstanding. No one wants to be seen as weak or inferior or cowardly. Some people continue to have these grossly mistaken beliefs. Taking charge of your life, opening up to your true person and the pain lying therein, and working to heal may actually be the bravest thing you can do. This means facing the brutal reality—recognizing your painful wounds, acknowledging a dreaded illness that the uninformed consider a weakness or character flaw, and taking the difficult actions to begin the healing, actions you never thought you'd have to take. It means looking down into the dark, bottomless pit that is the nightmare of depression.

Words cannot begin to convey the depth of the despair and dread that depression brings. And I feel fortunate in many ways insofar as my condition did not sink to the depth of suicidal tendencies or require hospitalization. I may have had glimpses, but cannot truly know what the absolute bottom must feel like. It's difficult for anyone to comprehend how a person like chemist and writer Primo Levi could have endured years of torture by the Nazis during the Holocaust, yet break under depression later in life and commit suicide. The power of depression to destroy is awesome.

'The opposite of depression is not happiness but vitality,' observed author Andrew Solomon. It's important to understand what depression is and what it isn't. In its essence, it is *not sadness*, although sadness is certainly a frequent accompanying mood. Even as we feel the unbearable burden of depression, we know that *it is not 'real'*, it doesn't accurately reflect our reality. Depression is totally irrational and illogical. For most of us are not uniformly unhappy with our lives, not disappointed in ourselves or in our loved ones, not bereft of a love of life. Depression does not indicate a dark outlook or futile view of life. Rather, it is an irrepressible force that surreptitiously seizes control of us from inside, much as a physical disease. It saps our energy, our strength, our very lives. It seems to happen almost mechanically, unconsciously. Depression is an insidious process that may have begun years earlier, with a loss or wound to your inner being that was never healed. Like an injury that is not treated, it invariably deteriorates and festers, spreading pain and infection that eventually demand attention. And it can kill if that attention isn't forthcoming.

Someone who's viewed depression from both the inside and outside, sociologist David Karp, interviewed 50 people to uncover connections among these depressed people in terms of the effects their illnesses had on their social lives. It is striking how the various personal descriptions of the feeling of depression reveal similar themes. An excerpt from one particularly articulate description:

> Depression is an insidious vacuum that crawls into your brain and pushes your mind out of the way. It is the complete absence of rational thought. It is freezing cold with a dangerous, horrifying, terrifying fog wafting throughout whatever is left of your mind...When you are in it there is no more empathy, no intellect, no imagination, no compassion, no humanity, no hope... Depression steals away whoever you were, prevents you from seeing who you might someday be, and replaces your life with a black hole.
>
> Subject interviewed in *Speaking of Sadness: Depression, Disconnection and the Meanings of Illness*, by David A. Karp

This same subject goes on to explain the value of learning how others experienced depression and managed to get through it, information that many report can be surprisingly difficult to obtain.

> I have searched and searched for articles or studies focusing
> on the perceptions of depressed people and have found very
> few… I do think that depressed people need access to the very
> real experiences of others who have survived it. You can't get
> that from psychologists, psychiatrists, drugs, or hospitals.
> The stories provide perspective, they provide balance to all
> the hype about drugs and 'cure', they provide information
> and background that may help other depressed people get a
> handle on their experiences, they prove that you're not alone
> with this monster. And they give hope.

This comment aptly captures the essence of my purpose for
writing this book. In the time leading up to my decision to write a
book, I had an unquenchable thirst for information and personal
stories about depression and the plight of children of alcoholics,
consuming several dozen books and numerous articles, essays,
and reports. And I've continually looked for more.

In the remainder of this book I will share my experiences and
learnings in a way that hopefully will be helpful and encouraging to readers. To anyone suffering from depression or other
such disorders, I would say, while depression in no way is your
fault, you do have an opportunity, some would say *responsibility*,
to fight back and regain control of your life. This is not just for
yourself, but for the sake of your loved ones.

Recalling the words of R.D. Laing: 'If our experience is
destroyed, our behavior will be destructive. If our experience is
destroyed, we have lost our own selves.' In the web of traumatic
emotional injury of which depression was but a part, I lost not
only myself, but also the pleasure of a peaceful and healthy life.
My family lost out too, and this hurts the most. And what was
destroyed was my ability to feel or express normal emotions, or
enjoy pleasures that other people enjoy, or relish the hopefulness

and freedom of a life unburdened by the weight of depression. But this terrible condition need not be permanent. With effort, strength and resilience, and help from others—an absolutely essential element of recovery—a victim can mercifully be freed of this unbearable burden, much of it at least.

2 Burning Out

The world is too much with us; late and soon,
Getting and spending, we lay waste our powers:
Little we see in Nature that is ours;
We have given our hearts away, a sordid boon!
The sea that bares her bosom to the moon:
The winds that will be howling at all hours,
And are up-gathered now like sleeping flowers;
For this, for everything, we are out of tune...
William Wordsworth, The World Is Too Much with Us

It didn't happen suddenly or surprisingly, and yet it shocked me to the core. I don't know exactly when it started or when I first sensed it, that my life was 'out of tune', *I* was out of tune. In the last year of my twenty-plus year career in a pretty good job, I truly felt like I had lost my heart and soul, like the insides were being ripped right out of me. And I had no idea how it could have happened. I was experiencing profound failure for the first time, and although there were numerous legitimate reasons why I could blame the impossible circumstances and not myself, I just couldn't forgive myself for letting it happen. That apparently was a big part of the problem, a common element in the fall into depression.

It's with mixed and conflicted emotions that I tell my story. At the fairly advanced age of 55 I can finally face my own demons and write about the intimate events and experiences leading up to my depression, having at last begun to rid myself of enough shame and guilt to acknowledge and express the pain; emphasis is on *begun* to rid myself of blame—I can't declare victory yet. And I could comfortably talk about my 'disorder' now, but with only one person, my loving wife Joanne, beside my therapist and psychiatrist of course. As caring, generous, and loyal as Joanne

27

has been through the volatile 33 years of our marriage, it required even this extraordinary person quite a few years to *begin* to understand my depression—what it is, how to deal with it, and how to stay sane herself. For a spouse to even begin to understand is a rare achievement, but even that's not enough, unfortunately. Not nearly.

Dealing with this most destructive and mysterious illness has been without doubt the most trying experience of our lives. It requires an openness and a willingness to see things differently and to change habits and beliefs, characteristics that seem to diminish as people settle into their middle age years. Just understanding something as enigmatic and devastating as depression is beyond the reach of most people, never mind having to deal with the many ordeals and hardships. Of course, understanding can't be given to you, but rather comes only through constant effort to examine yourself and your partner with open, loving and empathetic eyes, and with a willingness to reconsider preconceived ideas. For most people in such a situation, understanding will be a long time in coming, if it comes at all before one partner or the other gives up. That is the unfortunate outcome in so many relationships affected by depression, an insidious illness that destroys in silence.

If it takes a dedicated wife several years just to begin to understand a partner's depression, how could the average person understand it? This is a primary reason why I have always been reluctant to reveal my depression to others. They *never* understand, and why should I knowingly make myself the victim of another's ignorance and prejudice? Why have to deal with their skeptical, crude reaction? Furthermore, I'm a very private person who doesn't like to reveal inner thoughts, emotions or problems, which I've learned is actually an aspect of my condition, one of many byproducts of my checkered childhood. I could readily identify with psychotherapist Terrence Real's description of the telling characteristics of depressed men in his exceptional book, *I*

Don't Want to Talk About It. Among these characteristics are denial of emotions, reluctance to communicate feelings or acknowledge any possible weakness, and a powerful sense of shame and guilt. I could have been a poster boy for this.

It has gradually become apparent to me that I've carried an unbelievably huge, largely hidden burden—FOR FOUR DECADES! It wasn't until I was 48 that my symptoms suggested I might be suffering from depression. After a few months muddling along, this was confirmed in a clinical diagnosis of moderately severe depression. But I believe that a number of times earlier in my life I probably experienced episodes of depression; I just didn't know it, or want to know. I don't recall exactly when I first heard of depression, but I do remember having the belief that a depressed person must be making a 'mountain out of a mole hill' and was simply being too self-involved and swayed by emotional up's and down's. Naturally, I didn't want to be one of these 'soft' people, so denial took hold whenever I even slightly suspected I might have symptoms of depression. There's going to be good days and bad days, I thought, just deal with it. I'm still convinced that the great majority of people have this grossly mistaken notion and cannot begin to grasp the true nature or power of depression.

My 'official' depression diagnosed at age 48 was triggered by an accumulation of stress building up over a period of several years as a result of spiraling problems and conflicts at my workplace, producing an increasingly toxic work environment. I had been put in an impossible situation, culminating with a deceitful unit head who made me a scapegoat and was intent on forcing me out of the company I had served loyally for 20 years. It was essentially a type of 'burnout' on the job that did me in, I suppose with an assist from mid-life rumblings.

But there was much more to it than that; burnout is becoming very common these days. I've learned that a trigger such as job-related stress isn't usually enough to bring on depression for most people. You generally need a pre-disposition, a vulnera-bility, which can stem from prior experiences, often dating back to early childhood. More on this in a bit.

I had worked as a consumer market researcher at a large insurance company for 20 years, the first 15 of which were great. I enjoyed the work, my peers, and the overall environment. My work involved gathering and analyzing information about customers and prospects, largely done through surveys that we designed and conducted. During this time I met a number of terrific people, some of whom have remained friends of mine. While we worked together, we had lunch everyday as a group, played volleyball regularly after work, went out afterwards for a few drinks, and generally enjoyed each other's company. Having received several promotions over the years, the job was personally fulfilling, and, while I knew I'd never get rich, the pay was adequate for a middle class way of life. The job enabled my wife and me to own a decent home in a nice, family-oriented community where we raised our three children. Fair Haven, NJ was a quiet, friendly little town, idyllic in many respects. For about half my time with the company I managed a small unit of researchers, which included the corporate library for a few of the years. Back then the head of the research department was a former college professor who instilled a collegial atmosphere where creativity, autonomy and dissent were encouraged. In short, it was a great place to work.

Then everything changed. In my last few years with the company things went steadily downhill. The company was strug-gling financially, leading to cut-backs, reorganizations, and such rapid, unpredictable changes that things went from unstable to chaotic. A series of new executives with different work styles were brought in nearly every year to turn things around. Shifting priorities in the tough, new environment pushed consideration for employees further and further down the list of priorities. No longer did employees have a 'career'. Work became a daily struggle to survive, and my function was especially hard hit by the frequent changes and the conflicts between departments. Concern for employee welfare disappeared. Any semblance of trust disappeared. Many changes the company initiated made no sense, and some were actually complete reversals of earlier initiatives. The consequences to employees were no longer a concern. In fact, some of the changes and reorganizations were secretly *intended* to make people's jobs harder, for example, with longer commutes, in an attempt to reduce the workforce. Generating voluntary resignations is a lot easier and cheaper than layoffs and severance.

After so many years of stability and predictability, it's extremely unsettling to see your career suddenly turn precarious, leading not only to job insecurity, but also uncertainty as to how to do your job effectively. In this environment, I began to feel helpless and inconsequential, losing a sense of having any 'control' over events and circumstances in my job. The work environment in the company was rapidly deteriorating, stripping the joy and spirit from most of the people I observed. I could see it in their beleaguered, gray faces and their sad, deep-set eyes. People who used to smile and talk and joke were now seen with their eyes fixed downward at the floor or staring blankly ahead. How many times I thought this was a terrible shame, and then I realized how terrible I too must look.

The situation was especially threatening and insecure for me because the research area was undergoing frequent shifts from decentralized to centralized, and a new team of senior researchers was brought in from outside to lead and improve the function. I found myself reporting to a different person literally every six months. This required continual changes in priorities and in work styles. Some of the changes were drastic and confusing, and some went full circle, returning matters to an earlier structure when previous changes failed dismally. I felt jerked around by the chaotic, unpredictable and increasingly desperate executives brought in to save the sinking ship.

Compounding the strain was the fact that for a time I was reporting to two different departments in separate locations 50 miles apart, departments that had much different ways of operating. If you did the right thing in the eyes of one department, it was often the wrong thing in the eyes of the other, and you were told this in no uncertain terms. I was typically caught between the two departments to which I reported, and torn as to what to do. It seemed that I was expected by each department to talk the other into doing things the 'right' way, to get them to see the light. This was clearly impossible. The confused, conflicted situation brought continual frustration and a sense of being powerless to affect things. And just being under two separate departments meant twice as many meetings, half of them being an hour plus commute away, making it that much harder to get work done.

If this wasn't bad enough, conflicts also arose between one department I reported to and some of my 'client' departments, the users of the research I did. It had to do not so much with research practices, but with control over the projects and how they were reported. It was getting very political. Again, I was expected to simply make my clients see the light and conform to my department's ways, even though we were in theory doing the research *for the client department* and needed to fit *their* objectives and policies; you know, the 'customer is king' idea. Ironically, though my department did research on external customers and their needs and presumably understood the importance of meeting customer / user needs, they didn't see the hypocrisy of their mission to continually overrule internal customers. It was a mess.

One situation typified the problems. I couldn't understand why *I* was being held responsible by my department for the delayed start-up of a major new survey for a user department who had yet to agree on the survey design. Then I learned why—

in high-level meetings, the head of that department had been fighting off the new survey every way possible, but was obviously feeling increasing pressure to concede. So he gave in — publicly — and said the survey could go ahead, but privately he stonewalled and continued to quietly work on preventing it. I was the guy caught in between. Believing that the survey had been approved, my department head felt I should be moving aggressively to get it started. She apparently didn't believe me when I reported that the user wasn't at all comfortable with the survey. To me the incident was further evidence of the disappearance of trust and integrity from my workplace, which unfortunately seemed to be a widespread trend.

Largely due to the frustrations and conflicts at work, I was becoming more impatient, irritable, and easily angered at home. The problems at work would inevitably spill over into my home life, as my overall disposition was souring. More and more nights I came home feeling abused and drained, typically carrying a tight knot of tension in my neck and shoulders. It didn't make for a pleasant person to be around. At work, I was falling into a fog, and my declining ability to focus and concentrate made it harder and harder to perform effectively at work, although I tried gallantly.

No matter what I did, the situation only got worse. My struggles at work were compounded by a new director who, after several months of working together smoothly, suddenly became hostile and confrontational. She soon began to systematically misrepresent the facts in an apparent attempt to cover her own failures by portraying my performance as unsatisfactory. I acknowledge that my performance was starting to decline, but it was due to the deepening symptoms of what I would later learn stemmed from a formidable depression, with the usual generalized anxiety on the side. My director started radically altering the facts, for example on performance reviews, blaming me for late or erroneous reports and other problems that were not my responsibility.

I wondered for some time why she was doing these things, or if I was truly deficient and at fault. In my mind I continually reflected on my work product and methods to make sure they weren't inadequate or inappropriate in some way. The situation was beginning to really preoccupy me. For the first time, I was forced to seriously question my own professional competence. I became riddled with doubt—lingering, destructive self-doubt.

Eventually, I saw that my director was attempting to place blame on me to cover up her own problems and failures. In the first few months we worked together, it became apparent that she was an incompetent manager. She was disorganized and never met deadlines, although she'd insist that others meet them. She began alienating users of our research with her overbearing, self-serving style. You had to do things exactly her way. As a consequence of this stubborn, confrontational behavior, our major user department began refusing to work with her or even meet with her. This backlash affected all the projects in my unit and impacted me in particular, presenting serious problems trying to deal with other departments. My confidence had already taken a blow from the doubts raised by my director's accusations, so this was the last thing I needed. It seemed like each week brought another crisis or strain.

Another angle to the story developed, one that was totally unexpected, and kind of lurid. My director and I had gotten along very well for a period of several months following her assignment to head research in the business unit where I worked. She was appreciative of my work and seemed to be fair, honest and trustworthy. We frequently had lunch together and we were establishing a good working relationship. She often sought me out at meetings and conferences and we 'hung around' together—just at work.

Then she suddenly started telling me about affairs that were taking place between people in our division who worked in another location. Noteworthy in these affairs was that they all took place between people in a reporting relationship. And in one case the subordinate received a promotion while the affair was going on. This of course is a clear violation of policy in virtually any large company. It's unethical, exploitative, and just plain sleazy. She told me such stories a number of times and at some length, which was puzzling to me. On one occasion, I recall a long, awkward pause as she stared at me awaiting some kind of response to these affairs. I just shook my head.

I didn't think much about this until one night a couple weeks later when we were in Houston together on a business trip. We arrived at our hotel fairly late the first night and I just wanted to crash.

'Would you like to go down to the bar for a drink?' she asked.

'Not tonight, I'm really tired,' I replied, at which she seemed a little put out, but again I didn't think much of it.

For the rest of the two day conference I decided to hang around other people at lunch, breaks, and dinner. I was tired of being around her so much of the time.

That's when everything changed. From that day forward, her attitude and behavior toward me changed 360 degrees. She became critical, impatient, and unusually demanding, suddenly speaking to me in a stern, rigid tone in contrast to the previous collegial, pleasant style. Soon she even stopped inviting me to meetings, pushing me into the background of the unit's activities. And she started the fabrications about my performance. She would blame me for problems on projects that weren't even assigned to me. In several instances she denied having agreed with me on an approach to a project, and went on to be critical of it. She altered timelines from the past to make it appear that I was late on my projects. She seemed to have it in for me.

As my health deteriorated and I had the occasional rotten day at work, there wasn't a shred of understanding or sympathy. I remember one incident—after I had told her that I wasn't feeling well but would stay and try to get some work done. Later that day I wasn't able to remember some information she asked for.

'All you could say was you were tired and dizzy,' she commented with obvious dissatisfaction. I was shocked and offended by such a callous response.

The day of my first performance review with this director was a point where my mood sank to a new low. I had to sit in her office for a couple hours and listen to her endless criticism, much of it unfounded. This was my first poor review in 20 years, so that was hard enough to take. But upon seeing her become so hostile to the point of trying to twist everything to be my fault, I was devastated. I sensed that my long, proud career there was about to collapse to an ugly, humiliating end. Although I believed much of the criticism was based on lies and wasn't my fault, I feared I wouldn't be able to fight back against this new regime. My protests and rebuttals to her accusations got me nowhere. Even when I tried to defend myself, I remember her replying, 'you're so defensive all the time,' which she saw as a sign of weakness and guilt.

Since I also saw that my performance *was* declining in some areas due to my health, things suddenly seemed completely hopeless. I walked out of her office feeling as weak and small and helpless as I've ever felt. I was a shell of a man.

Nevertheless, I was able to rally shortly thereafter. Refusing to be victimized by these cheap lies, I spent a lot of time researching the events and circumstances in question, and was able to find evidence in emails, notes and other documents to refute each of her lies. It seemed to be a clear cut case, to me at least. I delicately mentioned this evidence to my director, to no avail, then to her Vice President, to no avail, and then to Human Resources, once again to no avail. To my amazement, no one wanted to look at the *evidence* of what had actually occurred! Not my unit head, or department head. Not even Human Resources. I had to resort to appealing to the company's dispute resolution channels and employee assistance programs. I was hopeful that these 'neutral' parties would pursue 'truth and justice' and help solve the problems that were enveloping me. How naïve! I eventually found them to be patronizing and covertly protective of management. It appears this is their hidden agenda.

After several weeks, as I thought more and more about the sudden shift in my director's behavior and discussed it with my wife, it became clear that the change occurred right after the Houston trip. I started piecing things together—all the lunch invites, the talk about office affairs, the stares looking for my reactions, the disapproving look after I declined having a drink with her, and then the sudden change. Was it retaliation? So, I decided to add *sexual harassment* to my complaint about the unfair treatment that I had filed with the company's dispute resolution unit. And I reported this to the company's equal opportunity office. Things were getting pretty complicated. (By the way, in case you're wondering, my director was definitely *not* attractive, not that it necessarily matters.)

I have to acknowledge that an initial reaction of resistance to changes being made in a company, a quite natural reaction for many veterans such as myself, can only work against you. I wasn't being flexible or adaptable enough, and this certainly compounded my problems. A part of me was blaming myself for the problems at work. However, I believe that if given enough time, I would have started to change and adapt, which I had done successfully before in my career. But the onslaught of lies by my director about my performance was an act of war in my mind, and I had to fight back, even though I suspected I could never win. Fighting the fabrications on my performance appraisal required such an effort that at times I lost focus on my job, which is never a good thing, especially when someone is looking closely for any minute thing that could be used against you. And my exaggerated indignation at being a victim of such deceit made my attitude that much worse.

My downward spiral began slowly and gradually accelerated from there. At first it was an occasional bad day when I found myself stressed, frustrated and fatigued. Over time the frequency and intensity of these feelings increased. I began finding it impossible to keep up with all the changes and the growing work volume. One of the first symptoms I remember that was a warning sign was the sensation of my head spinning at a time of unusual stress, often when things were happening very quickly, or when I was bombarded with information, or when I had more things to do than I could possibly complete in time. I began feeling lightheaded and dizzy. My mind seemed to start shutting down, and I'd have trouble just remembering what I was supposed to be doing. And the apprehension that someone was out to get me was starting to hang over me. Although I was justified in this feeling to some extent in view of my director's vindictive behavior, it was getting to the point of obsession, of paranoia. All the politics and the declining job security just made me feel worse.

Another symptom began to appear. When things started to become tense, difficult or frustrating, I'd often get an overpowering sense that I was sinking, deeper and deeper. I was being pulled down by an irresistible force. First it was once in a while, but eventually this heavy, sinking feeling became my constant companion. The kinds of stress and pressure that I previously was able to handle were now becoming overwhelming. Tension and anxiety built up daily within me while my health and mental state deteriorated. At work I often became dizzy, light-headed, fatigued, forgetful, and I was gradually losing the ability to concentrate. My stomach was often queasy, and I was more susceptible to a number of physical aliments, including digestive problems and contagious illnesses. And problems that I had been having with my back and neck began to deteriorate, producing frequent pain, stiffness and limited mobility. Much of this no doubt was tension-related. By the end of a typical day at work my neck would develop a painful knot at the shoulders that was almost paralyzing.

But this was nothing compared to the way I felt inside— empty, hopeless, weak. I felt like a failure, a loser. I found myself unable to handle change, stress, or challenges of any kind. The prospect of having to write a large report or handle a difficult client at a meeting, things I had done numerous times before, was beginning to grind me down. Increasingly, a sense of dread took hold of me, or at minimum was simmering just below the surface. If I had an occasional easy, smooth day, I'd still be appre- hensive, waiting for the next shoe to fall. My days became darkened with gloom and defeat. I often felt confused and distracted and my mind would go completely blank at times. Someone could be talking to me and, in the midst of the conver- sation, my mind would wander somewhere else, often out of anxiety about a situation, and I'd have no idea what the person was talking about. I had particular trouble dealing with difficult or conflicted situations or instances when I was unable to do what I wanted to do. I became easily frustrated and discouraged.

One instance exemplified my declining condition. I went out to a store at lunch time to buy a periodical for work. After a short time looking, I couldn't find the periodical, apparently because it was not on newsstands yet, which really annoyed me because I had wasted a lunch hour looking. When I walked out of the store and looked around the parking lot for my car, I couldn't remember where I had parked. That's actually not that unusual for me. But as I tried to recall, I couldn't remember what store I had been in, or why I even went there. Nor did I know the day or the time. My mind was *totally blank*. I looked around into the parking lot on a warm, sunny day, with people bustling back and forth, but had no idea what I was doing. I was momentarily stunned, feeling completely paralyzed and helpless. It seemed like it lasted for minutes, although I imagine it was much less than that. Only gradually was I able to recall where I was and what I was doing. This incident really shook me up—I was scared about what was happening to me and how bad it could become if my condition continued. I had experienced other incidents like this where my mind would suddenly go blank, but this was the longest and most frightening time.

Though these problems were very mysterious to me, it was becoming apparent that they were directly related to my work, which seemed to be quite simply making me sick. One not so subtle hint was that Monday's were almost always my worst day. The start of the work week would bring me down lower and lower every week. I naturally wondered if it was my doing—perhaps my inability to adapt or meet the new, tougher expectations of the job. In a time of rapid change, there may always be an element of failure to adapt sufficiently. But I sensed it was much more than this, that the environment was becoming toxic, inhuman.

I would later learn that my workplace was a type of 'depressogenic environment', characterized by tension, conflict, rigidity and lack of essential support for individuals. This environment can undermine individual judgment and self-esteem, according to Dr. Frederic Flach, often leading to frustration, anger, guilt and other stressors that often trigger burnout, depression or other disorders (Flach, 2002). If ever a workplace fit this description, it was mine. It was becoming stifling. No longer was there leeway or flexibility for the seasoned professional like myself who needed, and could handle, greater autonomy. In his book *The Secret Strength of Depression*, Flach describes a highly rigid workplace as especially depressogenic for the more 'self actualizing' person, in the terms of psychologist Abraham Maslow's hierarchy of needs. I suspect that many if not most professional people are of the self actualizing bent, and might have this kind of reaction to a workplace becoming unduly rigid and toxic.

My case may have been on the extreme side, but by no means was I in a small minority with regard to my feelings about work.

An estimated 20 million Americans stay in jobs they hate just to keep health insurance, says career consultant Dr. Barbara Bailey Reinhold. And less than ten percent are really satisfied with their jobs (see her book, *Toxic Work*). Stress at work causes untold health problems, from heightened cardiovascular disease to compromised immune systems that can lead to a host of ailments. The continuing decline of security and stability at the workplace contributes significantly to this heightened stress.

Looking back, it was clear that I had waited much too long before doing anything about my declining mental health. It was actually painful to think about my problems, and I was into denial big time. My instinctive reaction to the challenges I was facing at work was to do my best to meet them and succeed. So I just went to work everyday stubbornly determined to do my job effectively and survive the storm. I'd say to myself, 'I can take this, no problem.' And I ignored the warning signs.

It was just a matter of time until I could no longer ignore or deny my rapidly declining health. My job seemed to be wearing me down to nothing. Increasingly, I'd come home from work feeling completely drained. At the end of a day at work I often felt as if I had been forced through a meat grinder. I felt beat-up, hollow, anxious, unreal. The deteriorating situation at work was consuming me. Every day I would reflect on the day's events, desperate to understand what was happening and what to do about it. It was nearly an obsession with me, but nothing I did seemed to help in dealing with any of the problems. The only 'strategy' I came up with was to essentially fight back, deny the false accusations, and try to set the record straight.

Refuting one's management and even appearing to fight back it is one formidable task. Not surprisingly, the nightmare continued to hang over me, surrounding me. I was engulfed by it. Being preoccupied with my problems, I just couldn't focus on the work.

I reluctantly saw my family doctor and told him about my

numerous disturbing symptoms. After doing a physical exam to rule out certain conditions that could have accounted for my symptoms, he said in a soft, serious tone that it sounded like depression. While I was a little afraid that this would be the diagnosis based on warnings that I had read, it was nevertheless stunning to hear that I might be suffering from depression. I was kind of hoping it would be a physical problem, which is revealing in itself about my attitude insofar as a physical problem with these numerous symptoms could be very serious. Apparently, I wanted no part of the label 'depressed'. My doctor gave me a two-month supply of prescription antidepressants and said I should see a psychiatrist if I didn't feel better by then. To my surprise and disappointment, even my family doctor exhibited the stigma associated with depression.

'We'll just write fatigue on your chart,' he said softly, 'so no one knows it's depression.'

It surprised me that a doctor would think that way. I thought, 'Who's going to see my chart?' The office manager? Another doctor? If doctors can't be open about an illness like depression, who can?

Despite the high incidence and tremendous impact of depression in this country, it often remains undiagnosed, untreated or mistreated. Although more consumers are seeking help for depression and rates of antidepressant use are rising, fewer than 22 percent of people diagnosed with depression receive adequate treatment for their illness (Depression and Bipolar Support Alliance, 2006). Unfortunately, though treatment for depression is successful in half or more of the cases (depending on who you listen to), fewer than half of those suffering from this illness even seek treatment. According to Mental Health America, 'Too many people resist treatment because they believe depression isn't serious, that they can treat it themselves, or that it is a personal weakness rather than a serious medical illness' (Mental Health America website www.nmha.org).

To a great extent, the large number of people going without treatment, or without *proper* treatment, is due to the powerful stigma associated with depression and mental illness in general. And, judging by the high incidence of depression, when people are under treatment, it appears that they typically do not reveal their illness as depression, which helps perpetuate the stigma by hiding the true incidence of depression and the fact that it can strike anyone. Compared to the high current rate of depression, it is relatively uncommon that you hear of co-workers or casual acquaintances suffering from depression. This is because they believe there is reason to disguise it in order to avoid the stigma and the associated prejudice.

It's a sad irony of depression that the victims are put in a position of contributing to the destructive myths and the stigma associated with the illness. I came to the realization that I have been as guilty as anyone in perpetuating the ignorance surrounding depression—by failing to disclose my illness for most of its duration, and failing to educate others as to its true nature and cause. Quite simply, I felt ashamed, guilty and weak. At times I thought to myself, this would never happen to my father.

I was hoping of course that my problems would pass quickly. Maybe it was just a temporary condition as I adjusted to the new work situation. But over time I only got worse. After a couple months on medication, it was evident that this was insufficient to treat my deteriorating condition. I reluctantly saw a psychiatrist on the advice of my family doctor, and she indeed produced a diagnosis of moderate depression and prescribed stronger medication. So that was it; I had been clinging to some small hope that it was something other than this dreaded, mysterious illness. I felt another sensation of sinking still deeper.

Actually this was the second psychiatrist I had tried. The first was a man who during my initial visit did nothing but talk about himself. I tried several times to swing the conversation over to me, which seemed reasonable since I was the patient, but he wouldn't stop talking about himself. He was relentless and oblivious. Aren't psychiatrists supposed to listen, to empathize? Who's keeping an eye on this guy? I left his office reflecting on the irony that this man must have been insane himself.

Even though a part of me said I shouldn't feel that way, having to see a psychiatrist and take antidepressants left me feeling helpless and hopeless. Things were sinking fast at work, something that perhaps had been my primary source of self-esteem, which can be a very unhealthy situation. Without a sense of pride and accomplishment from work, I didn't seem to have enough to sustain me. It appears that too much of my identity, confidence and esteem were based on my career, and when my work life took a sudden downturn, a serious personal crisis ensued. My work had been my crutch, and when it broke, I fell down, very hard.

Depression can be both unpredictable and inexplicable. Although it may be more frequently triggered by burnout or other stressful problems at work, it evidently can also be triggered by *success*. Again, a common element is very often a *pre-existing vulnerability* without which depression probably would not have struck. Author and sociologist David Karp initially believed that his depression would ease if and when he got past the very hectic and stressful period of achieving tenure as a professor, which can create enormous pressure. However, to his surprise, his depression actually worsened when he became tenured, forcing him to look beyond the suspected genesis of his depression in social situations. He realized he now needed to look *within himself* for the causes, including examining his troublesome childhood. Perhaps the heightened expectations and pressures of his tenured position brought to fore his lack of self-assurance and his long-standing doubts about his capabilities. Karp has fought an up and down battle with depression for 20 years (see his book *Speaking of Sadness: Depression, Disconnection and the Meanings of Illness*).

Depression can be accompanied by a kind of personal 'identity' crisis. In his frightening yet poetic chronicle of his ordeals with depression, *Darkness Visible: A Memoir of Madness*, author William Styron writes about how the condition left him sometimes feeling that he had *two selves*. One of these selves seemed to simply observe his activities, largely unaffected by the madness. It's striking how I have felt much the same way, for a pretty long time actually, it's just more pronounced while seized by depression. One of the selves was a tough, enduring, shrewd individualist, very much like my father, and like the person he seemed to want me to be. The other self seemed to be the 'real' me, in many ways the opposite of my father—wounded, vulnerable, sensitive. This part of me would witness my ordeals and speak to me in my mind, much as a color analyst would comment on a football game. But often he would also assert himself and try to steer me in a certain direction. At times I vacillated between the two selves and didn't know which personality to let dictate my actions. It was almost as if two personalities were battling within me.

Despite these two selves, or maybe because of them, I seemed to lose any sense of a solid, continuing identity. I didn't know who I really was or who I was supposed to be. For a long time, even before my first manifest episode of depression, I have felt very 'existential', lacking a strong sense of meaning or direction in my life. Somewhat reluctantly, I generally followed more or less conventional paths in my life, not knowing what else to do. I always had a great deal of difficulty making major decisions in my life. People by and large viewed me as stable, levelheaded and practical, but I was actually uncertain and anxious to an extreme. I often felt myself 'wandering aimlessly' through a conventional, middle class life.

My situation at work was deteriorating by the day, to the

point where it was feeding on itself. Reflecting on the problems in an attempt to find a solution only made me feel worse, and I became totally preoccupied and overwhelmed. I'm a person who will compulsively analyze and re-analyze a problem in excruciating depth until I reach some resolution. I couldn't let it go. But for someone predisposed to depression, fixating on problems will only bring you down more. This made me even less capable of doing my work, making the job situation get worse and worse. The condition that began as occasional weakness, dizziness and queasiness from problems at work, became a paralyzing sickness at even the thought of work. By this point in time, I was feeling completely hollow, devoid of energy or substance, and utterly incapable of working, or functioning at all. I was falling into the grip of major depression.

3 Into the Maelstrom

We are all substantially flawed, wounded, angry, hurt, here on Earth.
But this human condition, so painful to us, and in some ways
shameful — because we feel we are weak when the reality of ourselves
is exposed— is made much more bearable when it is shared, face-to-
face in words that have expressive human eyes behind them.
    Alice Walker, Anything We Love Can Be Saved

My favorite contemporary folk artist, Dar Williams, wrote and recorded a song that aptly expresses the bleak, lifeless state that depression can bring. And hearing her perform this song, "After All', in her moving voice is so much more powerful than simply reading the words. My wife Joanne and I have seen Dar in concert four times in the past couple years. I'm mentioning this because she's not only an extraordinary singer / songwriter and entertainer, she's also an activist for environmental protection, community-based initiatives, and mental health issues, having experienced severe depression herself. I deeply respect and applaud her for what she does. Dar frequently does benefit concerts for one cause or another, and, among other activities, she's a founding supporting artist for 'Musicians for Mental Health', an initiative that uses the power of music to educate youth and to fight the myths and the stigma associated with mental health problems (see www.mpoweryouth.org). She is regarded as one of the most creative folk artists of the past decade (folk singers almost never become famous), and she's recently written two books for adolescents. She's also a wife and mother.

When you see Dar perform, her enthusiastic, self-assured, witty demeanor belies a personality that was highly fragile and torn by depression just a few years before her rise to success as a singer / songwriter. She speaks openly about her fight with depression in her songs, concerts, interviews and wherever else possible in order to show others that recovery is possible with proper treatment, which inevitably must include some form of psychotherapy. People like Dar can be a great inspiration to all of us.

I'm reciting some of the details of my fall into depression and my struggles to recover because I believe my story parallels the stories of millions of others and contains important lessons that others may find helpful, especially about the deep roots of these disorders. The specific elements of the story may vary somewhat person to person, but there seem to be so many underlying similarities and universal patterns in these stories of depression. I think we have to be careful not to miss the forest for the trees, the 'forest' being the widespread and growing incidence of mental disorders of all types. Depression shares many symptoms as well as origins with these other disorders, and in fact most sufferers of depression also have one or more of these other disorders. We need to look for the culprit, and the effects of alcoholism or drug abuse in the household would seem to be a primary suspect.

Having failed to reverse my decline at work, I reluctantly began seeing a psychotherapist weekly at the suggestion of my psychiatrist. Therapy is supposed to be the treatment that helps a person rise out of depression, since medication is primarily for *relieving symptoms* and for simply coping. This fact is not widely understood. Many people believe that medication alone will pull them out of depression, as the increasingly deceptive advertising of antidepressants seems to suggest.

My psychotherapist practiced the recommended treatment of the time, cognitive therapy. We'd talk about the problems I was having at work and he'd try to get me to think more positively. It was clear that my frame of mind at work was negative to an unhealthy extreme; I had come to routinely expect the worst, habitually engaging in what's called 'catastrophic' thinking. In a sense, I lost before the contest even began.

Although psychotherapy is something I never, ever thought I would need or want, I was optimistic initially that this would be the magic bullet that would stop my depression. I cooperated fully with the therapist and even tried to increase the number of weekly sessions, hoping to defeat the illness quickly. But after quite a few weeks of the same old thing, I actually felt worse than when the therapy started, becoming frustrated at the lack of progress. And, ironically, just going to the therapist forced me to think more about the problems, which only made me feel worse.

Cognitive therapy didn't do much for me, although it may have made me a little more capable of dealing with problems at work. But what struck me as troublesome was that increasingly, I was getting a strange, unsettled feeling, as if a force deep within was haunting me, conquering me. I thought about a lot of things as I tried to understand what was happening. It didn't take long for me to wonder if this may have to do with events in my childhood, events that were painful to think about. I hadn't thought about this in a long time. Since these things happened decades ago, for many years I assumed this was entirely in my past and I had completed any 'healing' that was necessary. A little part of me said this was wishful thinking. It wasn't over.

Many times over the years I'd get a vague sense that there were terrible wounds deep within me, like scars in my emotions. I sensed a tension below the surface. I just didn't feel 'OK' or normal, whatever that is. I felt unsettled, tense, wounded, incomplete. But the feeling generally didn't last long; I wouldn't let it, as I needed to go on with my business. Now the burden I was apparently carrying throughout my life seemed to be getting heavier and heavier.

Looking back, I can now describe this sense of feeling 'wounded' or 'crippled' at times earlier in my life. These are words I use now; but back then I had no word for it. I had never had to describe the deep, indistinct feeling, what I'd now characterize as 'wounded and afraid more hurt is coming'. But a child or adolescent cannot know what's unhealthy or abnormal, so I didn't put such a label on it back then. A child cannot know when constant inner tension and conflict and fear exceed the breaking point. You don't know what others feel and you grow accustomed to your own feelings, though they may be destructive, and you learn to adapt, at least outwardly.

Adapting, for me, seemed to mainly involve a strategy of coping and covering up, because you can't really change or wish away all those powerful, destructive emotions. They don't go away; rather, they take hold of you like a cancer. But I didn't know any of this back then, and I just wanted to be normal, or at least appear so. Appearing normal was the safe bet; who wants to be viewed as odd? Certainly not me. I never wanted to be singled out, often not even for something positive. In school I generally didn't like getting attention for my high grades; it made me feel weird compared to the other kids, and too studious, although I actually didn't study that much. Appearing normal was absolutely the way to go for me. I think I feared that attention might cause people to start to notice something odd about me, like my shyness, or my frequent nervousness. I definitely didn't want pity for what some might feel made me 'mental', or for having a dysfunctional family, or just for bad luck.

As I grew into my teens, I sometimes suspected that I carried a lot more tension, uncertainty and turmoil inside than other kids, but I didn't really want to think about it. So I tried to put it out of my mind. But hearing people describe you as 'really quiet', 'bashful' and 'introverted' eventually will make you wonder if it's true. Nevertheless, I succeeded putting the 'abnormal' label out of my mind for much of the time, maybe enough to give me a false sense of security. But severe inner wounds don't heal easily, if at all. I seemed to have had a deep, unconscious, vague paranoia—that some kind of catastrophe was about to hit. I didn't *think* this, but the feeling was often there, for no apparent reason.

As an illustration of my frequent mood in adolescence, I found this 'poem' that I had written sometime in my teens, probably late teens:

Time knows no mercy
Nostalgia dwells
I weep for yesterday
Savor its memory
Good or bad, joyful or blue
I crave to go back
To then, to you
But time goes on
And tramples my grief
Of many lost springs
Of hope and joy
One lifetime is not enough
To pick life's fruits
The past stands out, touches me
I cry for it
It beckons me
It's part of me
I cannot share.

The tone is painfully melancholy, particularly for a teenager. Reading this now, what really strikes me is the final verse, 'I cannot share.' That was me—as a child and adolescent I didn't share anything personal with anyone. Not my mother, not my father, not my sisters, no one. I'm not entirely sure why I didn't express or share strong emotions; maybe it was just too shameful and embarrassing. This unhealthy reluctance to express emotions, even powerful ones generated by serious issues, is not at all unusual for children of alcoholics.

Knowing very little about depression when it first struck, I naturally began to wonder how and why all this was happening to me. Clearly, severe workplace stress and conflict was a major factor in my illness, but I sensed that there had to be more to it. I thought more and more about that strange feeling of hurt deep inside me, and about my childhood. Someone once wrote that childhood is the biggest part of your life, despite the fact that it typically spans but a fraction of your years. This is because you become who you are in childhood.

It's difficult to characterize your childhood, having no basis for comparison. My childhood seemed fine insofar as I grew up in a loving family, in a home of our own, in a decent community. We were better off financially than most in town. From what I remember, and from what my mother tells me, I spent a lot of time playing alone in our backyard or in the basement. My sisters, Donna and Diane, are twins, 18 months older than me. It's an understatement to say they had a lot in common and did a lot together; they've always been inseparable. As a child, I was kind of a third wheel, and tended to keep away from their little-girl activities.

My mother spent most of her time on chores around the house. She was a fanatic about keeping a neat, meticulous home, preparing a healthy, tasty meal every night, ensuring everyone's clothes were promptly cleaned and ironed, etc. And my father wasn't around much, working long hours, and doing whatever else he did. I always had friends I'd play with, but being shy, I tended not to initiate things. So I was alone a lot.

My relationship with my mother was great, though a little distant. She's the prototypical mother, always attending to my needs, ready to take care of me. Doting on her children seemed to be her calling, as she was constantly asking me if I needed anything, if I was OK, or if I was hungry. I was 'the apple of her eye' and she boasted about me every opportunity she had. My sisters would get in trouble sometimes, but I was always viewed as a 'good boy' who did well in school, kept quiet, and didn't make trouble. My parents' view of me was actually a little more positive than it should have been, because I did get in some trouble, but was usually successful in keeping it unknown to them. My mom was a 'worry wart', always afraid that my sisters or I would be harmed in some way when we strayed from home. So I didn't want to alarm her by telling her all the things I did with my friends, some of which she'd undoubtedly find much too risky. Come to think of it, there were a lot of things I didn't tell her. She'd often ask about things I was doing, but I usually gave her a short, vague answer, which generally satisfied her. I wasn't one to confide in her, or in anyone for that matter. My mom tried, but I generally shut her out.

My relationship with my father was generally strained under normal circumstances, that is, when he was sober. When I was very young, he was distant and often disapproving toward me. I didn't know why, and I'm still not sure today. We did very little together, none of the things other fathers and sons did like playing ball, going fishing, going to the park, or watching a ball game. My Uncle Soup was the first person to take me to a ballgame, a Yankee game. My Uncle Nu Nu was the first to take me out to play ball, along with my cousins. My Uncle Willie was the first to take me crabbing, an old family tradition. My father didn't do any of these kinds of things with me, and as I grew older, this made me feel sad and unfulfilled, since I was missing out on things that could be fun and would make me feel closer to my father. As a boy I tended to be nervous around him, maybe because we didn't spend that much time together, and I was hoping to win the approval that never seemed to be there. I was constantly afraid of saying or doing the wrong thing around him. It felt like I was being tested when with him.

There was a distance between us, or maybe calling it a wall would be more descriptive. I remember one time when I was no more than nine and my family was staying at the Jersey shore with a few of my cousins and their families. Our fathers worked during the week and came down at weekends. When they arrived one morning while we were playing by the pool, all the kids ran to enthusiastically greet their fathers, except me. One of my cousins asked, 'don't you want to see your dad?'

I remember just standing there and wondering the same thing—why didn't I want to go see him, and why wasn't I excited? I don't know what I said, but I remember feeling uneasy or possibly a little guilty that I wasn't enthusiastic to see my father. Something seemed wrong. Of course, as a child I had no way of knowing what it was. Maybe I felt he wasn't usually excited to see me. Or maybe that was just the pattern we unconsciously settled into.

Still, looking back at my early childhood, I wouldn't say the relationship with my father was necessarily so bad that it would affect me in a severe way later in life. What I did wonder about was if the distance between us was somehow my fault. Did I do something wrong? Maybe it wasn't much fun for my father to be with me. I just didn't know. This bothered me, especially when I'd see my friends or cousins do things with their dads. They seemed so relaxed, spontaneous and loving, unlike the relationship I had with my dad. Lacking this kind of positive relationship, I felt cheated and jealous, and most of all, hurt. I felt rejected and unworthy; not all the time, but when I thought about it.

If that was the extent of the problem, it might not have been so bad. But there was much more. What was most unusual and dangerous about my father was his behavior after a night of heavy drinking. He was sheer terror. The rage he displayed came out of nowhere and absolutely petrified me as a young child. It always started with arguing and screaming at my mother, and often led to throwing things or breaking dishes, which my two older sisters and I would hear from our bedrooms upstairs. Although I was scared to death to leave the safety of my room during these rages, especially when I was very young, many times I was somehow drawn to get up and go down to where my parents were fighting. I don't know why; I couldn't really help in any way as a young child. I don't know if it was out of fear for my mother, or what the reason was. Maybe if I heard my sisters going down, I thought I should go too. The noise often pulled the whole family in, either as witnesses, or sometimes participants. My sisters or I sometimes were dragged into the ridiculous arguments my father started, and these could make one of us the object of his wrath. I was scared to death this could happen to me, and it sometimes did. I was especially afraid for my mother, who was my father's chief target. So I'd often try to be a peace-maker, at least when I was old enough to have this capacity.

This kind of thing happened on many weekends over a period of years. I don't know how many, but I'd guess close to ten years. It wasn't every weekend, but it was enough to make me worry that it could happen any time he was out late. The incidents could last one or two torturous hours or more. They began when I was very young, by age four in all likelihood.

I can't remember much about these incidents, but I do remember very well how they started. I would awaken in my upstairs bedroom and suddenly feel a sense of approaching doom as I heard noises downstairs. When my father came home at 2:00 or 3:00 AM, he was always drunk, and that could signal an ugly incident. I was a light sleeper so I could hear the first sounds of trouble, and the fear and dread would begin. I remember the pattern that signaled a rage was coming—the conversation between my mom and dad would get louder and louder. Then I'd often hear a crash—of my dad banging his fist on the table, or throwing and shattering a dish. I would cringe; it's happening again. After that, much of it is a blur.

I absolutely dreaded those nights. I'd lie petrified in my bed, sometimes for hours, hoping it would stop. But whatever emotions I felt as a young child—no doubt a lot of it being fear— I don't remember feeling much as I grew into adolescence. Oddly, I didn't feel much emotion at all at these times. What I did feel was non-feeling, total numbness. When feeling is so painful, particularly for a child, it can't be tolerated. Your feeling seems to go into hiding.

Sometimes there wouldn't be any trouble and my father would go right to bed. But many times he seemed to have some things on his mind he had to get out. He had such rage in him that would explode violently. I could never understand what it was or where it came from. This kind of thing is very strange and unknown to a young child. Typically he had some beef with my mother and the two of them would argue, sometimes violently. Often he called my sisters and me down, or we'd come down ourselves out of fear that something harmful could occur. My father rarely seemed to have any issue with my sisters or me that angered him. In fact, he'd often say he loved us very much. This was very confusing to me. I guess I didn't understand love if that's what my father was expressing.

My father would often draw me or my sisters into the argument somehow, by asking our opinion or by saying something we knew was outrageously untrue. He just seemed to want to argue. As best I can recall, my sisters and I tended to defend my mother, and that could make my father even angrier. It was impossible for me to figure out why he'd do these things, or how to stop them. It was odd and confusing to me that this person who at other times loved me and protected me, would do these horrible things. I was torn between respecting and obeying him the way a boy is supposed to act toward his father, and hating him intensely. Most of all, I was deathly afraid of him. These drunken incidents shook me to the core.

I remember at least a couple times when the police were called because the situation was getting completely out of control and it looked like someone would get hurt. I don't remember who called; it might have been me one time. Talking to the police about what had happened at my house was especially humiliating. We didn't want the humiliation to be compounded by having the police take my father away, so we settled for having them give him a warning. Of course, I was afraid that calling the police would make my father even angrier, but we were desperate.

As I grew into my teens, I became deeply ashamed of my father and was worried that my friends or cousins would find out my family's dark secret. With my feelings toward him dominated by fear and apprehension, I don't think I really felt love toward him until I was much older, after he had finally toned down his rages.

One thing I remember well is that these incidents made me feel small and insignificant, almost unreal. I'm not sure why; possibly because I was powerless to stop or even influence these events. Or, possibly because I thought that if I had been a 'real' person, my father wouldn't have done this in front of me. I felt almost as if I wasn't really there. The incidents were dream-like, as if they couldn't actually happen.

My twin sisters slept in a room together, while I was alone. I had no one to talk with to make sense of what was happening, or to share the pain with, or to provide needed support. I didn't know at the time, but over the next few years I came to realize that the more severe impact the events had on me as compared to my sisters was a likely result of their ability to talk about the issues with each other. I had to manage entirely *alone*, with no ally, no one to talk with to make sense of my dad's behavior.

Fear. Hurt. Isolation. Repression. It's easy to see now that this situation can be a recipe for disaster for an impressionable, confused youngster. My pattern of not wanting to talk about the issue seemed to become my overall pattern of non-communication. And although it makes sense that lack of social support and communication was a major factor in my being so impacted by these events, it seemed to me there had to be more reasons why I was so seriously affected. I had to know, and in time I would gradually learn why I was so impacted by my father's rages.

Considering the number of times these raging incidents occurred, I thought it strange that I could remember very little about them when I reached my adult years, aside from a few of the more traumatic incidents. I have a vague but painful recollection of my mother crying many times during these incidents, which left me torn with fear, sorrow and confusion. I just couldn't understand why these terrible things were happening in my family when we were supposed to love each other. It apparently is not unusual for victims of trauma in childhood to forget much of what happened. It can be too painful to remember, and becomes suppressed. A basic principle of psychology is that something suppressed will invariably come back, and in all likelihood much stronger than before, and potentially very damaging.

The tendency for most people is to deny there's a problem, at least until it comes back to slam you. Suppression and denial of the issues allowed the injuries to fester and grow within me, unknown to anyone and unchecked. My mother seemed to do the same, and she evidently was unable to see a problem brewing in me. For her too the pain, shame and humiliation were unbearable and may have blinded her to the truth. In those days people knew next to nothing about things like the need for emotional healing or counseling.

When I started to tell my therapist about these childhood incidents, he listened for a while, but didn't appear to want to get into it. This naturally surprised me. I expected more reaction, empathy, inquisitiveness, something. He said these events occurred long ago and I needed to focus on dealing with the *present*, beginning with the issues at work. So we continued with the cognitive therapy, which I was beginning to almost resent. But since he was the expert, I followed his direction. Several times I mentioned that I was becoming worried about the possible effects of events long ago. In particular, I wondered if my father's drunken rages may have affected me in some terrible way. But my therapist just ignored this, which mystified me. I thought, hadn't he ever heard of Freud and the whole idea of psychoanalysis?

In retrospect, I should have changed therapists. At the time, I only suspected something was missing from my therapy. This would later be confirmed in my second episode of depression. In connection with recovery from mental disorder, psychotherapist and author Alice Miller wrote that 'the truth will set you free' (Miller, 2001). You must face your demons, learn what happened to you, and thereby release the pain and guilt. Unfortunately, this basic knowledge seemed to be missing during my first episode, and consequently, my illness became prolonged. Dr. Miller argues that psychiatrists and therapists by and large are surprisingly reluctant to delve into childhood events and, as a consequence, frequently fail to address root causes of disorders. This can inhibit recovery significantly.

Getting back to the present, as the weeks became months my condition failed to improve. My mind was frequently in a fog and I was unable to do anything that required even moderate mental capacity. At work I became unable to focus on tasks and began forgetting things, important things sometimes. My awareness of this inability to work effectively compounded the problem by raising my level of anxiety and frustration as I persistently tried to continue to do the job in spite of the growing difficulty. Anytime I felt the fog and paralysis in my mind, I'd begin to sink into a state of worry or near panic, which generally brought with it dizziness, weakness, nausea, and the like. It was getting harder and harder to do my work. I'd often try to compensate by working harder and faster to get everything done. I gave it the old college try for several months, to no avail. I couldn't stop the downward spiral.

What bothered me more than the discomfort of working this way was the pressure and fear regarding my deceitful director and the new department I was under. I was well aware that when newcomers from outside the company take over a department, the changes they make often include getting rid of the veterans. I fought and fought to be successful in spite of it all, but the cards were clearly stacked against me.

All in all, my condition was such that I came to realize the circumstances made it impossible for me to perform adequately at work, and it was actually damaging me professionally to try, as my performance was coming into question. After discussing it with my therapist, I reluctantly went on temporary disability leave. Although I was told this would give me more time to focus on getting better and generally improve my chances of recovering, I felt like more of a failure having to go on disability. In a way, this seemed like a step backward to me. But sometimes you have to go backward in order to find a different path.

After 20 years of steady work, I had come to see myself as a solid, reliable bread-winner. But this sense of myself was abruptly shot down by the need to take a disability leave from work. It's a huge blow to one's dignity, particularly when your family sees you hanging around the house so much, in stark contrast to the 11 or 12 hours away from home every day for the previous two decades. I imagined that it would be much more difficult for children to respect and admire their father when they saw him out of work, lounging around the house much of the time. These concerns haunted me.

Particularly since I had more time on my hands while on disability, my mind turned to wondering why I reacted so strongly to the situation at work and fell so deeply into a mental paralysis. Granted the situation at work was taxing emotionally, I nevertheless felt I should have handled it.

Many times in my career I survived times of considerable stress and pressure. I'd made numerous presentations to groups of executives who often question and challenge your results, and while I tended to get nervous beforehand and in the early minutes, I'd make it through. In much of the time on the job, particularly the last five years or so, there was substantial pressure to complete a large volume of work with a tight deadline, and it seemed impossible to make it, but I did. I had changed positions a number of times and adjusted to new environments and different expectations. I survived several company reorganizations and lay-offs. For quite a few years I managed a unit that had its share of personnel problems, and some were difficult to work out. Once I had to resort to forcing someone to transfer, and one problem required a termination. And I had my share of difficult bosses, mostly in the past few years as the growing strains in the company produced more and more desperation. So, after all this, I thought I was 'strong' enough to endure this latest challenge.

However, having the vague suspicion that I had been weakened earlier in some unknown way, I found myself delving more and more into the past, in particular, my childhood. I was setting out on a mission to unravel the mystery of my demise, but didn't get very far during this first episode of depression. At this point in time, my mind could rarely move out of the clouds and fog of depression.

At times in my life, especially in childhood, I felt like I was walking around in a state of shock. While always attentive to what was around me, and feeling that I was fairly perceptive, I nevertheless felt a kind of numbness or separation, almost like being suspended in another dimension apart from the actions of other people. Life didn't seem real. It wasn't until several years later that I learned it was actually the case that I *was* in a kind of state of shock. According to research on children of alcoholics presented by Dr. Janet Woititz, therapist Wayne Kritsberg and others, traumatic incidents in alcoholic families can in fact produce a type of shock in children. Evidently, my father's alcoholic rages which I had witnessed repeatedly as a young child were actually a series of severe shocks, borne out of intense fear for my mother and for myself. There are some things that are simply unbearable for a child. Emotional trauma can shock a child into a kind of hiding, essentially as a defense. Repeated trauma can produce habitual hiding; the pattern of 'hiding' becomes ingrained in the personality.

What's more, if these damaging events are not discussed and explained by the family in a caring, supportive way, the problem is compounded — the shock can become severe and chronic. The shock condition reportedly can last for years if not treated, and often produces the emotional damage that is the foundation for subsequent disorder.

Could this really be the cause of my depression? So many years later? In my first episode I was barely beginning to learn about the dynamics of depression and other mood disorders. So, my instinct at the time was that this didn't add up. While I suspected that I had been harmed in some way, how could the witnessing of my father's repeated rages in childhood connect to a fall into depression in my 40s? I thought, wasn't depression sadness and despair? Is all this just a convenient excuse? I tended not to let myself off the hook very easily.

As often happens, a fair amount of anxiety accompanied my depression. A number of times I had what I call 'panic deja-vus'. These were like panic attacks, but for me there was always a return to an actual event or situation that had occurred earlier, but with a twist of sorts. Part of it was a real event, but part wasn't. In these dream-like episodes I usually encountered someone of authority, such as a boss, and felt an ominous sense of being controlled or manipulated. This was an absolutely dreaded situation for me to be in. It was perhaps my worst nightmare.

Reflecting on this, I saw in myself a fierce resentment of authority that I had not recognized previously. As I gradually learned about the history and roots of my personality, I realized that I detested being directed or controlled. It's now apparent to me that this was a major reason why my difficulties surfaced at work—that was where I felt 'controlled', often unfairly, and I deeply resented that. Connecting the dots here is not terribly difficult. This intense discomfort with a controlling type of authority can be related back to a father whom I loved but feared, and who could not be considered a fair or trustworthy authority figure. Almost unconsciously, I had to retaliate against attempts to aggressively direct or control me. Deep within, I felt seriously threatened, and understandably so given my history.

The panic-like attacks I often had really worried me. I shuddered and sweated during the attack, and came out of it with a totally blank mind. Everything seemed unreal. It took what seemed like a long time to re-orient myself to where I was and what I was doing. These attacks scared the hell out of me. They also made me feel weak and incapable of dealing with stress.

It seemed reasonable to expect help with these incidents from a mental health professional. However, when I saw my psychiatrist for the 15 minute sessions, she barely reacted. She rarely even looked at me. During my visits, she simply asked me how I felt at the time and took notes about whether to continue or adjust the medication. She seemed to see me as just another $100 of revenue, or whatever the fee was. I had insurance of course or wouldn't have been able to afford the treatments. It was actually difficult finding a psychiatrist or therapist within my insurance network who was taking new patients.

After a lot of phone calls, I was able to find another psychiatrist, one who was much more personable and empathetic. This was psychiatrist number three for me. Over a period of about a year I had to try a quite a few different medications to find the one or ones that would provide relief from the symptoms without serious side effects, which can sometimes be as bad as the symptoms themselves. I tried Lexapro, Zoloft, Paxil, Buspar and Xanax, possibly more— it's hard to remember. Later, in my second episode, I took Celexa, Wellbutrin, Cymbalta,

Lorazepam, and Lamictal at various times. For quite a while I took three or four medications at a time, and often I had to try varying amounts to see what worked best. Maybe I shouldn't complain too much, since the drugs took away much of the pain and despair.

In spite of disappointment with the slow progress, I stayed with my therapist. After about two months on disability, we agreed that I would go back to work and give it another try. I didn't tell anyone at work the true nature of my disability, except for a few people in employee assistance. Being afraid that outdated notions about mood disorders would undermine confidence in me and adversely affect my reputation and career, I made up a story that I had Lyme's disease, saying that it wasn't diagnosed immediately and therefore wasn't treated properly at first, requiring much more time to recover.

But the main reason why I didn't reveal my illness was the enormous shame and guilt that I carried, much more than I realized at the time. 'Carried feeling and carried shame are the psychological seeds of depression,' says therapist Terrence Real (1998). In damaged, dysfunctional relationships, shame and guilt can be 'carried' from father to son. If my father had truly felt the full burden of shame and guilt that he carried, he no doubt would have stopped his rages. But since he didn't fully feel them, it was carried over to me. I was beginning to learn the reasons behind my illness.

I quickly saw that not only did things at work not get better, they actually accelerated downhill. A couple of weeks after my return from disability leave I was given a mid-year performance review, which among other distortions, held me responsible for delays in several projects. The fact that I wasn't even *at work* for two months to keep things moving ahead apparently wasn't relevant. Almost nothing in the review was true. My director seized the opportunity to blame me for the problems and delays in her unit, many of which were due to her own incompetence.

On one project I was blamed for a delay in starting a survey that had been approved by my department, but the written review failed to mention the fact that the department that would use the results, and that needed to provide a customer list for the survey, had not yet approved the survey. So it was impossible to start it. But it was doing me no good to argue these points.

By this time I was feeling hopelessly trapped. It was during this time that I was working with the company's dispute resolution and equal opportunity people. This ended up going nowhere once I lost my case attempting to have the lies in my review corrected. Every day seemed to bring another disappointment or problem. My frustration and despair grew as the level of stress rose. I was learning first hand what burnout meant. Paraphrasing Wordsworth, I certainly felt like, 'the world was too much with me'. I felt a compelling need to detach, to *disconnect*. It wasn't so much that I wanted to detach, but that I felt I had to. Evidently it's a type of self-defense.

Disconnection is part of the great paradox of depression. As sociologist David Karp states, the paradox is that 'depressed persons greatly desire connection while they are simultaneously deprived of the ability to realize it' (Karp, 1996). Disconnection and withdrawal are common reactions to depression, since, as one of Karp's subjects put it, 'it hurts even to talk'. But withdrawal and increased isolation are likely to only make matters worse. The simplistic answer emerging from any analysis is for the depressed person to just reconnect. Not at all easy. Disconnection is likely to be an ingrained pattern brought about by response to emotional pain. Like all pain, the emotional variety demands action to relieve it, or it may be unbearable, particularly in the case of incidents so severe that the individual is essentially in shock. Emotional disconnection is often the response that relieves the pain. Of course, we see that this creates its own set of problems, which will become clear shortly.

Further complicating my problems on the job, the energy I

expended fighting back at work brought me down further and diverted my attention from doing my job. My job performance declined substantially. I realized this was an untenable situation. I made near enemies of my superiors, and took a stubborn, self-righteous position that burned critical bridges in my company. I knew better than to do this and was disappointed in myself. This was very naive—it's not enough to be right. It's all about power.

It was traumatic for me to admit, but I saw where things were heading—after 20 good years with the company, this was how it was going to end—I'd be terminated, probably in a matter of weeks or months. And because of fabrications and distortions!

Someone in my condition does not handle developments like this very well. What made it harder for me to take was that I had been an extremely devoted and loyal employee to the business line in which I worked. When the company was considering eliminating this business line, which had some 4,000 employees, I very boldly and forcefully presented evidence and arguments attesting to the benefits of our products to the larger enterprise. The disagreement between business units was becoming more tense and combative, and I actually risked my job several times by taking such a strong position. A number of co-workers confided that they would never have taken the chance that I took.

So this was the thanks I got. With this series of events, my outrage and frustration shot off the scale, and my mood plummeted further. I went back on disability leave, with much more work to do to get better.

Before all this, I had always thought that if I ever ran into a serious problem, I could count on getting help from caring, fair, understanding people, whether this was on the job or elsewhere. I had that sense of trust and confidence, I guess because that's how it worked when I was growing up, and even in my early adult years. But not in the late 1990s, at least not for me. My experiences at work once I began to suffer depression were worse than I ever could have imagined. At times I thought it had to be a bad dream. Not only was I not being helped in any significant way, I was getting screwed to the wall. This was as different as could be from the early days when I started my career in a very pleasant and supportive environment. I truly missed those times.

On top of this was the cold, uncaring attitudes of most medical providers that I encountered, not to mention the insurance companies. Even the initial reaction from my wife Joanne lacked any understanding or empathy, and actually bordered on blaming me for the problem. But I can understand this because it's not really possible for people to comprehend depression unless they've experienced it. Even my wife, as loving and caring as she is, couldn't begin to understand what depression can do to a person when I first announced my diagnosis.

Her response to me was essentially, 'If you just exercised more, this might not have happened.'

Exasperated, I could only reply, 'There's a lot more to it than that.'

Joanne meant well, but she just couldn't begin to comprehend this mysterious, complex disorder. She also questioned the need to take medication, arguing that it wouldn't help and would only become addictive. This lack of understanding, which is quite typical, causes people to minimize depression, which often leads sufferers like me to erroneously believe they may not have a serious problem. You tend to be influenced by the prevailing opinions, even though they may be based on faulty information.

I came away from that conversation feeling terribly misunderstood and belittled, that my wife acted like my problem was small and easily remedied. She might even be thinking that I was being *weak*, which for me was a real hot button. Joanne couldn't know that, unlike most illnesses, depression conquers every aspect of your being—body, mind, and spirit. I saw that she needed to be educated about depression, but at the same time I walked away with yet more doubts about myself and my ability to be strong enough to weather this storm.

One of the biggest problems with depression is that people just don't understand it. How can they? It's invisible, but insidious. And it's looking like even the medical community doesn't understand it well enough to recognize it consistently or treat it properly. This total lack of understanding of the condition and the resulting stigma isolates the victims of depression, in a kind of prison created by their despair and reinforced by a misinformed society. And what's perhaps most painful is that a depressed person can expect to encounter this stigma first among people *he knows and loves*, including his own family. This heart-wrenching consequence of the illness is one that is especially hard to take.

When I first read about stigma in sociology books, I never thought it would apply to me. Sociologist Erving Goffman, who studied the acceptance (or non-acceptance) of people with 'abnormal' characteristics such as mental illness, defines a *stigma* as any physical or social attribute or sign that so devalues a person's social identity that it disqualifies that person from full social acceptance. The operative words here are *devalues* and *disqualifies from acceptance*. These are strong, telling words. People with conditions such as depression clearly fit into the category of a stigmatized identity. To varying degrees you're viewed as abnormal, weak, or defective. You're not to be believed or trusted. You're seen as fatally flawed. In view of the powerful, pervasive stigma, it's no surprise that so many try to conceal their depression. Having to deal with the likely ignorant, suspicious and biased reactions of others only makes the prospect of recovering from depression that much more formidable.

What's particularly cruel and frustrating about the stigma of mood disorder is that it's not the result of any conscious choice by sufferers, who in many cases could have done little or nothing to have prevented the disorder. This is especially true when the roots of the problem go back to childhood. The stigma is placed on the victim by society, but it's *owned* by the victim, in the sense that he or she suffers the consequences and bears all responsibility for doing something about the problems associated with the stigma. It's the epitome of blaming the victim.

The labeling of people that takes place when this type of stigma exists creates conditions that present additional problems for the sufferer, and which are a gross injustice. According to sociologists, this is an example of a 'self-fulfilling prophecy'. When someone is labeled 'depressed', a whole set of characteristics is attributed to the person, most of which arise out of ignorance and bias rather than fact. The label causes the person to be viewed and treated in a way that inevitably leads to a conclusion supporting the original label. It is self-determined by the labeler, who is rarely able to see that he himself produced the outcome that he had predicted from the sufferer.

So, for example, in a work situation, it may be assumed that a depressed person must be incapable of normal, competent performance, and he is then required to spend substantially more time documenting, explaining and defending his actions, all of which reduces the time that can be devoted to actual work. The work then suffers, and alas, the prediction comes true! I've been there. Depressed people are routinely labeled such things as weak, over-indulgent, lazy, distorted in their thinking, and overly sensitive, among other flaws. It is difficult enough for a sufferer to battle the real, crippling symptoms of depression, which admittedly can affect one's work performance. Additional obstacles put in place by ignorance and prejudice are certainly not helpful or just.

In my particular situation, adding insult to injury was the behavior of my employer, a company for which I had worked loyally for nearly 20 years. Granted that many of the executives and middle managers were new to the company due to an ongoing shake-up, it was nevertheless a painful shock to be suddenly treated with suspicion and doubt. When I was out on disability and had to talk to people in Human Resources, I'd get sarcastic comments subtly questioning the legitimacy of my condition. In one instance I mentioned that I had to see a doctor about my back in addition to seeing someone about my depression.

A young and apparently untrained employee there replied sarcastically, 'So now you're saying your back is bad too?'

I lost it right there. The insinuation that I was looking for additional excuses to miss work really pissed me off. I never suggested that my back problem was so serious as to be disabling. It was just something that needed attention. But in what I came to see as a typical reaction, it was immediately viewed by the Human Resources employee as a sign that I might be using 'minor' problems to miss work, that because I suffered from depression, I might be some kind of hypochondriac. By the way, I instinctively ripped into the son of a bitch who made that demeaning comment; read him the riot act as it were. I was not about to take any more. The sad picture that was emerging was that the ability of depression to disable a person was simply not recognized, by anyone.

For me, one major upshot of this scenario was, *when I really needed help for the first time in my life, it wasn't there*. My faith in people was shattered, along with any sense of hope. I felt completely alone, and sinking fast.

If I had to choose one word to describe how depression feels, it would be 'empty'. Depression brought with it the apparently typical feeling of being drained of any energy or substance. I often felt as if my insides had been cut out; I was hollow. While out on disability, this led me to spend most of the days doing little more than a few things around the house, and waste a lot of time lounging or sleeping. Sleep can be a vital escape from the agony of depression, both the physical discomfort and the feelings of weakness and emptiness. But I always had mixed feelings about escaping into sleep, perhaps out of a sense that I was fleeing a problem rather than facing it and solving it. Part of me said I was entitled to the respite, while part of me felt that dogged companion of mine, guilt.

Although I was able to relax somewhat during this time, benefiting from the absence of work related stress, I always had the worry that I'd have to go back into the fire—whether I returned to my old job, or moved to a different one, which would have its own formidable challenges for someone with a compromised mental capacity, little energy, and an unhealthy, negative state of mind. It was extremely difficult in this condition to even look for another job. I was caught in a type of catch-22 insofar as I knew that changing jobs would likely be the surest way of recovering, but that it would be very difficult to find a good job in my condition. And if I did, it undoubtedly would have been very challenging and taxing in its own way, and I wasn't in a good position to handle this. Reflecting back on this situation, I was clearly trapped in a perpetually negative frame of mind, but of course that's the way depression is. It's next to impossible to cover up all of this extreme negativity on something like a job interview. I don't imagine depressed people have much luck finding new jobs. Realizing that I was so obviously down and discouraged, I hired a career consultant at a substantial fee to prepare me for things like establishing contacts, interviewing, and making a job change.

My moods seemed to swing between anxiety, despair and frustration. There was little true pleasure, and when I did experience a happy moment, a voice inside quickly ended the joy by reminding me of all my problems. When I went outside on a beautiful, sunny day, something I'd normally enjoy, the voice inside said this beauty wasn't for *me*, it was for others. The sun didn't shine for me. It was as if I wouldn't allow myself to feel pleasure.

Anyone who thinks depression is just a more severe or longer lasting case of 'the blues' could not be more wrong. You know this all too well if you've experienced depression. It is an all-consuming force that emerges from within you based on conditioning that is 'wired' in you. It's physiological and you can't stop it unless and until you understand the process and how it began.

I know this now, but at the time a strong sense that I *shouldn't* be feeling this bad continued to haunt me. After all, my childhood and my life in general actually seemed pretty good. I think one reason I felt so much guilt and shame about my depression is that I believed that nothing was ever terrible enough for me to fall victim to this illness. From things my therapist said and from what I read, I understood that many depressed people have this opinion, but they're actually mistaken. A largely pleasant and positive life can nevertheless contain events and circumstances that are sufficiently traumatic to do significant damage. This is especially likely with young, impressionable children, in particular when the damage is done by a *parent,* someone who is needed, loved, trusted and respected by the child.

I was enthusiastically taking in all this helpful, new knowledge, and it made a lot of sense to me. Still, I didn't fully believe it or understand how it applied to me, until my second episode. I'm not sure why this was the case. Perhaps I was not yet ready to forgive myself for falling into depression.

4 Recovery...and Relapse

Trust your wound to a Teacher's surgery.
Flies collect on a wound. They cover it,
those flies of your self-protecting feelings,
your love for what you think is yours.
Let a Teacher wave away the flies
And put a plaster on the wound.
Don't turn your head. Keep looking
at the bandaged place. That's where
the Light enters you.
And don't believe for a moment
that you're healing yourself.
Rumi, Childhood Friends

Unless drastic action is taken to make major changes in lifestyle or occupation, people tend to fall into the same traps over and over. Surprisingly, even a torturous episode of depression may not be enough to spur a person into action. I mean *major* action, the kind that may be necessary to achieve true recovery and wellness.

The concept of *'wellness'* sounds like a basic principle that should be central in any treatment and recovery program. Ironically, however, only in recent years has this begun to happen. The previously reigning medical model with an illness or deficit-based approach has narrowly emphasized the reduction of symptoms. 'Wellness is holistic and multi-dimensional, and includes physical, emotional, intellectual, social, environmental, and spiritual dimensions,' explains one of its leading proponents, Margaret Swarbrick, PhD (2006) of Collaborative Support Programs of New Jersey. Modest changes in but one of these dimensions will likely be insufficient to bring about the true wellness you may have been missing.

At the time I had no appreciation for the importance of this principle, and even if someone had bothered to explain it to me, which they didn't by the way, I probably would have been too deep in denial to do much about it.

In retrospect, I obviously didn't learn sufficiently from the past and was therefore doomed to repeat the same mistakes that helped bring about my first episode of depression. But it's easy to underestimate the difficulty of making a major life change; I had to make a living, and market research for 20 years was the one skill set that could put enough bread on the table. So I stayed in it, despite my fear that it could easily lead again to a problem, a kind of 'career depression'. I thought seriously about career change and the career consultant I hired helped me explore this, but the extent of change I was able to make was simply going from the corporate / client side to the supplier side. My move to a large market research firm, which had handled a project that I managed while on the client side, was a helpful albeit modest change. I knew many of the people, and the environment was more informal and collegial than the stilted, highly political corporate world. I found it rejuvenating and fulfilling, an especially welcomed feeling after the ordeal I had endured.

My 20 year corporate career actually ended in a rare stroke of fortune. After what seemed like years of continual misfortune and distress at work, I was able to work out a start date for the position at the research supplier the very *workday* after my severance package was effective. Upon receiving the job offer, I stalled a bit to wait for the severance offer so I didn't have to resign and get nothing. And I was fortunate to get a pretty substantial severance. My last months at the insurance company were tumultuous and precarious. I had threatened to go to the media to expose the treatment I had received at work following my depression, and I had the many documents in–hand that substantiated my case.

Maybe this was the impetus for the company to offer a good

package to shut me up and get rid of me. Despite the fact that I officially lost my appeal to overturn the fabricated performance appraisal, I suspect that behind the scenes it was felt there was enough evidence of wrongdoing that the company wanted this incident ended.

I don't know exactly what he did, but a senior executive whom I had known for many years intervened on my behalf, apparently to ensure that I was given a fair severance reflecting my many years of service. I had worked for this executive a couple of times and he was a user of my research over the years. I always had enormous respect and admiration for this man. Although he questioned my actions in fighting my superiors in research and he knew I had to leave the company, I think he looked back at all the years I worked devoutly and he appreciated my contributions to the company. He worked with Human Resources on arranging a sizeable severance, and I owe a great deal to him. My fortunes were clearly taking an upturn.

With ample time on my hands while out on a second stint of disability, this time for four months, I was able to put a lot of effort into finding a better job, which I managed to do a few months after returning to work from disability leave.

I was able to stop going to therapy and taking medication soon after changing jobs. I breathed a tremendous sigh of relief, feeling sufficiently recovered and essentially back to normal. My thinking throughout the ordeal was that finding a new, healthier work environment was the surest way of recovering. I had endured a long and painful experience, but things were turning out OK. For now at least.

I wondered many times if I would have fallen into depression if it weren't for the events at work. I don't think I'm being kind to myself by concluding that this was a very improbable and unfortunate series of bizarre events and vindictive actions. Many people around the company had to deal with new challenges and difficulties as the company went through rapid change. But I didn't see anyone else get hit with all the things that I had to endure.

On the other hand, I learned from therapy that I tended to have an extreme reaction to anything that appeared to be unfair treatment. When I responded to my work issues with outrage, self-righteousness and stubborn determination, I put myself in a situation that compounded the problem. I was my own worst enemy in some ways. And what's stranger, while I've changed and grown a lot in recent years, it's possible I would *do much of it all over again* if I was faced with the same injustices. It's likely that this kind of attitude inhibits recovery. You'd think that extreme persistence improves chances for recovery, but I guess not when it comes to fighting your employer. Most of the time, you can't win.

I'll never forget that first day on my new job. It was a beautiful, sunny, crisp spring day, and I was wearing a grey wool tweed jacket, which made me feel like it was a special day since the dress at this office was very casual. I think people select their attire not so much to fit the occasion and atmosphere, but to prompt in themselves the attitude they want to have. I walked in to work with a re-born enthusiasm and self esteem. It had been a tough last couple of years at my prior company, working in such a toxic environment. The new job gave me a fresh start and breathed new life into me. I felt valued, worthwhile, and productive again, for the first time in years. Though not one to be flamboyant or cocky, I nonetheless felt a kind of swagger coming back, manifesting a growing inner strength and confidence.

The first few years on my new job went very well. As early as the first few weeks, I was asked to go out with account executives on sales presentations to companies we were looking to penetrate, and I was part of several successful sales closings. Important projects were being assigned to me and it was evident I was becoming viewed with high regard. The clients I was working with on research projects gave high scores on surveys that they returned upon completion of a project and they seemed to be very satisfied with me. I felt vindicated following the ordeal in my prior position. After an accomplishment at work, I'd often think about my prior employer and say to myself something like, 'In your face, bozos.'

My mental capacities, which had been so seriously compromised during depression, returned essentially in full with my recovery, to my great relief. Once again I could concentrate, analyze, remember, and do all the other mental tasks critical to my job. No longer did I feel like the intellectual equivalent of a fourth grader.

My life outside work also improved dramatically as I was more energetic and confident. At home Joanne saw a huge change from the isolated, gloomy person I had been previously. A lot of activities became pleasant again, especially spending time with people. With recovery, my appreciation for people grew, with regard to both their character, and to outward beauty in the case of women. Both during and after my depression, I often felt attractions to women I had just met, or simply saw. I was easily captivated or infatuated, but this was short-lived in all cases but one, which presented a telling illustration of what depression can do to someone who is in dire need of revitalization. Back to this shortly.

I found my tastes and preferences changing in several ways. Professional sports were of less interest, but I maintained very high interest in watching my children's sports activities. Rob, Lauren and Steve were all outstanding, competitive athletes and I tried to go to their games as often as possible. I didn't get to see as many as I would have liked due to work demands, and I've always regretted this. Rob, who's my oldest, played baseball through high school and college. He played on a state-regional championship team and was co-MVP his senior year. Lauren played high school softball and field hockey, where she was co-captain and MVP her senior year. And Steve had an exceptional high school baseball career, having started at varsity all four years and making every all-star team in senior year. He's playing college ball.

What's great about baseball is that it's a such a microcosm of life. You have all the elements—hard work, honing of skills, teamwork, competition, performing under pressure, dealing with failure, sportsmanship, leadership, and much more. Using a game that kids love is an opportune way to develop skills in these crucial areas.

I coached my children's baseball and softball teams all though recreation and all-star levels, so it's gratifying to see them do well, and enjoy themselves at the same time. For all three of my children, many a coach has commented on what a pleasure it was to have them on their team. One great thing about coaching is that you have many opportunities to meet a lot of people and you can readily screen out who you want to know better and who you want to avoid. Joanne and I have met some of our best friends this way. I coached baseball for some 20 years and doing it with my great friends Jerry, Bob, Joe, Paul and Jim made it truly special.

This might seem obvious, but something I tried as a kind of self-therapy was to do more of the things I really enjoyed, and less of the things I disliked. Sounds like a no-brainer, but we all get caught up in the excessive activities of our rush-rush lifestyles, and coupled with the sacrifices you have to make working and raising a family, it's easy to lose sight of the importance of taking proper care of your own well being, which needs to include some enjoyable, meaningful activities. You need to be nice to yourself regularly, even spoil yourself once in a while.

One thing that I found myself doing much more was listening to music. I've always had a weakness for haunting, melancholy songs, and after my depression, this music resonated with me like never before. Rather than find these types of songs depressing as some people would say, they spoke directly to me in a way that was almost inspiring. Maybe this was because many of them contained themes of resilience and affirmation during difficult times.

At the same time I was celebrating my return to mental health, I sometimes felt uneasy down deep that all was not OK, that I hadn't necessarily done enough to restore my mental health permanently. Though I tried not to think about it, a part of me wondered ominously if I could again fall into depression. This feeling did not preoccupy me, rather it hung over me like a cloud that I could see only faintly if I happened to reflect upon my journey or wonder what the future might hold. Like Sylvia Plath's troubled character in *The Bell Jar*, I couldn't shake the foreboding that I might never fully escape my own prison-like bell jar of depression. I was only too aware of the bleak statistics showing that once you have an episode of depression, you're very likely to have another.

After four good years in this new job, I began to feel different. The work that I had heretofore found challenging and fulfilling was slowly becoming empty and meaningless. I often asked myself if this was 'all there is' as I approached my mid-fifties and what I considered the final phase of my career. At about the same time, the pace of work was accelerating, driven by escalating time demands from our clients, as well as an industry-wide trend to tighter and tighter deadlines. There was more and more work to do, and the numerous changes taking place in the company, most notably mergers and reorganizations, created heightened pressure to control expenses and be profitable.

I was once again losing a sense of having any control over my work life. I often felt it was becoming more and more difficult to do the job properly and keep up with the growing volume of work and the increased requirements. If I wasn't bored, I was frustrated and annoyed. My attempts to be reassigned as a way to revitalize my attitude were fruitless, as there were few openings that fit my background, and my unit wanted to keep me where I was. I was back to feeling helpless and hopeless, like a runner on a treadmill that goes faster and faster as you come to recognize the futility of trying to keep up. It was an all too familiar feeling.

My difficulties were compounded by a team leader who herself was struggling to cope with the pressure from all the changes and demands. The easy management style she had used for years, which seemed to work fairly well, didn't fit the new environment as well. In a state of desperation borne out of a sense of being overwhelmed, she became unpredictable, distrustful, and even paranoid. If I handled projects independently, she'd complain sometimes that I didn't run key decisions by her or keep her sufficiently informed. But if I got her more involved in projects, she tended to micro-manage, then complain that my projects were taking too much of her time. What's worse, more often than not the time she put into my projects did not help, and was sometimes counter-productive.

I remember times having to sit with her a couple hours discussing steps to take on a project, and then having less than an hour to do the work by the deadline. She was always painfully slow and deliberate, but she was now completely losing it, and as she felt more and more threatened by the changes, she seemed to also view me as a threat. As a researcher, I could do a lot of things she couldn't, and she knew it. So I had this to deal with too. Her unpredictable, paranoid work style was making it impossible for me to handle the increased demands, which naturally added to my sense of frustration and despair.

Within a fairly short period of time, my work environment went from good, to fair to horrible. While not as pathological as my prior position, the job by now met all the criteria of 'toxic work' outlined by Barbara Bailey Reinhold in her book of the same title—absence of trust and empowerment, weak, self-serving leadership, escalating demands accompanied by inadequate resources, feeling a lack of control or influence, conflicted roles, and more. Reinhold cites numerous stories of the increasing number of clients facing toxic work situations, produced by the changing, more competitive business environment, and the inability of managers to maintain or establish effective, employee-involved styles in the context of the shifting and heightening demands. For me, in addition to having an elevated, innate vulnerability to this type of stress, I was perhaps affected more than others because I was older than most and expected or even required more autonomy, respect and empowerment on the job. In any case, my job seemed to be poisoning me, once again.

As I felt myself sinking, I shuddered to think that it might be happening again to me. As in my first episode, there was stubborn denial initially that I might be falling into depression, and I essentially ignored the symptoms for the first couple months. I thought that it might just be a short-lived period of the blues, which I could weather. But it didn't go away. While different in some ways from my first episode, there were many parallels in terms of my symptoms, most notably my inability to concentrate, to reason, or to recall things. My mind was going into a fog again. There was that overwhelming feeling of sinking, a vague sense of impending doom.

Over several months I tried my best to work through this condition and outlast it. It was becoming harder and harder to motivate myself to do all the work, and even when I did, my compromised mental capacities limited my productivity. I realized that it had become impossible to do my job effectively in this condition. At minimum, the symptoms caused me to work more slowly, making me less efficient and productive. At the extreme, I was at times unable to function, forcing me to take frequent breaks to try to regroup. If I managed to focus enough to begin reading something complex and challenging, I might get through a couple paragraphs and realize that I hadn't absorbed a thing. My mind was somewhere else, often on how lousy and incapable I felt.

Having been through one episode, I certainly recognized the warning signs of depression. When I first read about the common symptoms, I was struck by how long the list was, and how many symptoms applied to me — poor concentration, irritability, difficulty tracking conversations, fatigue, insomnia, racing thoughts, difficulty making decisions, and of course, the old stand-by, depressed mood (Paterson, 2002).

The onset of symptoms of depression can easily have a snowballing effect, since the reaction to the initial symptoms is likely to be one of anxiety and near panic that it's happening again, which of course brings you down further. As in my first episode, among my major frustrations was the feeling that the conditions at work, while trying and 'unfair', were not so bad as to cause me to break down again. I felt that I should have been able to handle it. This kind of thinking made me feel weak and incapable, once again.

At the time, I hadn't yet fully appreciated the fact that *vulnerability* from early emotional trauma makes a person more fragile in a sense and more susceptible to stress later in life, often leading to emotional disorder. This vulnerability makes a person automatically go into a 'fight or flight' mode under even moderate stress, which triggers physiological reaction such as adrenaline release. The end result is often fear, anger, defensiveness or another type of extreme emotional reaction, followed by a feeling of being totally drained.

When I finally saw my family doctor and described the symptoms, he confirmed it was a recurrence of depression and put me back on medication, which diminished the adverse effects of the depression, but did not eliminate them entirely. We both hoped it would be a mild episode that would soon pass.

I began experiencing cycles of symptoms, usually consisting of one or two really down days followed by a few days that were not as bad. But the curious thing was that the bad days were often different from one another. On some of the bad days, I felt weak with a queasy stomach. On others, it was more of a lightheadedness and mental fog. Mondays were almost always bad days, but the other down days could come at any time. When increasing and then switching medication failed to provide sufficient relief, I began to fear that I'd have to take some time off again to recover.

Stress reportedly is the leading cause of illness in the United States, and most of this stress results from work. Workplace stress causes about 1 million employees each day to miss work. More than forty percent of all adults suffer adverse health effects from stress, and stress is linked to the six leading causes of death: heart disease, cancer, lung ailments, accidents, cirrhosis of the liver, and suicide. Chronic stress may double the risk of heart attack. Both depression and chronic stress can weaken the immune system and make people vulnerable to a host of illnesses. Researchers estimate that 50 to 80 percent of all medical illnesses reported to physicians have a strong emotional or stress-related component (Mental Health America website www.nmha.org).

Based on my experience, this is no surprise — depression and tension ravaged my physical health. My blood pressure and cholesterol were elevated and rising. Tension has tended to gravitate to my neck, and this exacerbated earlier problems I was having with my vertebrae and disks, including progressive arthritis. At one time I had two pinched nerves in my back, a herniated disk, numerous degenerative disks, and several vertebrae out of alignment. These conditions produced almost constant stiffness and frequent pain in my shoulders and arms, and numbness in my right leg. I had spent too many years sitting at a desk, hunched over the surface while working, and this wasn't helped by my 70 minute one-way commute during which I was trapped spending yet more time sitting. And, of course, there was the daily tension and stress. If I didn't get treatment soon, I was told I'd eventually lose the ability to move my neck.

I also found myself becoming much more susceptible to a whole host of digestive and contagious ailments, ranging from colds to flu to bacterial infections. And I had a ringing in my left ear that was getting progressively louder, signaling a gradual loss of hearing. I saw more doctors in a period of about a year than I had seen all my previous years combined. There were regular visits to a general practitioner, chiropractor and a psychiatrist, a number of appointments with gastro-intestinal specialists and a couple with orthopedic doctors and an ear-nose-throat specialist. Not to mention various lab tests and diagnostic procedures, which I'd guess numbered two dozen or more.

Though it may have that appearance, one should not conclude that I'm a hypochondriac—until I fell into depression, I was in the best of health and typically went many years without seeing a doctor. Nor did I ever take a lot of sick days. It's unlikely that depression and anxiety caused all of these health problems, but I have to believe it was a major contributing factor for most of them. The unfortunate truth is that depression increases the likelihood of developing so called physical illnesses ranging from heart disease and cancer to a wide variety of other conditions, including, to my surprise, back and neck disorders. But as stubborn and painful as conditions such as back problems can be, and I came to know them only too well, they pale in comparison to the other disorders that often co-occur with depression. This is a condition that can kill, in more ways than one, and too often does. People suffering with depression simply don't live as long as others. I've seen estimates that depression can take as much as a *decade* off your life. Does that sound like something that's just 'in your head'?

In order to get treatment for the various ailments I suddenly found myself with, I began missing a lot of time at work. For many years I had all but ignored warning signs of my deteriorating health, due largely to the demands of work on my time. I had not been listening to what my tense, fatigued body was telling me, that something was very wrong. But now I finally realized it was critical to take the time to get the necessary treatment. I was feeling miserable in many ways, emotionally and physically, and it was clear that it would only get worse if I didn't do something quickly. It may sound overly dramatic, but I felt that I had to view my health issues as a life or death situation, and act accordingly. My health became my top priority, finally. It had become abundantly clear that relapse into a second episode of depression was possible or even likely because I hadn't made my mental health a priority, or my overall health for that matter.

I think that as parents you can easily grow accustomed to a life of sacrifice. You get in the habit of going to work everyday regardless of how lousy you may feel. I needed to support a family and a lifestyle, and had to put three children through college. My day to day life was built around that. I never liked spending much on myself. Most of my earnings went to the house and family. In the past I didn't want to spend the time or money on me, on my health. All that changed. Despite a sharp decline in my income, I resigned to spend the thousands of dollars necessary to get better. I knew it had to be done. It's possible I had made too many sacrifices in the past and was suffering the consequences.

Unfortunately, the costs for my healthcare grew to be much greater than expected, and medical insurance only covered a portion of the healthcare needed to recover. Like many sufferers of so-called 'non-physical' illnesses, I faced numerous limitations and inadequacies in my coverage, including a limited number of in-network providers, a ceiling on the number of visits per year, and high co-pays for both visits and medication. Despite having medical coverage, I finished that calendar year with something like $10,000 in medical expenses, for my depression-related treatments, and the various ailments that no doubt were triggered or compounded by the depression. For someone with seemingly good insurance, not to mention a declining income, I understandably felt that this was way too much to be spending on healthcare. I thought, something's wrong here.

In addition to individual therapy, which now included some psychoanalysis, I began attending a men's support group for depression, alcoholism and anger. Although alcoholism was not one of my problems, these three conditions seemed to run together for many men. It was becoming very difficult to find time for the support group, psychotherapy, the many doctor appointments, and everything else I needed to do to restore my health, and still do my job. I had to travel a fair distance to the therapy and support groups, and to some of the medical appointments, leaving me too little time to handle the growing workload.

Since my declining productivity was apparent to my team leader, and my sporadic health problems and attendance were becoming an issue, I felt that I had to tell my superiors about my illness so they could understand why my work was being affected. I had serious reservations about revealing my depression and did so very reluctantly as I feared that the news could taint my reputation and undermine my career. But I felt comfortable trusting that my superiors would react empathetically and responsibly.

I soon saw that my trust was misplaced. Several instances occurred where my team leader wouldn't acknowledge the debilitating nature of depression and was insensitive to my need to get proper treatment. She said she expected just as much work out of me regardless of my health, which of course struck me as inflexible and callous. For five years I did my job diligently and effectively, and I deserved better.

At one point she asked me if I could get some sort of expedited treatment so the impact on work would be minimized. I was also interested in speedy treatment, but not so much because of the workload, but rather out of concern for my wellbeing.

'I did look into that,' I replied, 'and it's only possible for the most severe instances, such as suicidal cases.'

'Gee, it's too bad you're not suicidal,' she commented in a flippant tone.

I didn't know if that was a poor attempt at humor or what, but I was hurt and speechless. How could someone I worked with for five years make such an insensitive comment? Although I felt utterly belittled, I didn't think that a response was warranted for such a callous comment. When I do react in this kind of situation, I tend to become so outraged that it can only lead to further deterioration of the situation, which isn't a good idea when dealing with someone you report to.

Once again I was encountering a totally uncaring, even inhuman reaction to my illness. I have to believe my superiors would have reacted in a much different, more empathetic way if the health issue was a heart attack or cancer. Depression is no less serious. But people seem to view depression as minor or unreal, as a condition that can be controlled or easily defeated. As much as this lack of understanding of the condition upset me, what bothered me most about the entire situation was that the issues and stress at work were not nearly as bad as last time, and yet I again fell into the morass. I was blaming myself to a great extent, though I also felt that employers were far from innocent in the creation of this exploding but largely unrecognized crisis.

A report by the National Mental Health Association (now known as Mental Health America) indicates that business, government and families lose $113 billion a year from the cost of untreated and mistreated mental illness. This cost, which has nearly *tripled* in the past decade, is due to such things as 'discriminatory business practices' and 'unfounded fears and misunderstanding' of mental illness. Mental health conditions are actually the second leading cause of absenteeism from work. Depression alone results in more 'bed' days than many other medical ailments, including ulcers, diabetes, high blood pressure and arthritis. The report adds that, 'Business needs to help end the stigma against mental illness by adopting appropriate health insurance and human resources policies, and governments need to shift spending priorities.' Increased investment in the prevention and treatment of mental illnesses would more than pay for itself in stemming losses from disability, unemployment, underemployment, broken families, poverty, welfare, substance abuse, and crime (see the NMHA's *Labor Day 2001 Report*).

In spite of the enormous and growing economic costs of depression, the amount of money spent on diagnosis and treatment for it is dwarfed by spending on cancer, heart disease, muscular dystrophy, and other illnesses.

At about the same time I began to feel a decline toward possibly another depressive episode, I met a young woman who had just started working in my office. She was an unusually upbeat and friendly person, and oh yeah, quite attractive. She actually was very much like my daughter Lauren, glowing and effervescent. I stopped by her office from time to time for a friendly chat, or we sometimes ran into each other in the hallway or at the coffee machine. It was always a pleasant experience in an otherwise dreary day at work.

Then suddenly something changed. I felt a powerful attraction toward her as a woman, even though I tried hard to view her strictly as an associate and friend. The raw truth is that men tend to view beautiful women sexually, and this definitely happened to me. Especially because of her age, only 30, from the beginning I sensed there was something very wrong with this, viewing my attraction to her as indicative of a needy and unhealthy condition. Perhaps when your job habitually brings you down, you're drawn to seize something that shows promise for lifting you out of boredom and gloom. I suspected my attraction to her reflected a desperate weakness in me to grasp anything to lift my ego and bring some excitement to my life. Her youth and enthusiasm made me feel similarly, but just seeing this happen to me raised a serious concern for what it said about my declining condition. Looking back, I seemed to be trying to impress her or win her approval. I racked my brain to find a way to break this spell, but the only thing that worked was not seeing her during what was to be a six-month temporary disability leave.

This was my second disability leave in a little more than five years, and I didn't think I'd need the full six months. But I did. If my job didn't rely so much on my mental abilities, I could have worked most of this time. Physically, I wasn't that bad, but mentally and emotionally I was in rough shape. My mind was a broken-down, old machine.

It's curious that each of the other two times I experienced obsessive sorts of attractions was also during the crisis of a major life passage. The first, when I was 17 and about to go away to college, was with a girl I had dated briefly. I'm almost embarrassed to admit that my 'infatuation', for lack of a better word, lasted about two years. I might have made a move toward her if she weren't going out with someone I knew, which was very frustrating. So I was left with just thinking about ways we could get together.

The other time was when I was 32, which was significant to me because I had passed the median age. This may sound strange, but this meant that I was now in the *older half* of the population, which I found very disturbing. I had been married nine years and was going through a bit of an 'existential' crisis wondering if I was steering my life on the right course. A woman with whom I had worked for a couple of years and who was simply a friend, left the company. At that point I felt a sudden, overpowering attraction, which I found very bizarre and could only explain by the realization that I'd never see her again. It was a kind of symbolic loss. Although this attraction soon passed, I was disturbed by the way I was suddenly and unwittingly seized by a veritable spell centering on a woman I had only considered mildly attractive and of no real interest.

As fantastic as it might sound, I seem to have foreseen this obsessive aspect of my personality as a young adolescent. Watching the movie 'Of Human Bondage' with Kim Novak, whom I greatly 'admired', I actually foresaw a possibility that *I* had the type of personality that could develop the kind of obsession for a woman that afflicted the character played by Laurence Harvey. I remember saying to myself, 'That could be me some day.' I was maybe 14—how weird is that?

But it's not at all unusual for children of alcoholics to have obsessive-compulsive tendencies. The mystery of this type of obsessive attraction among people carrying inner wounds is explained by Dr. Charles Whitfield in his path-breaking book, *Healing the Child Within*:

> When we live our life in a shame-based and co-dependent stance, focusing inordinately on others, we naturally feel as though something is missing, that we are somehow incomplete. We are unhappy, tense, empty, distressed, feel bad and / or numb. But to be real seems threatening to us.
>
> ...But our Real Self, now alienated and hidden from us, has an innate desire and energy to express itself. Secretly, we want to feel its aliveness and its creativity. Held in for so long, stuck in such an approach-avoidance dilemma, its only way out is through a specific form of negative compulsive behavior...
>
> When we thus behave compulsively, we usually get temporary relief from tension, suffering and numbness, even though we might feel some shame about it. And even though of short duration, we feel alive again to a degree.

It's as if the submerged, stifled Real Self is longing to burst out and escape its paralyzing purgatory in order to feel the many joys of life, even if momentary.

Feeling that I had finally gained some understanding of

behavior that was so confusing and troublesome to me, this knowledge had a distinctly bittersweet taste. It was satisfying to learn what was happening to me, but the lingering feeling was that this was very abnormal and unhealthy behavior on my part. Little by little, this kind of knowledge would begin giving me some relief that there were valid reasons for my odd thoughts and actions—that I wasn't 'defective' and alone in my unusual and sometimes tormented behavior. I was seeing more and more examples of things within me that indicated lasting injuries to the inner child whom I didn't know was so vital and vulnerable.

A scene from a party I attended way back in eighth grade comes to mind when I think about the unusual need that children of alcoholics often have for approval and acceptance. Many of my boyhood friends were at the party, along with some girls we recently met.

Right in front of everyone a girl I barely knew came up to me and announced, 'There's two girls here who like you—Gloria and Janice.'

I was speechless and more than a little embarrassed hearing this right out in front of everyone. But at the same time, it was a tremendous feeling that two girls *liked me*, and pretty cute girls at that. I've always remembered this feeling, which may be telling given that it wasn't that big a deal, since crushes routinely come and go for eighth graders. But for me it *was* a big deal that I was liked for who I was. Perhaps I needed the acceptance to compensate for something that was missing in my life. While unusual and possibly significant, I think this needfulness was actually small potatoes compared to the direct damage from my father's alcoholic behavior.

By the way, I later asked Gloria out, given that rejection didn't seem to be a danger. We went together for about six months. At that point I broke up with her for some unknown reason. Years later I wondered if perhaps I had felt more strongly about the pleasure of having a girlfriend who liked me than about the girl herself. Don't get me wrong, she was great, but I think I was unduly caught up in just being liked, blinding me to other things. I seem to have had an unusual need for affection and approval, probably to compensate.

There have been countless incidents that demonstrate an unhealthy, fragile ego. Looking back now, I realize I'm a living legacy of the wounds and scars that can arise in homes made dysfunctional by the poison of alcoholism. And while I understandably felt terribly abnormal and inferior upon seeing my legacy, I learned that I share a fate with an astonishing number of others. If you suffer depression, or are a child of an alcoholic, you are in fact *one of millions*. We can take strength in this knowledge. At the same time, each of us is blessed with a wonderfully unique configuration of capabilities and gifts. We have come this far against all odds. Look within yourself and see your unwavering resilience in weathering a cataclysmic storm. Know that in your spirit, in your strength, in your humanity, you are *one in a million*. Despite the typically telling parallels, everyone's story is unique.

For me, it would require a second episode of depression to achieve any real recovery. The five year period in between episodes was essentially a period of temporary stabilization. I wasn't able to get past the denial, the pain and the suppression of emotion until my second episode. In retrospect, it now seems this was the inevitable progression I would need to work through.

Depression can strike suddenly at the most unexpected times. Author Andrew Solomon was at a point in his life where he was becoming established and successful in his career, was leading a fulfilling personal life, and was effectively managing his bisexuality, when depression abruptly struck. Feeling that he had had a fairly happy childhood and early adult life, he was stunned. But he began to recognize the accumulation of stresses in the years leading up to his breakdown—the death of a parent, failed relationships, struggles with his sexual identity, and more. Eventually, the accumulated stress led to a crash, then another, and another. Nevertheless, despite suffering from a severe, debilitating depression that produced attempts at suicide, Solomon steadfastly endured to, among other things, write one of the top-selling books about depression. He came to feel that depression had actually *enriched* his life, believing that it drove him to look deeper and appreciate the joys of life.

I would eventually come to understand this curious feeling, but not just yet.

5 Telling My Story

Telling our story is a powerful act in discovering and healing our
Child Within. It is a foundation of recovery in self-help groups, group
therapy, and individual psychotherapy and counseling.
Charles Whitfield, *Healing the Child Within*

One of the many dysfunctional traits of children of alcoholics can be preoccupation with past experiences that didn't turn out as hoped. No doubt you've noticed by now that I tend to reflect habitually on my experiences, especially the unpleasant ones. Actually, ruminate may be a better way to put it. No, make that obsess. That's just one of the many telling traits resulting from my particular development as a child of an alcoholic.

In any case, in the course of reciting the story of my journeys through depression, this book has been increasingly interjecting commentary about the lessons I learned along the way. This is the point in my story where I really close in on the core issues and come to understand the forces that shaped my illness. This is the essential *deconstructing* of my condition. I hope that the reader will excuse my frequent jump from a narrative, descriptive mode to an analytical one where I relate my ordeals to basic principles of psychotherapy and recent findings on depression. I seem to habitually segue into causal analysis before I'm halfway through a story, even in therapy sessions. Maybe it's a result of my long career as a market research analyst, or maybe that's just who I am. My inclination to intellectualize appears to be yet another legacy of my checkered emotional history. It was actually the source of my drive to write this book and I suspect that the universal lessons I relate here are of much more interest to the reader than the intricate details of my experiences. Beside, my inclination to analyze and understand my situation is an integral part of my story.

I should add once again that, while I've tried to properly apply what I've learned about the science of the mind to my experiences, I am by no means an expert in this area. If any of this information piques your interest, try some of the recommended readings.

As with many people suffering with depression, for me a vital element in my recovery was trying to *understand what had happened to me,* and become able to talk about it—finally. I absolutely had to learn the origin of my condition, and this turned out to be good in a way. Learning how and why a mental disorder befell you helps to remove the guilt and shame, since many sufferers feel a profound sense of responsibility and fault for having the illness. I certainly did. And talking about it surfaces painful emotions from deep within, eventually enabling healing to occur.

In my second episode, I took it upon myself to learn as much as possible about depression—about its origins, about the impacts of alcoholism in the family, and about the various treatment programs out there. During this time, my enthusiasm in researching and reading material was in stark contrast to my first episode of depression, when I preferred to put the condition completely out of my mind. It was too painful to think about back then. I felt that my new attitude was a positive step toward healing. The extensive reading I was doing and the understanding it brought felt beneficial, possibly as therapeutic as the actual psychotherapy. The activities of reading about your illness, its possible causes, and how to recover have come to be known as 'bibliotherapy', and therapists are increasingly recommending this for patients. I was beginning to learn what had happened to me and why—why I fell into this morass. In short, I learned about *emotional trauma* and its effects, something I had never thought much about. Writing this account of my experiences has helped me a great deal to surface the traumatic issues that I had repressed for many years, and to complete the essential process of grieving, which is necessary in order to heal.

The types of books I found helpful were *not* the best-selling, self-help books with the six or eight or ten 'easy steps' to recovery. These strike me as shallow and gimmicky, tending to be more marketing than psychology. I was interested in three basic things: seeing how others experience depression; learning what steps they took in recovering; and, discovering the roots of my own condition. To me, this kind of self-knowledge would be more therapeutic in reducing destructive fear, guilt and shame than any superficial formula that ignores personal history.

For example, from what I have read and experienced, it seems to me that *cognitive* therapy is not an effective way of dealing with depression caused or influenced by some form of childhood trauma, which recent evidence suggests may account for the majority of incidents of depression. I can see cognitive therapy being a useful *supplement* to a treatment program, to provide a focus on dealing effectively with the present. But this therapy seems to completely ignore the individual and his unique characteristics, as well as his personal history, which may include deep wounds that people carry with them for years. Cognitive therapy seems to be largely a 'one size fits all' technique that says, 'regardless of what may have happened to you in the past, here's what you need to do in the future.'

An example of what strikes me as a simplistic assertion comes from David Burns' best-selling book on cognitive therapy, *Feeling Good: the New Mood Therapy*. Dr. Burns says, 'Every bad feeling you have is the result of your distorted negative thinking.' Does he really mean *every* bad feeling? Are the thoughts always *distorted*? Are the feelings always the result of *thinking*? Or might they sometimes result from the effects of severe trauma that occurred previously? Emotion can spring automatically from within, not necessarily as a result of thought. Burns goes on to write, 'Intense negative thinking always accompanies a depressive episode, or any painful emotion.' But isn't negative thinking merely a symptom of depression? What's most important is to look for the *causes* of the illness.

Having said this, I must add that my experience definitely shows that habitual negative thinking tends to accompany depression, and it needs to be minimized for your own good. While I would certainly concede that ingrained negative thinking brought on by depression can serve to prolong or compound your problems, what I object to is the simplistic notion that one can dispense with depression by simply deciding to think positively. Despite the best-selling status of Burns' book, I believe that a more accurate and comprehensive account of the deep-seated nature of depression comes from the work of psychotherapist Terrence Real, who in *I Don't Want to Talk About It* asserts, 'In a way, trauma memory is not memory at all; it is a form of *reliving.*' Using the example of a boy who was abandoned as a young child and in later years encounters the stress of rejection, Real says the man again becomes that young boy, and looks at the world 'through the lens of that abandoned child.' The tragedy of early trauma is that it repeatedly compromises later reactions to stress.

Real expounds on this point, adding a summary account of research on trauma done by pioneering researcher Bessel van der Kolk, who found that traumatized people don't react to stress the way other people do. More precisely, 'under pressure they may feel or act as if they were being traumatized all over again.'

This is a simple but powerful statement. People in situations such as mine do not simply *feel* stress as most people do, you can actually *relive* the original, severe traumatic emotions. It is completely unconscious, invisible, and insidious. You do not choose it. It's almost as if you become that wounded, innocent child again. Curiously, many times I have felt as if I had never matured emotionally beyond the level of a child. I couldn't imagine myself doing the things that my father's generation did, like having to work fulltime as a young teenager, or fighting hand to hand combat, day after day after day. I'm beginning to understand why.

The fact that this phenomenon of reliving trauma is observed in animal behavior also suggests that it is an inherent and unavoidable part of the make-up of a wounded individual. You can work with it, but you can't deny or ignore it. And you certainly can't be 'blamed' for it.

I could understand now why the stress I felt leading up to my burnout impacted me much more than it would have affected most other people. In effect, you're already carrying substantial stress around with you all the time, which is the tension and burden of emotional wounding that you experienced earlier. Any stress that you encounter day to day is on top of that. The mind and body are 'hard-wired' based on earlier events to react in a certain way to stress. Unless steps are taken to remedy the problem through means such as therapy, the extreme reactions to stress by a previously traumatized person appear to be automatic. It is programmed inside of us.

Learning this was a bittersweet moment of eureka for me— now I see! It was also a consolation of sorts—that I was not in some way weak or inferior for having collapsed, even temporarily, under the weight of events and circumstances that can be unbearable to those with a built-in vulnerability to depression or anxiety disorder. It is the body as well as the mind that is reacting so intensely to the stress, in a way that is virtually automatic, beyond the reach of willpower or determination or strength as we normally conceive.

Depressive behavior is so much more than negative thinking. Cognitive therapy seems to ignore the powerful dynamics of the mind-body subjected to repeated, intense stress from an early age. Based on my experience with cognitive therapy, I would have no objection to using it to re-focus negative, destructive thinking as long as it is supplemented as needed with techniques to surface and resolve any deep-seated issues or scars. People who haven't had the misfortune of suffering with severe traumatic wounds cannot appreciate their devastating power and resilience, and this applies to professionals as well.

The most credible analyses of depression for me are the ones done by people who are both students of the illness as well as sufferers, who know the experience as only a person who has lived it could. For one, I've found the tone of a book written by a mental health 'consumer' (sufferer) to be noticeably different than others—there's a depth and understanding and sensitivity that's usually missing from books written by someone who hasn't experienced the unbearable anguish of the disorder. As a result, advice from the latter can sometimes be superficial and off-target. And frankly, I'm offended by flippant comments and attempts at humor such as those in the book *Feeling Good*. Perhaps the book would have had more credibility with me if the author could have spoken first hand about how a mood disorder feels, but then he probably wouldn't have been so inclined to joke. The greater sensitivity and credibility of fellow consumers / sufferers are reasons behind the move by support organizations such as the Depression and Bipolar Support Alliance and Collaborative Support Programs of New Jersey to increasingly use mental health 'peers' to assist in recovery efforts.

Similarly, without having experienced the torment of depression, it's possible for author Thomas Moore to write about the wonderful 'gifts of depression' without adequately conveying the terrible downside. Granted that depression can lead to positive changes for a victim and fuller realization of his potential, but this is *only if* the victim endures and achieves some recovery. That's a pretty big 'if'. Until then, he must suffer through the horrific symptoms. Fierce and devastating, these symptoms can conquer the psyche and obliterate the soul. Rarely is this recognized by those fortunate enough to have never suffered these symptoms. Moore's *Care of the Soul* is an exceptional book in many respects, but just because it's a best-seller doesn't at all mean that it's accurate and balanced throughout. In fact, I think best-sellers are often books that simply sound nice and comforting. The truth is often confusing, complex and disconcerting. As a matter of fact, based on my formal education and my learnings from consumer research that I've done, as well as my general observations, when everything seems to fit together in a nice, neat way, leaving no unanswered questions, it most likely is *not* the truth. It's just never that simple, especially when we're talking about human behavior. Reality is far richer than simple concepts.

I never thought something like post traumatic stress disorder (PTSD) would apply to me. One day while reading a description of it, I was startled to see how I could identify with so many of the symptoms, for example, a paralysis or numbness of emotions, feelings of guilt, and worry or anxiety about the future, a type of 'hyper-vigilance'. And I wondered if the way I often become unduly startled by a loud noise might trace back in some way to my father's drunken rages, which were typically signified by a crashing sound that I'd hear from my bedroom. However, most of the descriptions of PTSD referred to a single obvious trauma or series of traumas within a limited time, rather than repeated, less blatant traumas occurring over a period of years. These criteria for 'qualifying' seem very arbitrary insofar as the symptoms are most important.

Physician and psychotherapist Charles Whitfield defines PTSD more liberally and broadly than most therapists and psychiatrists. In his pioneering book on recovery and inner growth, *Healing the Child Within*, Whitfield contends that PTSD may result from what many people would consider less severe traumas that may have occurred *repeatedly* over a period of time, possibly many years earlier. What is significant is that when the traumas take place in childhood, and at the hands of a *parent*, the devastating effects are multiplied. Since young children are so impressionable and vulnerable, and so totally dependent upon parents, emotional trauma caused by a parent can be overwhelming. Emotional and mental trauma may carry a serious threat of violence even when there is no actual violence. A child simply has no way to know where a threatening event is going.

I saw myself jumping off the pages when I read Whitfield's analysis of PTSD. It began to explain a vague sense I sometimes had of reliving some horrible event. Although I could not pinpoint anything specific about the trauma—what it was or exactly when it occurred—the sensation was like a sudden mental flash of a terrible event that happened long ago and shook me to the core. It would pass so quickly that I couldn't get a handle on what had actually happened. These incidents were like after-shocks of a powerful earthquake. The 'panic deja-vus' that I described earlier were one type of aftershock.

Dr. Whitfield's most recent work presents a wealth of compelling evidence about the role that childhood trauma plays in subsequent mental or mood disorders such as depression, generalized anxiety, addictions, personality disorders, and more (see his books, *The Truth about Depression* and *The Truth about Mental Illness*). This evidence, based on a review of hundreds of studies conducted by numerous, independent medical researchers and scientists worldwide, indicates that childhood trauma is a much more important causal factor than previously thought. Although the biological / genetic model of mental illness continues to prevail, somewhat inexplicably, the latest research is revealing that childhood trauma is the predominant causal factor in depression and other mental disorders.

While I'm not a degreed health professional and in no position to evaluate this argument, it definitely rings true for me, being consistent with my own experience. For a long time, I have felt wounded deep inside, and this wound crippled me emotionally and brought out anger and frustration. I would have no way of knowing if depression sometimes occurs in people who did not experience earlier trauma, but I can certainly attest to the damaging effects of early trauma on me. Evidently, mental health theory has been slow to recognize the full impact of trauma and its link to depression and other emotional disorders, but the work of Charles Whitfield, Terrence Real and others appears to be changing this.

Most people can easily appreciate how a highly traumatic event such as violent physical abuse, rape or sexual abuse can have devastating effects on a child. But with the invisible effects of less blatant, non-physical traumas that are repeated again and again, generating continual fear in a child, the damage is not easily appreciated. Possibly biased somewhat from my own experiences, I would think that the repeated, non-physical trauma, though possibly less harmful at any one time, could do more harm over time. As opposed to a one-time event, each time the child is subjected to the threat, there is a return of overpowering emotions of fear, dread, shame and guilt, triggering an emotional shut-down. There is a reaction of, 'No, this cannot be happening again!' But it does happen again and again and again. A child can't help but feel that nothing can be done about it. Through the continually repeated pattern, the dread, fear and emotional shut-down are thereby reinforced and can become entrenched as part of the child's personality. Increasingly, evidence is emerging that demonstrates the cumulative effects of emotional trauma.

In a curious way, learning of this argument about the primary role of early trauma leading to emotional disorders was more good news than bad to me. I thought, how could I be responsible or guilty about my fall into depression if the major causes were way back in childhood? To me it was like suddenly getting a perfect *alibi* for my condition, relieving some of the perplexing, stubborn guilt I've felt for in some way being responsible for my illness. At the same time, I was a bit skeptical at the outset and needed to learn more about how exactly these kinds of childhood incidents could be so damaging.

That was my initial reaction, which exemplified my difficulty grasping the magnitude of what I was learning. The knowledge that *I* might be a victim of some kind of chronic post traumatic stress disorder slowly hit me, and a number of emotions began to surface as I emerged from the confusion and disbelief. Can this be true? Isn't this a serious disorder? How could I have lived with this so long—more than 40 years? Why wasn't this diagnosed much earlier? I had seen so many physicians with so many specialties. I had taken so many tests, and described my symptoms ad nauseum so many times. Maybe I'm mistaken, but I had the sense that no one really cared enough to look closely and diagnose me properly.

This may have been somewhat of an overreaction, to which I feel entitled, by the way, in view of the seriousness of the issue. I learned from my therapist that the treatment for depression is essentially the same as that for PTSD. That is, you try to recall the traumatic events, get in touch with your feelings, try to open up and resolve the issues, and you can begin to heal. So, as it turned out, it was in a sense academic that I seemed to have a kind of long-term PTSD in addition to depression, because I was in essence being treated for it anyway in conjunction with the depression. Still, I would really have wanted to know the whole story. Having PTSD isn't exactly trivial.

Actually, thinking about this kind of long-term shock reaction to childhood trauma, for at least the hundredth time, I still can't fully comprehend it in terms of it *happening to me*. I do grasp a little more each time I consider the symptoms, which fit me to a tee. It's takes a long time for this to sink in.

One thing that is confusing and unsettling is that the symptoms of PTSD are so similar to depression that it's possible many people are being misdiagnosed as depressed. This is suggested by Charles Whitfield in his latest summary of the extensive research on the relationship of trauma to depression, contained in his book *The Truth about Depression*. Whitfield's review of the research found that, 'PTSD can mimic nearly every diagnostic criterion of depression.' Granted that many depressed people also have PTSD (as many as 4 in 5 according to studies reviewed by Dr. Whitfield), the whole situation leaves me bewildered about what disorder or disorders I truly have, and does it really make any difference if I have *both* PTSD and depression?

I have to say that my own interpretation is that my symptoms fit closer to PTSD than to depression, for what that's worth. Whitfield explains that 'depression' is a common element or symptom of PTSD, which is much more widespread than previously believed. Curiously, none of the eight or so psychiatrists and psychotherapists I've seen ever mentioned PTSD, only depression. It was only upon reading about the effects of trauma that I discovered how my symptoms suggested PTSD, which Whitfield calls the 'great masquerader'. Thinking back to my repeated incidents of distress, this makes a lot of sense to me. For one, when I think about the way I react to sudden loud noises, especially during times of stress, I realize that my extreme reaction is way out of proportion to the noise. My insides suddenly jump and, it's hard to express, but I often feel immediately possessed by darkness and dread. Although this doesn't last long, I have noticed that my mood afterwards would be less pleasant, for example, I'd be annoyed, irritable, or withdrawn. This could very well suggest PTSD. And this is likely just one aspect of my reaction to stress that might indicate PTSD—the other reactions probably being so subtle or invisible that I'm not even aware of them.

It may be commonplace that people are walking around with a type of PTSD and have absolutely no idea. Again, this extreme reaction to possible danger, which is instinctive and automatic, is a process encoded in the *body*; it is not a voluntary mental choice that we make. Brain research has found that it reacts to fear and threats much faster than it could possibly think or reason

(Cozolino, 2002; Johnson, 2004). And severe or repeated emotional trauma, especially in the early, developmental years, can cause exaggerated response to danger. It seems to me that since the brain commands the overall nervous system that first reacts to perceived danger, disorders such as depression cannot simply be 'in your head', certainly not in the sense that it's in your thoughts. It's wired into your nervous system.

I don't know exactly what to think about the confusion in diagnosis, but a person in this situation would be understandably upset by the inability of mental health professionals to properly diagnose, explain and treat these disorders. It's a shameful mess. And, unfortunately, a trauma sufferer's plight can be still worse, as in the case of the many young men returning from risking their lives in the middle-east only to find an uncaring military bureaucracy unwilling to recognize and treat the mental and emotional wounds caused by service to their country. This disgraceful failure to respond to traumatic stress disorders in such situations is perhaps the ultimate injustice.

It's become apparent that the main element of my childhood trauma was *fear*, primarily fear for my *mother's safety* when my father had one of his many drunken rages. We never knew what he was going to do once he started throwing things around, breaking dishes or glasses, or repeatedly banging his fists on the table, all the while screaming about some issue or another I didn't understand. This rage and verbal abuse was usually directed at my mother and it could go on for hours. No doubt fear for myself was also a factor. Never knowing where these rages would lead or how long they'd last, I became paralyzed with apprehension and dread. It was a living nightmare. I felt powerless to do anything. Fear is an incredibly powerful and damaging emotion, and when repeatedly reinforced, it can produce a conditioned response. It becomes biochemical, the release of stress hormones effectively removing reasoned response from the arsenal of weapons. The body effectively seizes control from the mind.

I think these incidents produced damage over and above that caused by a child's intense fear. My memory of these events is very spotty, but I recall incidents when my father's verbal assault on my mother as a wife was so vicious that I felt my mother's terrible pain and humiliation. And I felt a shame hanging over my entire family for being associated in any way with such a disgrace. When I became old enough to know and to take some kind of action, I sometimes tried to comfort my mother after my father's attacks, or even try to stop them. I hated and feared my father during and just after these incidents.

Looking back at my childhood, I feel a haunting and painful *loss*—of a relationship with my father, of innocence and hope. Early on I sensed a poisoned character to my childhood, in contrast to the seemingly easy, unburdened experiences of friends. As I reflect on those days, it's clear now that I was much different from other children, wounded or defective in some way. As a youngster I was extremely shy and solitary, always uncertain and timid about dealing with people or trying new things. I tended to worry a lot. I didn't know then, but my condition was beyond borderline and must have been nearly pathological. I never really knew what carefree or secure felt like.

As I grew and matured, I began to overcome many of these constraints, but unfortunately, not completely. In sports, in school, and in dealings with other kids, I was determined to be strong, persistent and respected—in my *behavior*. I was competitive in most sports I tried, and very successful at one, track and field. I was a top student throughout school, always had a group of friends I'd hang around with, and many of us were elected class officers or student council officers. I was elected several times to positions on the student council, and was even voted 'most likely to succeed' in my class. But all this time, doubt and anxiety simmered *inside*, which I always kept to myself. It was silent turmoil.

As I learned more about depression, an unsettled sense grew in me that I had not yet let go of these problems. Unresolved issues remained; I had not come to terms with all the events, not by a long shot. For one, it appeared that I hadn't completed all the *grieving* that needed to be done. I may have repressed this for a long time, and now I suspected that I needed to feel and grieve for myself—my wounded Inner Child, for my mother who suffered years of anguish trying to hold the family together, and even for my father. We were all terribly wounded, and we denied the pain and the shame.

Yet, despite everything, in my confused emotions I retained a deep love and respect for my father, and a profound sorrow for the difficult, sometimes tormented life he had. I think of my father often, and mostly with admiration and awe for his strength and individuality. I don't remember him ever wavering. He never doubted or second-guessed himself. He was who he was, for better or worse, and I can't help but envy that kind of self-assured, rock-hard character, despite the wounds in me that resulted in part from this very attribute.

No doubt the very trying times my father had to endure made him the kind of toughened, self-reliant person he was. At a young age, he dropped out of school during the Great Depression to work in his father's business. Talking with him, you'd never guess that he didn't finish high school. He was self-educated and managed to become a polished, successful businessman who wasn't at all afraid to take a chance investing in a new idea. His spirited, entrepreneurial style often clashed with his own father's rigidly controlling style. My grandfather ran the business strictly his way and didn't take kindly to suggestions or differing ways of operating. Nonetheless, my father always worked very long hours, generally six days a week, with little vacation.

Back in World War II, he served as a medic for the Army infantry in North Africa and Europe. I can only imagine the horrors he must have seen. He was a hardened individualist who, despite appearing confident and on top of the world most of the time, seemed to enjoy few pleasures, and became lonely and depleted in his later years. When he was diagnosed with lung cancer at age 63, he didn't seem overly upset—it's almost as if he'd had enough. He wasn't interested in whether any extraordinary medical efforts might save him or prolong things. And it was just like him to forego long stays in the hospital or treatments to prolong his life, preferring simply to stay at home as if nothing extraordinary was happening. He passed away at home at the age of 65. I cried more than any time in my adult life. (But since I almost never cried as an adult, this perhaps is not saying much.) Shortly after my grief at his death came my signature emotion of guilt—that I wasn't there when he died, or that I hadn't seen him in the days before.

Although I can understand the difficult nature of my father's life, I'll never know all the reasons why he had such demons inside him, torturing him and many of those around him. Those demons probably injured him at least as much as they injured others.

It was more than 20 years ago when my father died. And the emotional damage I suffered in childhood was as much as 45 to 50 years ago. Nevertheless, I realized that I needed to go back to those times to address the trauma. I decided to change therapists from someone who practiced strictly cognitive therapy to one who used more diverse techniques to fit the need, including psychodynamic techniques. All I knew was that there were overwhelming, unresolved issues deep within me.

By the way, it's imperative that a person be completely comfortable with a therapist and leave the sessions with a sense of accomplishment and confidence. If not, you should not let inertia or loyalty or fear of insulting the therapist make you stay. With your health at stake, you're entitled to expect progress and results. Do not be too polite or patient, particularly if the therapist invalidates your experience. And do not be reluctant to screen a therapist or psychiatrist before setting an appointment. I did this a number of times by phone or email; otherwise you may waste time on someone who will be unhelpful.

With my next therapist, well-meaning and competent though she was, the depth of our weekly sessions was essentially, 'So how are you feeling this week?' And, 'Why do you think that is?'

It didn't take long for me to see that I needed much more than that, and I set out to learn and find the treatment right for me. That determination and drive was one of the first sparks on my road to recovery. It gave me a cause, a purpose. I changed therapists again and sought out a type of treatment that would be deeper, more effective, and wouldn't completely ignore the past, which I sensed could not be as irrelevant as some therapists seemed to believe.

With my second therapist during this episode, third overall, we focused primarily on bringing out and dealing with my hidden demons. I selected this therapist in large part because he practiced a number of different techniques to suit the need. And he believed in psychoanalysis, which seemed to be essential in my case based on everything I had read. He used 'psychodynamic' techniques such as free association to uncover my hidden beliefs and feelings about childhood events and about my parents. I kept track of my dreams and we talked about them, but it wasn't so much him analyzing the dream as it was the two of us together making sense of them. He used psychodynamic techniques to surface unconscious reasons for my feelings.

In spite of my reservations about cognitive therapy, he used some aspects of it productively, for example, giving me 'homework' to track positive or negative experiences, or to record early childhood experiences as I recalled them. And while I don't understand all the techniques and how they're classified, I believe he often practiced what's called humanistic psychology to show empathy and support for me in view of my ordeals. The variety of techniques and approaches used was fruitful and welcome so that we didn't sit around and wonder what to do with all the time we spent together. That was the feeling I had with my first two therapists—they didn't seem to know what to do in our sessions. You can get only so far with, 'So how do you feel this week?'

At first it was uncomfortable and difficult trying to bring up the trapped emotions—I definitely sensed there was guilt—a lot of it, I suppose regarding the flawed relationship with my father. Shouldn't *I* have done more? I carried a lot of shame. But I was unable to truly feel much of anything in the present. My emotions were always difficult to pin down. During the therapy sessions, my therapist frequently said it was strange that I wasn't showing any emotion when I recalled the painful experiences.

I replied, 'That's just who I am. Isn't that what happened to me as a result of those damaging experiences?'

Many times he'd reply to a comment of mine about how I felt, repeating his mantra, 'That's a thought, not an emotion. Give me some emotion.'

But my emotions were largely shut down, and they apparently are very difficult to turn back on. My therapist constantly pushed me to look at the painful emotions brought on by the childhood trauma, to truly *feel* them, and begin to deal with them. This requires a great deal of difficult, painful work.

From the comments of my therapist I deduced that mine was one of the more extreme cases of emotional shutdown. I've often felt paralyzed emotionally, unable to express normal feelings. Even a simple smile can be impossible to muster. It's not that I didn't actually *feel*. The primary problem seemed to be *expressing* emotion.

In fact, based on my memory of childhood, I didn't seem to express much of anything. I didn't share important events in my life with anyone. My recollection of a typical dinner at my house when I was in middle school and high school was my two sisters going on about something or other that happened that day, my mother and father attentively listening, and I'd just sit there eating. Even if something noteworthy happened to me that day, I didn't talk about it, unless someone asked specifically about it. Apparently I was content with this, I don't know why. Later in life I would feel considerable guilt about not doing more to open up and communicate with my family. Reportedly, it's not unusual for men to be less expressive than women, due largely to the way we're socialized. Nevertheless, I have to believe that my innate reluctance to express myself is an extreme case, driven to a great extent by the hiding of my inner child during those frightful alcoholic rages.

What started there was probably reinforced by other things, like my father's distancing himself from me and his disapproval when I was very young. When I was disappointed or sad as a child, I don't know how many times I heard him say, 'I cried because I had no shoes, until I saw a man who had no feet.' I felt chastised for feeling bad. It was as if I wasn't allowed to express those kinds of emotions. No doubt I took many of his comments much harder than he intended.

My difficulties expressing emotions and personal matters continued through adulthood, up to today actually. In nearly all instances the most I'm able to do is drop a hint or a subtle clue to a friend or family member about a personal issue or emotion I'm feeling. Nor do I show much reaction to an unusual or surprise event, at least that's what people tell me.

Maybe a reflection of this repression of emotion is the fact that I have recently had a lot of nightmares, only some of which I can remember. But according to Joanne, there are often several each night that cause me to groan or quiver or even push or hit her in my sleep. There seems to be a lot of violence and turbulence in me, which may reflect repressed emotions and unresolved issues. Often I'd wake up in a sweat. In many of the dreams I was being chased or threatened by beasts, animals, hoodlums, or other people out to cause me harm. Sometimes it was gang members with knives, sometimes gunmen, and sometimes it was some sort of big, monstrous man. Many times when I was being chased, something slowed me down, preventing me from running away at full speed. I can remember nightmares like this dating back to adolescence. When I was young, I was one of the fastest kids in school and could always out-run anyone chasing me, so my inability to run away in my dreams struck me as strange. As I became older, the dreams sometimes were more subtle, but they nonetheless centered on my struggle to escape someone's power or control.

Dream analysis is not an exact science and it can be difficult to identify what's driving the dreams. Who, for example, were the beings chasing me? Did they represent a single person, or were they symbolic of threats from people in general or life in general? I think it's easy to read too much into dreams and I'm a little skeptical about any simplistic analysis. In any case, when my psychotherapist analyzed my dreams, they generally suggested a deep fear, tension and resentment of power and authority, which conceivably could have stemmed from my relationship with my father. Who else could be chasing me?

The dreams also indicated a resentment of being controlled or managed in a way that was not in my interest, which may also connect to my father. I had a fundamental ambivalence about my father—he was the ultimate authority, but I learned early on that I couldn't respect and trust his authority because of its destructive and unpredictable nature. So I developed an innate suspicion of authorities, sometimes even resentment.

This explains some of the difficulties I had at the workplace when I had a boss with an over-bearing, directive style, as opposed to a softer, consensus-building style. I really didn't like the directive types, and I eventually had to let them know this, which of course isn't a good idea career-wise. I suppose it's possible that, in adulthood, the creatures chasing me in my dreams were my superiors at work. Particularly in the last ten years or so, I have found it counterproductive and quite annoying when someone, even a superior, who does not and cannot know as much about my projects as me, attempts to give me direction that is contrary to my own ideas. More so as I get older, I just don't like being told what to do. I don't know how much of this attitude traces back to my father, the original authority figure in my life, and his lack of credibility and trustworthiness in my eyes. But it's very likely there's a connection.

My therapist, noting that my discussions of these early experiences and my feelings about them were distant and strictly factual, observed that I had gone 'from the heart to the mind', where I was more comfortable. My account of these traumatic experiences was analytical rather than personal and emotional. I didn't reveal the hurt, and therefore, it was much more difficult to surface the emotional pain and deal with it. I don't know if this was a completely unconscious act, or if there was substantial conscious intent. But I do know that revealing hurt to others made me very uncomfortable, possibly because it implied *weakness* to me, which was unacceptable. My father always expected *strength* from a man, a trait that probably resulted from his need to work during the Depression, his role as a medic in the infantry during World War II, and other aspects of his challenging life. And I tried to show the strength my father expected, despite the inner uncertainty and pain. Consequently, the last thing I wanted from people was pity.

I had thought I was a pretty 'easy' patient for psychotherapy because of my research on depression and my ability to understand the issues. However, I was actually proving to be a difficult subject, because I was staying 'in my head', and shutting off my heart, where the pain lived. This requires longer, more intensive therapy to once again truly *feel* the pain inside, which is prerequisite to healing. This is hard for me. My first instinct is to figure out what happened and why, which, of course, is staying in my mind, not my heart.

Anyway, I feel much better when I understand what happened to me, so I'll continue to examine and analyze, even as I work on my feelings. In *The Adult Children of Alcoholics Syndrome*, therapist Wayne Kritsberg fills in more pieces to the puzzle. When I witnessed my father's drunken rages all those times as a young child, it brought tremendous, unbearable fear. The fear may have been more for my mother's safety than for myself. Since a child cannot deal with that kind of intense fear and trauma when it occurs repeatedly for years, the shock left me emotionally shut-down and numb.

People simply cannot live in constant pain. If there is a means of ridding themselves of the pain, people will tend to seize upon it. Through therapy I learned that my emotional shutdown was a *defense mechanism* whereby I would repress emotions that brought pain and discomfort. It helped me survive. As a result of countless times witnessing verbal abuse to my mother and uncontrolled rage from my father after drinking, compounded by an unhealthy and tense overall relationship with him, my emotions were brutally assaulted. This is an intense shock to the system, which in turn leads to defense mechanisms that closed me off from the fear and pain. However, when painful emotions are cut-off in defense, *all emotions* are apparently affected similarly. Severe emotional numbness can result. It certainly did for me—I was left almost totally numb emotionally.

If the traumatic events are dealt with openly and fully, the child can recover from this shock. But openly handling such problems is rare in alcoholic and dysfunctional families. So, the child can carry the wounds for many years, and may *never* recover. The shock stemming from the trauma becomes chronic and may represent PTSD. You may suspect something is amiss, but you apparently can walk around your whole life with this latent condition of shock without really knowing it, since you've never felt any other way. You don't know how other people feel, so you just don't know any better. As with countless others who suffered childhood trauma, the condition of chronic shock was the initial vulnerability that resulted in my depression when significant stresses occurred later in life, which is bound to occur to most people. In a nutshell, all the indications are that witnessing my father's numerous, uncontrollable rages as a child was the foundation of my adult depression, no doubt compounded by a degree of fatherly neglect and disapproval.

Still, I long wondered why my father's drunken rages had hit me so hard, harder, for example, than they seemed to have affected my twin sisters Donna and Diane, although I know they were certainly impacted as well, having to endure more than their share of burdens and heartaches. They just seemed much more relaxed and comfortable with my father, for whatever reason, while I almost always felt a wall, a tension between us. I seemed to look at every interaction as another test with my father, and that I had better pass this one because I was failing overall. In short, as a young child and into adolescence, I was afraid of him. And if there's one thing I've learned it's that fear can do untold damage to a developing child, especially when a parent is the source.

The answer turns out to be quite simple—at least what I believe now is the answer. A key factor that likely reduced the impact on my sisters was that they had each other for support, while I was essentially on my own, unable to talk about these frightening incidents with anyone. Being twins, my sisters were extremely close and did everything together, making support for problems readily available. In the language of author and psychotherapist Alice Miller, my sisters served as 'helping witnesses' to each other, enabling them to deal openly with the traumatic incidents rather than repress them. When you talk about danger and fear with someone in a supportive way, you can temper the effects. I now realize this was a huge factor in softening the impact for my sisters. Largely due to my profound sense of shame and the severe emotional suppression caused by the incidents, I wouldn't or couldn't talk about it. Consequently, I could receive no empathy or support regarding the traumatic events, which compounded the damage.

The fact that I was a year and a half younger than my sisters must have also factored into the way the incidents affected me. I also wonder if the effects of the alcoholic rages were magnified for me because, up to my teens, I was never really sure if I had my father's approval. In the feud between my parents, I was sometimes caught in the cross fire, since my father always considered me to be Mommy's son first and foremost. Lack of a sense of approval could only compound the strained relationship with my father and exacerbate my insecurity. This I imagine would tend to prolong or even add to the existing shock from the earlier trauma. According to best selling author Janet Woititz, the constant tension and anxiety present in families of alcoholics are internalized in the children, who may carry the burden for many years.

It seems to be human nature that when we feel victimized in some way, we ask questions like, 'why me?' or, 'how could this happen?' Preoccupied with our problem and its damaging effects, rarely do we seem to consider the possibility that it could have been much worse and that we actually may have been fortunate in some respects. It's not that this bit of fortune could offset the overall problem, but I think it's something important and helpful to think about.

In my case, it was years before the realization hit that I actually could have been much worse off—if I didn't receive the love and affection from my family that prevented the trauma from having much more destructive effects. Granted that I didn't discuss the extent of my fear and shame about my father's rages with anyone, I nevertheless benefited from the love, affection and support of my mother, and really my whole family. While not a true 'helping witness' in the sense that Alice Miller defined it, my mother did try to shield me from my father's anger and fury to the extent possible, and in some ways she seemed to try to compensate for it. What's more, I always felt love and affection from my whole family, including my father, despite my obvious bewilderment about how he could do such horrible things. It wasn't until I began reading Alice Miller's work that I realized my problems could have been much worse.

Miller's analysis of the childhoods of a number of famous people has revealed the profound effects of how childhood trauma is handled. It can make the difference between a Picasso and a Hitler. The absence of a positive, loving, supportive response can lead to destructiveness and violence on a massive scale, as in the cases of Hitler and Stalin (Miller, 1990). So, I've come to recognize the positive things that helped to somewhat reduce or limit the damaging effects of the early trauma.

Sometime in my mid-teens, my father's drunken rages started to become less frequent and intense, and they eventually stopped. Our relationship improved over this time, as we started to do more things together, such as keeping tropical fish as a hobby. My father was then more generous to me and to my sisters, making me suspect at times that he was trying to somehow compensate for the terrible things he did when we were younger.

One particular example of his rare generosity, and astuteness, comes to mind. My father was one of the original investors in a golf course in the early 1960s. His investment rationale wasn't the golf per se, but the land. He recognized the economic equation of a growing population demanding land and housing, and a fixed supply of land, which of course will generate ever rising land prices. His investment grew many times over 20 some years, and he wanted to share the wealth with his family.

One Christmas my father made a gift of 50 shares of the golf course to me and my two sisters, at a time when we were all recently married. Having no idea of the value of the shares, I assumed that I might be able to buy something like a television with the money when the course was sold. I wanted to know the value of the shares, but didn't want to be crass and ask outright. So I tried to be clever. Knowing the approximate total value of the course, I figured if I learned the total number of shares, I'd do the math and get my answer.

During the breakfast conversation I delicately interjected a question, 'Dad, about how many total shares are there?'

My father caught on immediately, answering, 'If you're wondering what that's worth Son, you can pay off your mortgage with it.'

I was stunned— my mortgage was $45,000! That was a lot of money in the mid 1980s. And although we had bought a house a few years earlier, I didn't realize my father even remembered my mortgage balance. He could be full of surprises.

Sadly, the damage had been done long ago and it was too late to have a normal, healthy relationship, although I think we both tried. It's not that there was animosity. In my mind I forgave my father and acted like everything was pretty much OK during my adult years. But the injuries deep within cannot necessarily be undone or healed. For me, there was always a wall between us. I will always regret this terribly, and not just because he was my father. He was an incredible person. There were many times when I found myself envying him—for his unique, powerful personality and his supremely confident, nonconforming character.

In arguing that my childhood wounds were most severe among my siblings, I am not minimizing how my sisters were affected. While it's not appropriate to disclose details here, suffice to say that both of them have developed health conditions that may have been caused or compounded by my father's drinking. I do have the sense that their conditions are not as directly traceable to my father's rages, and they do not appear to be as far-reaching psychologically.

I certainly cannot claim to understand this process. Why, for example, does childhood trauma lead to depression in some, and in others it might lead to alcoholism, drug addiction, violent or criminal behavior, personality disorder, panic attacks, or eating disorder? How could trauma produce so many kinds of disorders? What I do see after all my time contemplating these issues is how, in my case, the early traumatic wounds were intimately linked to my later depression. It is impossible to explain the indistinct sense, but I've come to realize that the two things—the traumatic wounds, and depression—actually *feel very similar*. The primary difference is the degree, depression being much more intense but over a shorter time period (for most, hopefully), while the symptoms of PTSD seem to be more numerous, subtle and permanent.

Again, it's important to remember that for many, depression is not primarily sadness; it is largely a loss of *vitality*, which is easy to see being a result of emotional wounds. Depression is emotional destruction. It is a loss of key tools that enable people to cope. Clearly, there are different types of depression, and mine was borne out of intense fear and the resulting emotional shut-down in childhood. Many people suffering from depression seem to feel similarly, while others may be unable to recall or connect the early traumas that could have scarred them. It is common for these painful memories to be buried deep within and forgotten.

One way to look at the benefits of telling your story is to view the emotions paralyzed and shut-down in children by the 'chronic shock' caused by the family trauma of alcoholic parents as negative energy deep within that needs to be released. Therapist Wayne Kritsberg (1998) succinctly describes the essential process of emotional discharge:

The client in chronic shock has intense and deep emotions that have been repressed for a long time, sometimes decades

119

and longer. As these emotions are experienced and recognized for what they are, the energy behind these emotions is discharged. It is the discharging of this energy that releases the client from the effects of chronic shock. When discharge takes place, healing can occur.

Telling your story activates discharge of the energy of the original shock. It allows resolution and healing. For me, the energy of the childhood trauma and shock was carried with me below the surface in my unconscious mind for *four decades,* until a large enough stress came along to manifest it in depression. That stress was the decline of my career and the threat of losing it completely, which was unbearable to me. It seems that life's small stresses that occur along the way can produce minor incidents of irritability, anger or melancholy, but it may take a mega-stress to bring on real depression.

In therapy I learned that my emotional wounds were compounded by my extreme reluctance to admit them to anyone, which was a result of the particular complex of damaged emotions stemming from my early trauma and from childhood experience overall. These characteristics included shame, guilt, a sense of being defective, intolerance for being judged, and a fear of being seen as weak. All these factors make it extremely difficult for one to open up and acknowledge emotional wounds. The fact is, I spent a good part of my life *covering up* what I feared were abnormal feelings or thoughts. I kept the turmoil and tension inside. Needless to say, these traits can only serve to complicate an illness like depression, through such things as heightened disconnection and denial, inability to face the problem, and the paralysis and destructiveness of guilt and shame. And all this makes recovery that much more difficult.

The recognition, treatment and release of severe emotional wounds are essential steps toward recovery that many experts endorse. The benefits of this process extend well beyond mood disorders. Dr. Martha Beck, an author and life coach who has steered many clients through recovery from burnout and other crises, calls this process, 'emotional surgery', analogous to the physical removal of diseased organs or tissue. In her book *Finding Your Own North Star*, the specific steps that Dr. Beck recommends for healing emotional wounds are:

1. Identify what hurt you
2. Find a reliable, sympathetic audience
3. Tell your story, in full, including your feelings
4. Accept the listener's compassion and extend it to yourself
5. Give yourself time to heal.

Interestingly, these steps parallel the essential actions that many psychotherapists recommend for the healing of deep emotional wounds. If my experience demonstrates anything it's that ignoring the problem, trying to bravely move on without dealing with the toxic issues deep inside, may enable temporary coping, but will never produce true healing.

So, tell your story, no matter how fearful or ashamed you may be at the outset. Release it from deep within. Free it and it will help free you.

And in case you're thinking that the telling of a story such as this could bring shame and disgrace to your family-- realize that it's not the telling of the story that brings shame, it's what happened.

6 Wounded Boys...Angry Men

*Holding onto anger is like grasping onto a hot coal with the
intent of throwing it at someone else. You are the one
who gets burned.*
Gotama Buddha

This is a chapter I didn't decide to write until after the first draft
of this book, out of fear that it would open a huge can of worms.
It would be easy for Joanne to misconstrue and become upset. But
problems relating to communication, intimacy and relationships
are at the very heart of depression, and therefore, overcoming
these problems is vital to recovery.

It's not at all surprising that maintaining strong, healthy
relationships would be problematic for a person experiencing
emotional numbness, disconnection and other wounds
associated with depression. These characteristics are almost the
exact opposite of the traits critical to healthy relationships. As a
consequence, depression can compound problems in a
relationship and may become the last straw. Relationships that do
survive can be rocky and volatile, requiring unrelenting, loving
effort to hold things together.

In my case, an unhealthy reluctance to acknowledge my
childhood traumas to *anyone*, and the tendency to view any
discussion of possible wounds as a sign of weakness, were most
likely major factors in the failure to deal with my wounds until
decades had passed. I suppose this was a type of denial, exacerbated by a refusal to open up to another person even after I
strongly suspected that something was seriously wrong. One
consequence is that my road to recovery has been especially long
and difficult.

For many, the very wounds leading to depression can prevent
one from doing much to deal with the illness and achieve

recovery. Denial of emotions, shame, a sense of weakness, and inability or unwillingness to express oneself are all byproducts of trauma and depression that conspire to prolong the illness, particularly for men inasmuch as they are often socialized to repress emotion and to appear strong no matter what. Consequently, many men tend to be reluctant to express emotions or acknowledge weakness.

Many of the characteristics associated with depression tend to inhibit communication and undermine relationships. As a result, the relationships and support structures that the depressed need in order to recover are that much more difficult to develop due to the very symptoms of the condition. It's a kind of catch-22—it may be impossible to recover without supportive relationships, and supportive relationships are difficult to establish or maintain while suffering the symptoms of depression.

The disconnection alone that accompanies depression can be painful and damaging, stifling the normal development of a person's capacity to live to his potential. In this regard a noteworthy lesson can found in Herman Hesse's classic novel *Siddhartha* about a young man's quest for wisdom and fulfillment. The title character spends the better part of a lifetime in his quest, only able to begin realizing his goal upon reflecting on the endlessly flowing waters of a river, symbolic of life. As he again contemplates his existence, Siddhartha sees in the flowing river an innate connection of all people, all creatures, all things on earth, and a one-ness that had eluded him, a sense of linkage to things much larger than himself but of which he is part. This realization alone can enable him to achieve his life long goal to obtain peace and wisdom.

What psychologists call disconnection is essentially the same phenomenon as what sociologists call alienation—absence of a sound relationship or bond with your social and cultural world. I believe that for all of us, connection to people and to the world that depression inhibits is the only path to peace and fulfillment.

According to Terrence Real, *reconnection* is central to the process of healing from depression, especially for men since they tend to be more disconnected than women. Having experienced disconnection a number of times in my life, to varying degrees, I have felt the intense loneliness, a sense of being lost in a dark jungle, of being a lone foreigner who's morbidly different from everyone else. As I begin to understand the need for connection, I am feeling myself move toward it slowly but steadfastly, a most gratifying development. Unlike my earlier years, I can now walk into a store or diner or social setting and feel an immediate connection to strangers, a sense that any one of them could be me but for a negligible difference. Our genes, our values, our fates are essentially the same. We are part of all things.

Connection doesn't necessarily mean you have to be gregarious or socially active. It just means you don't feel isolated, excluded, or disinterested in people. It means you recognize others as being like you in sharing values, understanding, and common experiences.

Terrence Real is someone who speaks of the damaging effects of early trauma not just from the professional perspective of a therapist, but also from the viewpoint of someone who suffered terribly for many years. For much of his childhood, he had to endure countless, severe physical beatings at the hands of his father, which forced him to completely withdraw deep inside himself in order to withstand the pain. These defense mechanisms, which often lead to disconnection and isolation, may do as much damage as the original trauma itself. According to Real (1998), early trauma 'creates both the wounds and the defenses against the wounds that are the foundation for adult depression.'

By time he was 30, Real had gone through years of drug abuse and depression, had been expelled from school, had a number of run-ins with the law, faced financial hardship, and became washed up in his pursuit of psychotherapy. That he later became a successful therapist, author and faculty member at a prestigious institution is a remarkable testament to the ability to persevere and recover. Real's *I Don't Want to Talk About It* is a successful and highly regarded book exposing the hidden dimensions of male depression. I've found this book invaluable to the search for the roots of my illness, due to insights such as, in depression, childhood trauma 'takes up permanent habitation within him.' And, the depressed man then 'adopts a relationship to himself that mirrors and replicates the dynamics of his own early abuse.' So telling.

My own depression wasn't diagnosed until my late 40s, but it has become evident that I had the telltale signs far earlier, possibly my whole life. I never took bad news well, not even relatively minor setbacks. I can remember many times as a child sitting alone or with my dog Lassie, feeling sadness or regret over one event or another. In retrospect, I habitually blew these setbacks out of all proportion. What's worse, I don't recall ever going to my parents or my sisters with a problem or with any issue that might remotely suggest weakness or failure. This would be embarrassing to me, even shameful.

One strange occurrence that I happen to remember was when as a freshman, I was trying to transfer from a satellite division of Rutgers University to the main campus. Based on my strong grades and test scores, I fully expected this to be a cinch. So, when I received a letter of rejection one day, I was utterly devastated. I remember sitting alone for hours trying to figure out how it could happen, feeling like a total failure. My total despair was way out of proportion to the event. Ironically, a couple days later I received another letter from Rutgers—a letter of acceptance— written as if the first letter didn't exist. Apparently, there had been a mistake in the records, indicating that I had failed a course, which in fact I never took. The bottom line is that I over- reacted to such an extent that I made myself sick, and for nothing.

That was pretty typical for me. What's more, consistent with my disconnection, I talked to no one about this matter in spite of how serious it was. Maybe I was too embarrassed, I don't know. Incidentally, I ended up transferring to Lafayette College instead. Not surprisingly given my nature, this decision and in fact my entire college search process, was done entirely on my own. My family had no role (except to later pay the bill!) because I didn't include them in any discussions or decisions. Granted they knew little about college and couldn't be of much help, but I certainly should have included them more.

If a person doesn't show emotion or open up and communicate personal issues with immediate family growing up, can you expect him to suddenly do it in marriage? At best, it's a slow, gradual process. Handicapped with paralyzing numbness and extreme disconnection, even alienation, it requires great effort to overcome these obstacles to maintaining a marriage. I'm not sure that people suffering with depression are in a good position to make the considerable effort that's necessary. Personally, I know in my heart that I tried very hard, but I didn't do as much as I could have. I have only a vague sense as to why, and it's difficult to articulate.

This is a very complex issue that defies simple analysis, but I have a few observations and theories. One is that when you experience so much discomfort, uncertainty, apprehension, and similar unpleasant experiences, and so little joy because of underlying depression, you need something positive, something that isn't taxing and difficult like everything else in your life. Consequently, such an individual may not work at marriage as hard as necessary. After all, your childhood was difficult, work is a struggle, friendships and dating were troublesome—marriage should be better, right? Aren't you entitled to something stress-free, some real pleasure, something that doesn't require yet another huge effort, for which you probably lack the energy? Actually, I can't say I love this theory, but it may have some merit.

Another theory, which I like better, is that working harder at marriage to overcome the emotional obstacles brought on by depression requires *acknowledging* the depression, or at least acknowledging that you are a major 'problem' in the marriage and therefore need to adjust and compensate with extra effort. As we established, acknowledging these things is difficult to near impossible for many depressed people. It surely was for me.

Possibly the best explanation as to why a depressed person may not work hard enough to sustain a problem marriage is that he is so preoccupied with the overwhelming struggles and pain associated with depression that he has too little energy left for his partner. He is spent. Living with depression takes all you have.

Compounding the problem is the need for the pain and turmoil inside the depressed person to surface, to be discharged. This inner pain, unfortunately, seems to frequently come out in the form of *anger*, irritability and frustration, particularly in men. Anger is no more pleasant for the person erupting than it is for the targeted person, but the former is always viewed as the guilty party, the perpetrator. This is despite the fact that in the case of a depressed person or any severely wounded person, he was originally a victim, someone who has suffered terribly. That is why he explodes, but of course no one understands this, or excuses the outburst. And I'm not saying they should. The point is that the depressed person is caught in a trap—he is prone to anger because of his inner pain that knows no other outlet, but the anger undermines the marital relationship and, most importantly, precludes the spouse from seeing him as the *victim that he is*—he is seen as a tyrant, a perpetrator. The displays of anger prevent the spouse from feeling the understanding and empathy one would receive for most other serious illnesses. People tend not to feel sympathy for an angry person. The depressed person is further upset at the lack of empathy, and he resents being viewed as the guilty party in the troubled marriage. After all, isn't he suffering enough? It's easy to see how this situation can spiral downward.

The prevailing treatment for this problem seems to be programs to cope with anger. This is much easier said than done. More importantly, this seems to be treating the symptom, not the underlying disease, which is an inner self wounded by trauma, and unable to deal with it. Speaking from experience, when you know few emotional outlets other than anger, what do you do? If you're successful in the Herculean effort to control your anger, you still have the daunting task of finding another way to discharge trapped emotional energy. In my family, my father never showed 'soft' emotions such as grief, sorrow, or fear. But he surely did show anger. As a role model, albeit a negative one, he no doubt influenced me a great deal. But I'm not sure that's the main reason why anger often seems to be the prevailing emotion among severely wounded people, particularly men.

Anger is perhaps the most immediately extreme and intense emotion, which alone can express the tremendous intensity of emotions trapped inside. Possibly the magnitude of pain within cannot be adequately released by more moderate emotions such as grief or sorrow. When the pent-up inner pain explodes, it's the equivalent of a super-volcano.

It seems to me that anger is an expression of the destructiveness that is produced when a person is prevented from living a fulfilling life with a full range of emotions. Childhood trauma can produce such stifling effects on the emotions and on the capacity to enjoy a full, rich life. As much as a half-century ago, Erich Fromm, the psychoanalyst, philosopher and author, described essentially this same phenomenon in his classic exposition of humanistic philosophy *Man For Himself*, albeit in a less clinical or precise way:

> If life's tendency to grow, to be lived, is thwarted, the energy
> thus blocked undergoes a process of *change* and is trans-
> formed into life-destructive energy. Destructiveness is the

outcome of an unlived life.

In this book, Fromm expands on the ways in which stifled or damaged experience can later produce destructiveness and alienation. Parallel to the ideas of other experts, the contention is that the severe stifling of individual development also creates negative energy which, unless treated and released, will be destructive, most likely to both the individual and to others in his life. Given all the time since Fromm made this connection between a type of trauma and subsequent destructiveness that characterizes emotional disorder, it's surprising that more progress hasn't been made in isolating and treating trauma as a factor in subsequent illness. Maybe it's just that the experts can't agree. I for one find it compelling that Charles Whitfield, Terrence Real, Alice Miller and others have observed a preponderance of traumatized childhood experiences among patients suffering disorders such as depression, anxiety and addictions.

In the simplest terms, when emotional or mental trauma inflicts repeated wounds, a child finds protection by submerging deep within the unconscious. The 'child goes into hiding.' As described in the prior chapter, the child becomes disconnected, alienated and emotionally numb, which obstructs normal development and can lead to depression or any number of disorders. The pattern of hiding can become an innate habit throughout life. Recovery must consist of 'discovering and unearthing the true self', which is the child within (Whitfield, 2003).

There appears to be a striking commonality between the core ideas of Fromm and R.D.Laing developed decades ago, and the recent work of Alice Miller, Terrence Real and Charles Whitfield. Though these psychoanalysts started from somewhat different places and employed differing terminology, the common underlying theme is that thwarted experience and emotional injury, which can most harmfully occur in childhood, will lead to stifled development as a person and wounds that will bring repeated destructiveness to oneself and to others if not treated. It is a compelling concept that allows us to begin to understand much of the extreme behavior we've always found mysterious, ranging from depression and personality disorder to violent crime and murderous dictators. And the wounds are not simply 'mental':

> Our brains are sculpted by our early experiences. Maltreatment is a chisel that shapes a brain to contend with strife, but at the cost of deep, enduring wounds.
>
> Martin H. Teicher, MD, Phd, *Wounds That Time Won't Heal: The Neurobiology of Child Abuse*

We have been talking at length about how childhood trauma can lead to depression and other disorders, but thus far the exact way in which this happens hasn't been broached. As I was writing this book, I happened to be reading *The Truth about Depression,* one of Charles Whitfield's latest books that presents compelling information on recent studies about the relationship between trauma and emotional disorder. As it turns out, and this is quite stunning, the latest studies indicate that the mechanism by which emotional trauma affects future behavior is essentially through 'disruption of neurodevelopment', including damage to the brain and its functioning—i.e. a form of *brain damage.* Dr. Whitfield reports:

> I have found forty-one studies that show a significant association between the history of childhood trauma and abnormal brain structure, functioning and chemistry...What these tell us is that repeated childhood trauma damages the brain and some of its functioning.

I suspected for a long time that I was damaged in some way by my father's drunken rages, but I never, ever could have imagined anything like *brain damage.* Dr. Whitfield goes on to describe some the specific effects on the brain, which include reduced mental capacities, atrophy, and a reduced size of certain parts of the brain and of the brain overall.

Brain damage—this kind of chilling information makes you really stop and think. The next time someone minimizes depression or suggests that it's not real, just mention brain damage. Mention brain atrophy, stunted development of critical parts of the brain, damaged hormone and neurotransmitter systems, and neurological dysfunction. Or mention that people who experienced unresolved childhood trauma are more than four times more likely as others to suffer depression; seven times more likely to become alcoholic; and fifteen times more likely to attempt suicide. These are telling numbers.

The findings on the effects of trauma on brain chemistry may explain why the psychiatric profession for years has been viewing depression as primarily an illness induced by brain biochemistry, presumably transmitted genetically. But the focus on brain chemistry has been to the neglect of actual causes, most notably trauma according to Whitfield. If it is true that brain chemistry is different when a person is depressed, the latest research indicates that *trauma is what produces* this unusual biochemistry that is present during depression, along with the impaired brain functioning resulting from early trauma. Apparently behavior can affect biochemical functioning as much as the biochemistry can affect behavior. The evidence is revealing that any imbalance in brain chemistry, which has not even been conclusively demonstrated, may be much more an *effect* than a cause of depression. Perhaps this knowledge will lead to changes in the ways psychiatrists treat depression, which is largely through drugs.

Don't get me wrong, antidepressant medication appears to be vital in stabilizing a person while receiving other treatment—it can elevate you from unbearable to just lousy, which is progress. But proper treatment needs to address *causes*, rather than simply symptoms such as serotonin imbalance. Causes relate to earlier experiences such as trauma, and to lifestyle. An indispensable part of effective treatment must include *understanding* what happened that led to the depression, which is why I feel that psychoanalysis and learning about depression can be crucial to recovery. Isn't this one of the critical lessons we learned long ago from Freud? Unfortunately, psychiatric training today focuses on administering medication and increasingly ignores significant childhood events that often underlie illnesses (Miller, 2001).

Can it be that the damaging effects of emotional trauma are simply being underestimated or unrecognized? Fortunately, the issue is getting increased attention of late. Terrence Real has extensive experience treating traumatized, depressed patients, and has examined the research on the effects of trauma. Real (1998) comments that our culture, historically dominated by male values of masculinity and strength, has caused us to deny vulnerability, and therefore deny the effects of trauma, particularly with regard to the more subtle forms of trauma as opposed to outright abuse. This is especially true for men in our culture.

Like Whitfield, Real has identified considerable research linking trauma to long-term physiological effects. Similarly, psychoanalyst and author Alice Miller has identified research that links trauma, particularly childhood trauma, to damage to the brain. For example, she points out that newly formed neurons and their interconnections can be destroyed (Miller, 2001).

Increasingly, medical research is finding that early trauma or abuse may result in altered brain development and functioning. This has become an accepted fact in neuroscience (Cozolino, 2002). As a result, the trauma that people frequently think of as 'only emotional' becomes hard-wired into the body's neurological processes. For one, early trauma appears to create a low threshold for subsequent stress and a vulnerability to disorders such as depression. A 2008 study published by the U.S. Centers for Disease Control and Prevention reports that:

Brain circuits are especially vulnerable as they are developing during early childhood. Toxic stress can disrupt the development of these circuits. This can cause an individual to develop a low threshold for stress, thereby becoming overly reactive to adverse experiences through-out life.

Middlebrooks J.S., Audage N.C. The Effects of Childhood Stress on Health Across the Lifespan

There are many possible sources of 'toxic stress'. For one, having a parent who for years abuses alcohol or drugs can expose a child countless times to severe toxic stress — trauma, essentially — that can result in this type of damage.

Research has shown that even primates suffer these physiological and neurological effects as a result of traumatic 'emotional' events. Leading trauma researcher Bessel van der Kolk (1987) looked at the effects of early maternal separation on monkeys and found that 'long-term neurobiological alterations' occurred, which were behind the psychological effects of the trauma. Another parallel with human behavior is that the monkeys traumatized by maternal separation were more vulnerable to both physical illness and depression when faced with subsequent stress. Similarly, for the monkeys having suffered earlier trauma, any subsequent stress impacts them much more severely. They are in effect carrying around additional stress daily, the result of that earlier trauma.

As an aside, while I by no means want to appear to belittle what's obviously a deadly serious issue, when I hear 'brain damage', I can't help but recall a scene in a Woody Allen satirical movie, I think it was *Sleeper*. When Allen's character heard that his brain would be frozen, he protested, 'Not my brain! That's my second favorite organ!'

I hate myself when I become angry, absolutely hate myself. After a verbal outburst of anger, I feel profound regret, guilt and failure — that I couldn't deal with an issue in a mature, civil way.

Anger is weakness and failure, and the sense of failure creates frustration that can feed further emotional eruption. I wonder sometimes if anger may be a desperate attempt to present a façade of strength to cover up a profound and shameful feeling of weakness.

Excess anger is but one of the destructive emotions that can result from the wounds of trauma, along with irritability, anxiety, low self esteem, and more. Anger is not simply a momentary emotional explosion over one incident in time. It's a long-simmering reaction of pent up hurt and frustration that may reflect psychological damage done years earlier.

A critical feature of anger is that it is an emotion born out of a felt need to maintain some *control*. Men are socially programmed to seek and keep control. That's how they are raised, that's how they are rewarded in sports, in business, and elsewhere. To lack any control, or heaven forbid, to be dominated, is just not manly. It is seen as weak, a sign of failure. And one of a man's greatest fears is to be controlled by a woman. I don't like saying this, but again, that's how men are raised and it's what they come to feel. If all this is true, it's easy to see how the tendency to seek more control can lend itself to displays of anger, particularly in the case of a person who feels like he's losing any semblance of control in his life overall, as a depressed person often feels. The anger may begin as hurt feelings, but being *hurt* suggests no control, while anger asserts some control. Perhaps this is why anger tends to surface often in a man / woman relationship such as marriage, more so than in other relationships. I see anger as an unconscious, desperate attempt to maintain some control in an environment perceived to be out of control.

Indicative of the desperation associated with anger, it seems to me that the person becoming angry is possibly damaged more from the episode of anger than the person at which it is directed. You suddenly become tense and tight, you can feel your pulse increase and your blood pressure skyrocket, and you lose control of yourself. This is not at all pleasant. Then, immediately after the display of anger, comes an overpowering sense of guilt and shame. This is definitely not the way you want to deal with people or with problems. For me, following such an episode often is a period when I feel upset, lose my appetite or energy, and ruminate about how I could have handled the situation better. The ruminating can be nearly obsessive and can last for hours. This at least is how it often happens with me.

Many experts say that depression is 'anger turned inward', because a depressed person cannot feel or express emotions normally. I would say that even for a person who tends to show a lot of anger, it's likely that the anger turned inward is much *greater* than the anger displayed outwardly. This certainly does not diminish the hurt of the person targeted by the anger, who feels small, disrespected, and unloved. But for what it's worth, it's likely that the *angry person* is in more pain.

I learned most of this the hard way—for both myself and for Joanne—by experiencing many of these problems. And if there aren't enough challenges, depression presents yet another—it's such an enigma. If you think you understand it, you're probably just scratching the surface. One of the problems for people dealing with depressed loved ones is that they tend to see depression as simply sadness or despair. Many times when I hear news spread that someone is depressed, invariably someone says something like, 'What is he/she so unhappy about?' Or worse, 'What made her lose it?' Well, depression is not sadness, and it's certainly not insanity.

Due to the gross misconceptions associated with depression, most people have difficulty understanding why *anger* often emerges from the depressed person. They expect sadness and despair, not anger. People could easily empathize with sadness, but not anger. They simply see anger as evil, not the product of inner wounds that also produced the depression. People don't seem to view the depressed as victims, but as accomplices in their own crime, not deserving of compassion.

I don't know if anger is a serious problem for the majority of depressed people, but I believe it is for countless depressed men. I'd like to learn more about this, but from what I understand, deep, inner rage is a very common condition for depressed men. It is not easy for people to see these symptoms being intimately connected with an illness known as 'depression', which again is equated with simple sadness by most non-sufferers. For four months I participated in a weekly support group that consisted of 10 men. As I heard each man's story emerge over several weeks, I was struck by how many men were alcoholics, children of alcoholics, and had bouts of depression. But the main problem they all had that was threatening their marriages and their jobs was powerful, destructive *anger*.

The other common misconception about depression is the sense many people have that the person should be able to handle it, since 'it's all in your head'. A lawyer I once spoke to about discrimination in the workplace, upon hearing that I suffered from depression, replied with a casual but demeaning comment.

'Everyone has bad days from time to time,' he said.

Bad days? I thought to myself, how about a bad *year*? No, make that *horrible*. Ever go through that? The lawyer's comment really bothered me, but I wasn't about to waste my time trying to educate an insensitive, arrogant person.

All of these distinctive characteristics of depression add up to the most unfortunate situation that depressed people tend not to get the empathy and understanding that victims of other serious illnesses get. This is very disheartening. You feel that people just don't care enough to recognize this unbearable burden that you carry.

Before I was terminated from my last job, I had told my team leader and division vice president that I suffered with depression, so they'd understand my inability to keep up with the work. There was absolutely no empathy forthcoming. All I heard from my team leader was concern for how the work would get done. And I heard nothing from the VP. These were people I had known more than six years, people who I liked and respected, and who seemed to feel likewise about me. Several years ago this lack of support would have devastated me. Now, knowing what I know, my expectations are much lower and I'm only slightly disappointed. (But I am definitely *pissed off!* I'm still working on my anger.)

I'm not sure how true this is, but one thing about anger that strikes me as a positive is that it indicates the depressed person is still *fighting*. At least he hasn't given up. If he had, I'd imagine the level of energy would be well below that of anger, more like quiet submission—Why bother? Who cares anyway? For loved ones of depressed people: take some consolation—anger may be a good sign that depression hasn't defeated this person.

Lately I've come to feel that, in our society, victims of depression are lepers, suffering with an illness that society cannot or will not understand. The great majority of people have no idea. It seems that the only people who have a chance of understanding it—as a human *experience*—are those who have suffered from it, and perhaps those care-givers who truly listen to and empathize with their patients, which sadly seems to be a small number.

Regarding the *science* of assessing and treating depression, it appears that a similarly small number have a basic under-standing—the handful of professionals who have studied it and have seen beyond the propaganda of the pharmaceutical and insurance managed-care industries. The evidence suggests that the majority of psychiatrists, medical doctors, psychologists and other therapists do not understand it very well either. There is currently widespread disagreement among the 'experts' about essential issues such as the causes of depression, the most effective treatments, and how antidepressants actually work. These are drugs being prescribed by the millions, and often for numerous conditions other than depression—anxiety disorders, PTSD, obsessive-compulsive disorders, substance abuse, and eating disorders—to name a few. But I've yet to read an account of exactly how the drugs actually reduce depression, or how they address all these diverse disorders. Every book and article I've read acknowledges that this is not yet understood. What's more, the techniques for diagnosing depression are widely assailed for being arbitrary, subjective and lacking the basic elements of science.

Given all this uncertainty, it's very difficult for me to accept many of the assertions you read—that depressed people think they're failures, or just need to stop all the negative thinking. It seems to me the problem starts not with *thinking*, but with wounded emotions deep within that can cripple your capacities or erupt uncontrollably. These things are deeper and more far-reaching than your thinking. They precede and pre-empt thinking. You can accuse me of negative thinking for this very comment, but it seems to me that much of the 'change your thinking, change your life' talk you hear today is a simplistic marketing ploy, ignoring the true nature and depth of depression.

Many times my reaction to something adverse or threatening has been an immediate sinking feeling in the stomach, sometimes accompanied by lightheadedness or dizziness a moment later. This begins to happen before I could even begin to formulate a thought that might have been able to avert the sense of disaster. This is very common among trauma victims. The human brain has been found to have multiple systems or modules and the one that plays the key role in handling fear is the amygdala, which is part of the limbic system and reacts to danger and fear very quickly, well before the 'thinking' module can begin work. So, there are immediate and often exaggerated physiological reactions to fear based on prior events such as early trauma that precede any ability to reason or analyze (Cozolino, 2002; Johnson,

2004). It is not the *thinking* that triggers symptoms, although I'd certainly acknowledge that negative thinking can compound the problem. But this is the point where issues get far too technical for anyone who isn't a professional in this field.

Apparently you can work toward controlling or altering these reactions, and I feel that I've made some progress, but it can be a long, taxing effort trying to alter the body's automatic reactions programmed over many years. Fortunately, our truly amazing brain is actually being constantly 'rebuilt' by our experiences through changes in its neural circuitry due to the remarkable 'plasticity' of the brain. (Cozolino, 2002).

In a sense, positive experiences can gradually replace the negative. But even when I've managed to temporarily forget my illness and move on, there are just so many reminders that you're different or defective that can set you back. It could be any number of things—a comment someone makes stigmatizing depression or other mental illness, or one of the many times you just don't feel well and you wonder what's causing it or how much it might bring you down, or when you're unable to concentrate as your mind habitually wanders off somewhere, or when you see one of the omnipresent advertisements for antidepressants. Or the trigger can be completely outside of thinking— perhaps just a loud noise that sets off a type of exaggerated 'fight or flight' reaction instilled long ago by trauma. 'Fear memory' is powerful and intractable, able to produce unpleasant symptoms without your awareness of what's happening.

I'm now much more aware of these triggers, and there are other reminders of your illness almost everywhere you look. Depression touches everything you do. While you don't want to dwell on your problem or allow it to make you perpetually feel like a victim, nor can you simply deny or ignore it. It's a delicate balance acknowledging and owning your condition without letting it dominate your life.

Yes, very few people understand depression. Early in my first episode my wife Joanne insisted she understood enough to not need any further explanation. She had no idea how such a cavalier comment could sound insensitive and even offensive— by seeming to belittle the scope and complexity of this illness and thereby failing to recognize the true depth of suffering. Comments like this come across as, 'I get it, it's not that complicated.' It can even sound like, 'no big deal,' even though that was never the intent of the message. When that person goes on to offer advice on how to deal with this perplexing illness, especially if it's advice such as, 'you don't really need medication,' this only makes the matter worse.

Imagine speaking to someone whom you recently learned has liver cancer. Would you say something like, 'You don't need radiation or chemotherapy for that?' Most people recognize that they have virtually no knowledge of the body or of cancer, but in the case of depression, it's different. 'Just suck it up' is a common reaction. 'Stop being so self-absorbed.' This trivializing of the illness tells you that the majority of people *do not believe depression is a real, debilitating illness.* They simply cannot comprehend the depth of despair and defeat, the horrific symptoms.

Even today, there is widespread doubt about the validity of depression and other mood disorders. This doubt extends all the way to insurance companies, elected representatives and policy makers, evidenced by the inferior benefits for mental illnesses versus physical disorders. It's great that there is now progress toward achieving 'mental health parity' in insurance benefits, but the simple fact that this had to be a fight demonstrates the stigma and ignorance associated with mental disorders. Maybe when people learn about the brain damage behind many emotional disorders, the misconceptions about depression will change.

Incidentally, Joanne saw my disturbed reaction to her comment that she understood depression as indicative of the highly sensitive nature of depressed people. It's very frustrating to see all your observations dismissed as simply a result of your illness and not considered for their possible merit. It's a kind of invalidation.

Once a person learns that his / her spouse is depressed, it's easy for that person to begin blaming most of their marital problems on the depression, or on the depressed person. After all, the depressed person isn't 'thinking straight'. He's frustrated, irritable, overly sensitive, and so on. It's not surprising that this happened with us.

Joanne began to say things like, 'Now I see why you were nasty to me all those times,' or, 'It's not right that I've suffered so much because of your condition.'

While true to some extent, you cannot suddenly attribute all problems to someone simply upon learning they suffer a disorder such as depression. This strikes me as a 'cop out'. The result is the depressed person is no longer an equal in the marriage, having been relegated to an inferior, less credible status. Along with his opinions and wishes, he is dismissed, *invalidated*. Clearly, marriage cannot work this way. And personally, I have to say, I'm so very tired of being blamed. Of course, it's the *depression* that's really being blamed, but the carrier bears the brunt. I actually believe there are ways in which a depressed person can be *more* understanding and empathetic as a result of dealing with the trials and tribulations of depression, although it admittedly can make a person volatile, unpredictable, and just plain difficult. There is some research to suggest that depressed people may actually perceive situations *more* accurately and realistically than others.

It appears to be yet another of the ravaging effects of the *labeling* of the depressed that they are routinely invalidated, which can further compound their struggle for the self-esteem and peace crucial to recovery. Behind this virtually automatic labeling and invalidation of the depressed I believe lies the widespread, deep-seated ignorance and misinformation—that depression is not a real, legitimate illness with severe physiological symptoms, which cannot be simply willed away. The uninformed public seems to see depression as faulty thinking, laziness, self-absorption, and the like. The issues keep coming back to this singular point.

It is not unexpected then that, to a considerable degree, all these problems have occurred in my marriage, beginning before I even told Joanne of my depression. Little by little over the years I started spilling out stories of my father's drinking and his reckless behavior, gradually suggesting the damage it may have done to me and my family. She never seemed to grasp how I could carry severe emotional wounds all these years, and she appeared to minimize or dismiss these ideas. But she did seize upon my father's incorrigible behavior toward my *mother*, and how this may have made me do some cruel things to her, though on a smaller scale. I suppose it's natural for people to think first about how they themselves are affected by a problem, and think less about others. While I surely realize that depression is extremely difficult to understand, you have to hope that loved ones can show efforts to understand and make some kind of progress.

Equipped now with much more knowledge about what this destructive condition can do to a person, I can appreciate the difficulties a spouse might have in trying to understand a depressed partner and show empathy. I've tried to educate Joanne about depression in general and how it's affected me in particular, and this has done some good. And she has taken it upon herself to learn. This is part of the hard work that needs to be done to maintain a marriage under very difficult circumstances. What with the many pitfalls, it's not surprising that marriages where one partner suffers with depression appear to be particularly challenging, and often dissolve.

The differences in the ways that men and women communicate don't help the situation. A man may make a statement thinking he has adequately described what he meant to say, whereas the woman seems to feel the topic has barely been introduced. Many times after I felt I had said something pretty clearly to a woman, her subsequent reaction indicated that she didn't hear or grasp half the things I tried to express. Men often have a common understanding that requires few words, but this doesn't seem to work so well between men and women. Different wavelengths I guess.

With all these forces lined up against a marriage, it might appear it is doomed once one partner experiences anything more than a brief depression. Though many of the years have been rocky ones, the fact that a marriage such as mine has lasted 34 years, the last eight being burdened with my overt depression as opposed to the earlier covert variety, demonstrates that it is indeed possible to endure. Clearly, love between the partners is the essential ingredient. But I don't think love is enough. There has to be much more—loyalty, dedication, resilience, compassion, and willingness to learn and understand. I don't really know what the key is, but peppered in with my feelings of frustration, I've felt tremendous gratitude and fulfillment in this journey with Joanne striving to get through such a trying ordeal. It makes for a most bittersweet experience. In spite of the difficulties I've described living with depression and maintaining a marriage, I appreciate Joanne immeasurably for her love and dedication. I truly cannot blame the partners of the sufferers for the relationship difficulties any more than I can blame the sufferers.

This kind of struggle could easily present the challenge of a lifetime for both partners. Regrettably, there may not always be a fairy tale ending. Marriages today are hard to maintain under the best of circumstances, so the addition of a condition such as depression may be the last straw. I certainly recognize that I've been difficult at times to live with, and the fact that I haven't always been able to be 'normal' seems to be something many spouses might have trouble tolerating. Given the difficulty of grasping this complex illness, I can't entirely blame Joanne for her difficulties appreciating my condition. I know that trying to find blame is counterproductive, and yet I can't help but feel like the target of the blame in our relationship, and I don't need another burden like that.

And even if your partner does gain a solid understanding of this illness, that still may not be enough. It's just no fun for someone to be around a depressed person. Hey, maybe the problem is that simple.

7 A Symptom of Our Time

Our moral problem is man's indifference to himself. It lies in
the fact that we have lost the sense of the significance and
uniqueness of the individual, that we have made ourselves into
instruments for purposes outside ourselves, that we experience
and treat ourselves as commodities, and that our own powers
have become alienated from ourselves. We have become things
and our neighbors have become things. The result is that we
feel powerless and despise ourselves for our impotence.

Erich Fromm, *Man for Himself: An Inquiry into
the Psychology of Ethics*

As a result of my battles with depression, I developed an interest
in its incidence in my family and in the wider community. The
unfortunate fact is that my family has been contributing more
than its share to the rising incidence of depression. It was often a
well-guarded secret in the family, but as best I could tell,
depression afflicted two uncles, an aunt, and a cousin—just on
my mother's side. I didn't know my father's side very well,
although I doubt if there was much depression. The one possibility was my father himself—he may have done such a good job
covering it up with alcohol that we cannot know for sure. It's
striking how much time he spent alone in his den when I was
growing up. He practically lived there, just lying on the couch
sleeping or watching TV, that is, when he wasn't out.

If Erich Fromm's observations shown at the opening of the
chapter accurately described the direction in which our
civilization was moving in 1947 when he wrote it, and I believe
they did, then these statements are even more applicable today.
In spite of numerous, mind-boggling achievements in
technology and parallel economic advancement not thought
possible a decade or two ago, people increasingly seem to feel a

vague discontent and emptiness. Regarding man's situation, Fromm wrote:

> By virtue of his reason he has built a material world the reality of which surpasses even the dreams and visions of fairy tales and utopias ...Yet modern man feels uneasy and more and more bewildered. He works and strives, but he is dimly aware of a sense of futility with regard to his activities. While his power over matter grows, he feels powerless in his individual life and in society.

While the past few decades have seen an acceleration of the decline, man's modern predicament has very deep roots. For at least a century now philosophers, writers, and poets as well as social scientists have been chronicling conditions that diminish man's individuality and the possibilities for fulfillment. Although my focus in this book is on the many inflicted with various mental or mood disorders, the issues extend well beyond that, touching essentially everyone. But first, the facts about the outright 'disorders'. The numbers from the National Institute of Mental Health regarding mood and anxiety disorders are staggering:

- Approximately 19 million adult Americans suffer from depression in a given year, and 15 million of these suffer major (clinical) depression. The median age at onset of major depression is 32. It is more prevalent in women than in men.
- Rates of depression have been rising sharply. Roughly 10 percent of Americans will experience major depression at some time in their lives, and as many as 50 percent will experience some symptoms of depression.
- The number of Americans suffering from some type of anxiety disorder is about 40 million. A significant number

of depressed people also suffer anxiety disorders, which include generalized anxiety, panic disorder, post traumatic stress disorder, obsessive-compulsive disorder, and phobias. For the majority of those having anxiety disorders, the onset occurs by age 21.

The facts on alcoholism are no less disturbing (source: the National Institute on Alcohol Abuse and Alcoholism):

- Approximately 30 million Americans grew up in families having one or more alcoholics. A significant number of Children of Alcoholics suffer from depression, anxiety disorders, alcoholism, addictions, and other disorders.
- An estimated 8.2 million adults and 3 million youth in this country currently suffer from alcoholism (alcohol addiction).

The devastating effects of alcoholism, which extend well beyond the individual sufferer, are but one example of the countless ways in which our activities and institutions betray us. I believe that we live in a society that is becoming increasingly harmful to the true needs, values and welfare of individuals. Just as work is becoming 'toxic' for more and more people, our society and culture comprise a deteriorating, toxic environment in which to live.

The conditions created in a society where technological and economic progress steamroll the individual can only be expected to generate more cases of depression, anxiety and similar disorders. People's communal and spiritual needs come to be secondary to the imperatives of the marketplace. And by 'spiritual' I don't necessarily mean religious. Various organized religions may or may not support true spirituality, which is a sense of awe, wonder and connection to some power beyond oneself. True spirituality is in contrast to the obligatory posture most people today seem to have toward their church, which too often spews out empty values and platitudes disguising the hypocrisy, arrogance and intolerance of many religions today. For me, the primary takeaways from a childhood of enforced Catholic mass and catechism were reinforcement of the guilt and fear that were building inside.

The trends and patterns in our society are unmistakable—a sense of community is disappearing; constant, disruptive change leaves people struggling to adapt; work hours grow longer and longer, preempting family time; jobs are becoming increasingly impersonal; employee / employer loyalty is disappearing; workers are coming under intensifying pressure to produce more and do it faster and faster; people are becoming transients in their jobs and their communities, disconnecting them from fulfilling and stabilizing social ties. The role of limitless consumer, collector of expensive but useless material goods, grows to fill the void left by the increasingly harried and meaningless lives.

Conditions in today's global society produce growing isolation and disconnection, diminishing the nurturing and support that might prevent or temper mood disorders such as depression. People today are subjected to many more stresses that can trigger depression, particularly in those with some prior vulnerability. Ironically, people in the western world are reportedly subjected to more stress than in any other time period, despite our many advances, exemplified by innumerable time and energy saving devices.

Much of the heightened stress today is on the job, as workers strive to keep up with expanding workloads and an ever-accelerating pace, in the face of threats to their health and well-being (see *Toxic Work* by Dr. Barbara Bailey Reinhold). These changes have crept up on us gradually and insidiously over the past few decades, and in the interest of doing our jobs diligently, we have allowed ourselves to be overused and abused. In the past several years I have personally witnessed more and more people approach or succumb to job burnout. Beyond this is the growing number of people I see whose signature smiles have been wiped off their faces, replaced by a beleaguered and gloomy look that perhaps only another victim of burnout can recognize as a sign of serious trouble. This is in stark contrast to my initial years in the business world in the 1970s when I saw or heard of no one burning out. I didn't even know what burnout was until the 1990s.

And by no means is it just corporate employees who are suffering from the evermore stressful, toxic workplace. I see telltale signs of burnout in countless others including those we view as being at the 'top' rung of society, ranging from doctors and lawyers to business owners and executives. What they all have in common is the appearance of being caught up in a storm of change that has removed any meaning or pleasure from their work. They feel trapped; but are they really?

I don't know to what extent the causes of this demise of the work environment are a runaway work ethic; or an overly materialistic culture not balanced by more traditional, people-centered values as in other countries, including many European ones; or an inevitable result of technology advancing at a geometric rate; or social disruptions brought on by ever-accelerating change; or what. I suspect that all of these factors play a role to a degree. What's certain is that they are taking a serious and often deadly toll. In addition to the devastation of depression itself is the numerous diseases it can lead to or compound.

It is certainly the case that people *do not have to allow* technology and the marketplace to dominate their lives. However, it *is* the case that the great bulk of people, in western societies at least, historically *have* allowed this domination, even welcomed it, in the name of 'progress'. We have been seduced by a never-ending array of products that do little more than feed our vanity. We're racing faster and faster while becoming less and less able to see that we're going nowhere but in circles, and draining our spirit and vitality in the process. We buy countless products in the desperate hope that they'll somehow compensate for our increasingly hollow existence.

The current inability of individuals and governments to make the changes necessary to forestall the catastrophic effects of global warming is testimony to the powerful addiction we have to our way of life, despite the knowledge that it is poisoning our world and threatening the lives of every creature on the planet. It may seem unnecessary to note that we are included among these threatened creatures, but I get the sense today that people by large do not view themselves as *biological* creatures, susceptible to the same forces, needs and threats as other creatures. Our way of life is simply not sustainable—not for the planet, and not for our physical or emotional wellbeing. We live with an arrogance and sense of invincibility that has put us on a path to destruction and at the precipice of disaster. And yet we cannot change on any kind of meaningful scale. We have distanced ourselves from our roots in nature and forgotten our place as living, needful, vulnerable beings. We have become the machines we invented to supposedly improve our lives.

And so it goes. By his recent death, I'm reminded of that novelist of the counterculture, Kurt Vonnegut, whose dark humor and barbed satire exhorted people to assert their freedom of thought and action to fight the dehumanizing institutions that have come to dominate our way of life. Himself a sufferer of depression, Vonnegut displayed profound contempt for the mechanization, commercialization and brutalization we have become numbed to of late. He was a self-described free-thinking humanist who longed for a communal life centered on respect and compassion for all. These, regrettably, are disappearing values.

With all the increases in productivity and wealth in recent decades, workers are actually in a position to reduce their hours.

But they don't by and large, and while the accelerating pace of work produces yet more numerous and more serious health problems, workers continue to put in the long hours. This goes on while workers' children spend less and less time with their parents, who provide irreplaceable love and nurturing. What kind of emotional stability can we expect to see when these children become adults?

The longer work hours alone demonstrate our addiction to a harried lifestyle and the continual accumulation of more and more worthless consumer goods. Despite significant gains in income over several decades, work hours have failed to decline. Workers have made a choice. While everyone decries the hastening pace and lack of time to do what's meaningful to them, the overwhelming majority nevertheless stay in the race. It's clear that this is not a conscious choice, but a blind addiction. Workers today seem to be motivated more by *fear* than by a sense of professionalism or pride, and the fear drives the decision to put in more and more hours in jobs that are increasingly pressured and toxic.

This is a prescription for disaster. While tolerable in the short run, it will catch up to you in the end. Two-earner families are now considered a necessity. Really? Why wasn't it necessary 20 or 30 years ago, when productivity was much lower? It's telling that we even call it a 'necessity'. The increased incomes resulting from the long, hard hours may enable consumers to obtain more and better products, which are purported to enrich their lives, but in the final analysis we see this is not at all true. I don't believe that many people in their final years feel they should have worked yet longer or acquired more cars or boats or houses. Rather, I believe they wish they had spent more time with loved ones, or more time just enjoying their lives and doing what is meaningful and fulfilling to them. Recalling the words of Wordsworth:

Getting and spending, we lay waste our powers:
Little we see in Nature that is ours;
We have given our hearts away, a sordid boon!

Technology creates an insidious process that has turned the original man-tool relationship on its head — man created technology as a tool, and man was the master. With today's highly intricate technology that demands precise execution of numerous, specific rules and procedures, people no longer are the master. It is the *person who now must conform* to the requirements of the machine — be it computer, cell phone / camera, kiosk, iPod, yet another technical development in television, or any number of new, 'convenient', time-saving devices that are supposed to improve and simplify our lives. The problem is, we must adapt to *them*. This represents a dangerous loss of control, a loss of purpose, a loss of meaning, and a further loss of community. Though it was no one's intent, it is quietly elevating machines over people. It is a subtle but symbolic perversion of the role of man versus tool. As Fromm commented on modern man:

> While becoming the master of nature, he has become the slave of the machine which his own hands built. With all his knowledge about matter, he is ignorant with regard to the most important and fundamental questions of human existence: what man is, how he ought to live, and how the tremendous energies *within* man can be released and used productively.

On top of this, the various new forms of electronic communication have the effect of separating people and threatening communities by removing face-to-face interaction. Communication is becoming little more than electronic messages, a growing amount of which is automated.

The compelling issues of our present times suggest to me a dire need for a new humanistic perspective. Humanism is built on a conviction that man is and rightly ought to be the center of all our institutions and actions, and his well-being, freedom and dignity are paramount. Man is not a means to an end, a cog in an ever-growing techno-economic machine, but rather man is the end in himself, the centerpiece, the purpose.

If you walk through a typical corporate office today, you'll see hundreds of cubicles in row after row, each cubicle with a single person who will generally be sitting in front of a computer monitor. It's not unusual for a worker to spend the great majority of his 8-10 hours of work sitting in a cubicle in front of a monitor. Everyone works *alone*, since there is access to almost anything via the computer network. Email, instant messaging, text messaging, phone, fax, and the like are threatening face to face communication with extinction. What a way to live! The implications are most unsettling. For one, it's far less difficult and troubling to be unkind or unfair or dishonest to someone *you don't see*, someone who isn't part of your community, if you even see yourself having a community. There is no human contact, no group dynamics, no building of team spirit or community, no understanding of others, no open communication, no solidarity. Disconnection and alienation become the norm under these conditions.

In the two companies where I worked in the past decade, and in the many companies I've visited, the majority of employees eat lunch alone at their desks, usually while they continue to work. Apparently there's no longer time for sitting down with co-workers, taking a break, socializing. We are social creatures who evolved in groups and communities, but as employees we're pushed harder and harder, and any 'community' is lost. Community really exists in our heads and actions, but it appar-ently cannot be part of today's driven, high-tech workplace; the transformation of man to tool takes another significant step forward. When a tool breaks, it is often thrown away, as is a worker who is suddenly unable to work. Though this may be temporary, no matter—there's no time or money for such charity. I've been there. The workplace of the 21st century is not a good place for a human being, particularly not for the millions wounded and weakened by prior events out of their control, making them susceptible to a whole host of illnesses.

The argument that conditions in a mass consumer society exhibiting rapid change can take a toll on individual well-being is certainly not a new one. One of the founders of sociology, Emile Durkheim, linked his era's rising rates of suicide and it's preponderance in particular social segments to a lack of social cohesiveness, leading to a disconnection and loss of purpose for many. Durkheim's research found that high rates of suicide were symptoms of large scale societal problems. As community and traditional forms of meaning declined, people were becoming more isolated and alienated.

None of these arguments about the power of social forces should be interpreted to mean that individual, psychological forces are not also at play in the rising rates of suicide or depression. On the contrary, social forces appear to compound or activate problems such as the psychological effects of trauma. This was certainly the case for me. Aspects of my increasingly stressful and unhealthy lifestyle activated an old, deeply entrenched vulnerability to depression caused by early trauma. I suspect the same can be said for millions in similar circumstances.

The various forms of ever-present 'machines' that dominate our way of life are symbolic of our subverted values. The machine's mastery over man begins with the programmed logic, 'I have to get one of those.' Our unshakeable attachment to consumer goods and our blind faith in technology compel us to desire every product purporting to be a technological advance or improvement. These *things* come to supersede people. They have come to have more credibility than people. The first research studies to come out of the computer age were typically highlighted as path blazing 'computer studies', which endows a kind of unquestionable validity. Machines are viewed as being superior to people, even though, as we know, man is theoretically directing the machine. But are we? In whose interests?

This is not to say that technology is inherently evil or that it does not produce many worthwhile benefits. The point is, as Lewis Mumford, Jacques Ellul and other social critics have written, that we have placed technology in a predominant position by organizing our culture and society around it, and thereby allowing it to virtually control our lives. Technology is seductive and insidious in its conquest. The means have become ends, and our very ideals and values are subverted. The effects are dehumanizing as man falls from master of his society with noble ideals, to a pawn in a pathetic, meaningless competition for more and more things that are better, faster, and more powerful, ad nauseum. This way of life does not feed the spirit, or nurture the young, or enhance our capacities. It stifles and subjugates and demeans.

As a society, had we paid as much attention to mental health—to a person as a whole, fragile creature in need of proper care—as we have paid to products and technology, the terrible effects of abuse and dysfunction stemming from alcoholic families would have surfaced much earlier. (Dr. Janet Woititz's trail-blazing book, *Adult Children of Alcoholics* wasn't published until *1983*.) It is shamefully barbaric that children on such a massive scale could be subjected to abuse and neglect to the extent that their lives could never be normal and healthy. This is a civilized society? This is progress? We need to pay more attention to people, and less to products and machines.

There is perhaps no better illustration of the distortion and perversion of our values than the way we celebrate our most significant holiday, Christmas. Originating as an observance of the birthday of Jesus Christ, it once celebrated the cherished principles and values that this heroic figure embodied—love for fellow man, the life of the spirit over and above material things, courage of conviction, simplicity, forgiveness, and sacrifice. Today's chaotic, decadent celebration has totally corrupted these values and turned them upside down. The occasion has been so thoroughly commercialized that the central figure is no longer Christ, but that gift-bearing symbol of today's materialism, Santa Claus. We barely recognize this perversion of the principles we supposedly hold dear. Of course, we give lip service to those traditional principles to comfort and delude ourselves, but who are we fooling? What I'd like to see one time is a Christmas built around the simple values of peace, community, and generosity of *self*, without *purchased* gifts, but rather gifts of the self, of time and friendship and affection. Maybe we can then turn this stressful, shallow, decadent holiday into one of enrichment and meaning, the way I believe it was originally intended.

When I was a child, I received a modest number of gifts at Christmas, but each one meant a great deal to me. I felt fortunate and cherished each toy. It's much different today, when a child might receive numerous gifts that are often unappreciated or even ignored. Whether child or adult, when someone has a proliferating number of possessions, they tend to lose their meaning and value, and the owner's thoughts habitually drift to what else he can acquire. It's not clear how much of this is due to the many forms of advertising we see that creates demand for all these dubious products, but what is clear is that we are inundated in nearly every facet of life today by the subtle and insidious messages of corporate marketing.

One of the many adverse consequences of our consumer addiction is the way we have shifted so much power to the greedy organizations producing and marketing these endless products, the multinational corporation. It is ironic that the very same party, the *consumer*, who is buying these countless products and should be in command—if the 'customer is king' as we've been told—is the same party in most cases who is the *employee* of the companies depending on the consumer purchases. And the employee today is increasingly being squeezed in the workplace to produce more and more, faster and faster, in an evermore stressful, toxic and inhuman environment. The consumer-employee should be king, being both the prime asset of the corporation *and* the ultimate buyer of the products, but has unwittingly forfeited the power to this corporate dominion. There is immense, insurmountable power in the hands of the consumer-employee that we are simply not using. The idea of a union, for employees and / or for consumers, doesn't seem to have much appeal in this country, where the spirit of individuality and freedom reigns supreme. But organizing appears to be the only way to begin to counter-balance the immense power of large corporations today.

Our civilization is creating an environment in which a condition such as depression can flourish. And the trends strongly suggest that the future is likely to be much worse. Again, this assuredly *does not have to happen*, but there is very little evidence to indicate there exists the will and courage and humanity to stop the steamroller of modernization and globalization.

My own experience in the business world followed the pattern of burnout and deterioration of morale experienced by untold millions as our society sped along with economic and technological advancement and an evermore unquenchable appetite for products. The first dozen or so years of my career were extremely fulfilling. I liked the work, the environment, the co-workers, the company, everything. But with the intensely competitive, cut-throat era beginning to take shape in the 90s, my company along with many others metamorphosed into an impersonal, highly pressured, un-empowering, and fragmented entity. My own job satisfaction declined dramatically with these broader changes in business and in society overall. I felt completely trapped, having to run faster and faster on the treadmill of business today.

For me a toxic and conflicted workplace was the primary trigger of a fall into depression. And it's happening to more and more people, most of whom don't want to acknowledge or admit it. Granted that a disproportionate number of these victims likely had a vulnerability or predisposition to depression based on their history. But perhaps they would have averted depression if their workplace had been a healthy one. More importantly, we can only expect more vulnerability to depression as increasingly harried parents sacrifice the nurturing and bonding that could provide their children with better defenses against future stress.

Thinking of the many job listings I've seen, it seems that the great majority these days make reference to a 'fast-paced', 'results-oriented' environment where 'multiple priorities' must be juggled. Job postings generally understate any difficulties in the job, so it's likely that the pace in those jobs is indeed extremely fast. Aside from the question of how humans fare in this type of environment, I have to question the work product. Many times I've seen quality and consistency sacrificed for the sake of speed, not to mention a disregard or neglect for learnings accumulated through history. Workers today seem to live blissfully in the present and only the present, speeding through their tasks aided by the finest technical tools, but with little or no sense of what happened yesterday, why it happened, or what we should learn from it. They are truly doomed to repeat the mistakes of history.

There is in fact widespread evidence that the incidence of depression is increasing throughout developed countries. The increased rate of diagnosis does not account for this increase—it is a real phenomenon. In this country there has been a significant rise in depression, particularly among baby-boomers, and it is striking victims at earlier and earlier ages. With the unmistakable trends and the powerfully destructive forces we see driving our way of life, one cannot be optimistic about the prospects for stemming the rising rates of depression and other disorders in the future.

It is doubtful that man evolved to handle the challenges and pitfalls we see in our modern, materialistic, technological society. People surely sense this, that we live an unnatural, unhealthy life. As Wordsworth lamented, 'we are out of tune'. But we are so caught up in this destructive way of life that we feel we can do little about it. We have been seduced, perverted, subjugated by the very products and tools we developed for our comfort and convenience. The temptation of magical technology and unlimited consumer products has seized our souls and diverted attention from what is truly important. When asked, most people give similar answers regarding what is most important to them—family, friends, a sense of accomplishment and fulfillment, living in a pleasant community, leisure activities, time to relax and appreciate what we have. Nevertheless they continue to allow themselves to be preoccupied by the things that are *less* important. We have created a Frankenstein's monster on a massive scale, one which threatens to destroy us.

Is this freedom? Are we any freer than a rat in a cage running round and round a spinning wheel? The answer, of course, is yes we *are freer*, but we do not *act* as if we are. We do not exercise our freedom, but rather unwittingly exchange it for enslavement through the seduction of luxury and wealth. Existential philosopher Jean-Paul Sartre called this mindset 'bad faith'—the view that something in our lives is necessary when in fact it is voluntary. We forget that our way of life is free and voluntary. Existentialist philosophy reminds us that we have much more freedom and choice than we realize day to day.

Every day we can see more and more signs of a dehumanizing society and culture as we steadily move away from the values that are hallmarks of what we think of as 'human'. Does this not conspire to create conditions for the acceleration of disorders such as depression? Among the many therapists I've spoken with or read, it's striking how many describe the typical person in this country as poorly adjusted and characterize our society as dysfunctional overall. Some therapists say that as many as eight of ten people can benefit from counseling due to existence of emotional wounds, psychological maladjustment, or other condition that could interfere with a functional and fulfilling life. Most people don't want to hear this, which is quite understandable. It is significant that the incidence of depression is on the rise despite more widespread knowledge of the damage that alcoholism, drugs and family dysfunction can do.

The higher incidence of depression among women warrants comment. Men are much more likely to hide depression with alcohol, drug abuse, violence, and workaholism. This helps to explain why men are four times as likely as women to commit suicide in spite of women's higher rate of diagnosis of depression. Disdaining any seeming preoccupation with feelings, many men are so indoctrinated into an extreme macho-masculinity that they are unwilling to even consider the notion that they may be falling into the grip of an invisible illness like depression. In this sense, it seems to me that such a man is little different from the dedicated hunting dog who has been bred to routinely risk his life for his mission. Neither realizes what he is doing and at what risk. Our dedication to a work ethic might be admirable were it not overzealous and predicated in large part on a desire for more and better products that in the end fail to enrich our lives.

Ours is an 'extremist consumer culture', according to a recently released book by clinical psychologist Bruce E. Levine, which has sapped the meaning and morale out of the lives of countless people, creating an environment conducive to depression. Dr. Levine's book, which is aptly titled *Surviving America's Depression Epidemic: How to Find Morale, Energy and*

Community in a World Gone Crazy, in many ways follows in the line of thought of social critics such as Erich Fromm. It is essentially a humanistic piece pointing out how our current lifestyle is not sustainable in the long-term because it fails to protect and sustain people's mental and emotional wellbeing. Levine shares one particularly revealing statement from an unhappy high school student:

> There's nobody who really knows me—so of course how can I feel anybody really cares about me or truly loves me?

I would think that in order for a person to truly know and care about someone else, she has to *be known* and cared about herself, ideally by a parent. So if that's missing, the child carries and passes along this deficiency, and a vicious cycle can easily develop. With the declining time that parents spend today with children, you wonder how many children feel truly 'known' by their parents.

The recent, continuing rise in rates of depression is linked to declines in levels of social support and overall connectedness, or 'social capital', according to sociologist Robert Putnam. In *Bowling Alone: The Collapse and Revival of American Community,* Putnam argues that the resulting dearth of this social capital today is inhibiting society's ability to address critical social issues and solve the kinds of problems that typically can be managed by a healthy society. For decades social scientists have commented on the 'decline of community' and 'lonely crowd' phenomena that have diminished the benefits of the 'social' and in our social lives.

As a clinical psychologist, Levine also has a particularly useful vantage point for evaluating the state of psychiatric *care*, which he concludes is sadly failing the bulk of sufferers, being more concerned with expeditious, low-cost treatments than with the long-term wellbeing of sufferers. The treatments he has found to be most effective focus on restoring energy, meaning and sense of community to the lives of sufferers. This rings true for me. Although I trace the deep roots of my depression back to childhood traumas, I can't help but think that depression would not have been visited upon me years later, at least not to the degree it was, had I not followed the meaningless, materialistic path presented to us by our mainstream culture.

Depression is your mind and body screaming out to you that your life is becoming dangerously unhealthy, and a radical change is needed.

Escalating rates of depression are but one symptom of a dangerously unhealthy society and culture. Most people would be surprised to learn that suicide accounts for more deaths each year in this country than homicide, substantially more actually (National Center for Health Statistics, U.S. Dept. of Health & Human Services, 2005). Compared to most other developed countries, both suicide and homicide have unusually high incidence here, and they are a byproduct of our way of living. It is increasingly vital that we remind ourselves that social institutions are not handed down from above or predetermined. We should not blindly allow customs and social institutions to run our lives, often to the detriment of our physical and emotional health. It is within the power of people to *alter or replace institutions* that do not serve them well, whether they are religious, governmental, economic or communal.

You can change your life; *we* can change the world.

We need to slow down. Simplify. Embrace our families, appreciate our neighbors, connect with colleagues, and rebuild a community and lifestyle compatible with our values and our basic human needs. This could vastly improve both our mental and physical well-being and the overall quality of life.

It is worth reminding ourselves of the timeless wisdom of Thoreau:

Most men, even in this comparatively free country, through mere ignorance and mistake, are so occupied with the factitious cares and superfluously coarse labors of life that its finer fruits cannot be plucked by them....He has no time to be anything but a machine...The finest qualities of our nature, like the bloom on fruits, can be preserved only by the most delicate handling. Yet we do not treat ourselves nor one another thus tenderly.

Most of the luxuries, and many of the so called comforts of life, are not only not indispensable, but positive hindrances to the elevation of mankind.

In the midst of this chopping sea of civilized life, such are the clouds and storms and quicksands and thousand-and-one items to be allowed for, that a man has to live, if he would not founder and go to the bottom and not make his port at all, by dead reckoning, and he must be a great calculator indeed who succeeds. Simplify, simplify.

Henry David Thoreau, *Walden*

8 I Who Have Died Am Alive Again

I thank You God for most this amazing
day: for the leaping greenly spirits of trees
and a blue true dream of sky; and for everything
which is natural which is infinite which is yes
(I who have died am alive again today,
and this is the sun's birthday;this is the birth
day of life and of love and wings:and of the gay
great happening illimitably earth)...
E.E. Cummings, I Thank You God

Originally I titled this chapter, 'One More Time to Live', after the Moody Blues song by the same name, and I wanted to show some of the poetic lines from the song. But it can be difficult and costly to get approval for reprinting excerpts of lyrics. So I looked for something else and found the excerpt above from an E.E.Cummings poem, which captures the mood just fine. (And no, those aren't typographical errors—he wrote with little regard for convention, which I really like.)

Speaking of music, I find it can be very therapeutic, good music at least. Possibly this is because music can surface an emotion that's trapped deep inside. In my own situation, it's clear that I've needed more help than most in feeling or openly expressing emotions. I find that music—at least music that is genuine and touching—can immediately cut through the normal defenses to release emotions that are deep within. No doubt because of the entrenched barriers to openness, for me this tends to happen when I'm alone listening to music.

One day not long ago when I was driving to work, I was listening to one of my favorite songs on a CD. The song, 'Making Pies' by Patty Griffin, is a very poignant, melancholy story of a woman who grieves the loss of her lover, but who goes on to reaffirm her life by enduring in her dreary job at a pie factory. Patty's voice reaches a crescendo during this reaffirmation, and her voice is so full of emotion throughout the song that I played it over and over all the way to work as I found myself in the very unusual circumstance of being on the verge of tears. How strange that I could feel such powerful emotion listening to a song! Maybe it was because I could relate so easily to the song. This is where I happen to be now—grieving, dealing with the burden of depression, but ready and willing to reaffirm life, just not quite fully able—not just yet. Though perhaps with less intensity, this kind of emotional release upon hearing a touching, well-done song has happened to me a number of times, mostly during an episode of depression.

Part of this evolution in my emotions has been a recent shift in my tastes from rock music to folk, which in its lyrical content and use of voice and sound to reinforce the mood and theme, is much deeper and richer than rock. Folk songs are often poetry put to music. The elements of voice and instruments added to the poetic lyrics bring you into another dimension, resonating with the emotions.

My shift in musical taste has happened largely since my first depression. But as I look back at my favorite songs over my lifetime—I have kept lists of these songs—it's curious that I've always had a weakness for haunting, introspective, melancholy songs, even when I was listening primarily to rock. My all-time favorite singer / songwriters are all artists whose music is highly moving and rich in meaning—long-time favorites Justin Hayward of the Moody Blues, Neil Young, Joni Mitchell, and contemporary folk artists Dar Williams and Patty Griffin. It's fitting that the Moody Blues would be my all-time favorite musical group, since, as the name suggests, their music leans toward the somber, reflective, and existential.

I think music can be very therapeutic even if it's sad, disturbing or tragic. It can get you in touch with emotions that are difficult to reach, and I would recommend the use of music to anyone trying to reach repressed emotions. Again, this idea is based on the recommendations of experts who say you must surface and deal with repressed emotions, rather than ignore them. Like reading, music is increasingly being recommended as a form of therapy. For me, what is striking is that despite my shifting musical preferences, when it comes to my top songs of 40 years ago, I enjoy most of them just as much today. This I see as symbolic of a constant in me that endures even as I evolve through the healing process into someone quite different.

After about a year into my second episode, I was doing a lot of things to recover, and they started to pay off, although it was a long, slow process. Through weekly psychotherapy, I was gradually becoming able to again feel the pain of the original wounds, which needed to come out. The two support groups that I joined provided opportunities to hear about similar problems that others had, to share my story, and to enjoy the mutual empathy and encouragement of the group. I'm more reluctant to share detailed, personal issues in a group setting as opposed to individual therapy, so I had to gradually 'warm up' to each group. I ended up dropping out of both support groups after four or five months, feeling that they were covering the same ground over and over, as the groups consisted almost entirely of attendees describing the problems they had since the prior meeting. Each group had become unproductive in my opinion, but I definitely got something worthwhile out of each one before deciding to leave.

I then decided to try an Al-Anon group consisting of adult children of alcoholics. The meetings are very structured around the widely used 12 step program for recovery. Tending to be averse to rigid rules and structure, I wasn't sure how well Al-Anon would fit me, but I thought it was worth a try. After six or seven meetings, I felt I was getting nothing out of the group. What I wanted was open discussion of people's real problems, and what solutions worked best. But what the group discussions consisted of was mostly the reciting of one passage after another from the organization's handbooks. The people were great, but it just wasn't right for me, so I dropped out.

One major factor aiding my recovery was the absence of work-related pressures. The escalating time pressure alone had become very taxing. As in many jobs these days, I was compelled to do more and more, faster and faster, and could never see the light at the end of the tunnel. Looking back, I've never done well when there's constant, extreme time pressure, just as I don't seem to do well when there are excessive 'stimuli', such as several people demanding things at once, or even just a lot of background noise when you're trying to have a conversation. Research is showing that people with mood disorders such as depression are more prone to being 'highly sensitive' to their environment and tend to disdain noisy, chaotic situations. So it's not surprising that I've come to prefer and value a certain amount of peace and quiet, and being away from the frantic atmosphere of business was a welcome change, even if I did carry some guilt and anxiety about not working full-time.

Somewhere along the way I came up with a pet label for the frequent, abrupt jolts I experienced— I called them 'pangs' of depression. I think I just said this to myself. It seemed like a fitting and descriptive term. They were like a sudden blow to the head that would leave me weak and dazed, sometimes near collapse. At best it would take several minutes to catch my breath, regroup and try to continue whatever I was doing. In a worst case scenario I was shot for several hours and could do little more than try to sleep it off. Little by little over a period of months these overpowering pangs of depression that I had felt almost constantly were beginning to decline in severity, duration and frequency. I now feel occasional, weak versions of these symptoms, which seem to come in clusters that I can't predict or understand, then go away just as mysteriously.

Curiously, this sudden blow to the head sensation was actually very different from another distinctive sensation I often got during depression—the slow, sinking feeling, like I was caught in the currents in a gigantic toilet bowl being flushed. That sensation seemed to be more predictable, usually being tied to the experience of an impossible, hopeless problem, some sort of bad news, or the like. I got to the point where I knew it was coming. But the blow to the head sensation just came out of nowhere. Maybe there's some kind of subconscious force I'm not aware of that causes it.

A couple months into my disability leave I decided to try something different and attend a weekend retreat at the Omega Institute for Holistic Studies, which helped me to step back, look at what's truly important to me, and to simply *relax*. I needed to slow down. It seemed like an unlikely remedy when I first heard how important *breathing* is to controlling tension, but I thought back to times when I was stressed out and saw that I indeed lapsed into taking short, shallow breaths, which compound the physical effects of stress. I see now that I was too easily pressured by stress to ratchet up my pace to a point that could not be healthy, constantly feeling the need to race, but never reaching the end line. We need to unlearn the bad habits brought on by stress, and learn to practice natural, slow, deep breathing.

It was becoming clear that relaxation was an essential part of recovery for me. I almost always felt turmoil inside, which wasn't necessarily visible on the outside. Even when I wasn't feeling depressed, this inner turmoil had a number of elements—a troubling uncertainty or anxiety, a sense of needing to constantly hurry to do things, and a frequent experience of racing, almost random thoughts. The latter was so disturbing that I once thought I had Attention Deficit Disorder. An online test that I took produced a score that suggested a strong possibility of ADD. I recalled that over the years I have often had trouble concentrating or following directions, as my mind was prone to become easily distracted and wander.

Thinking back to my school days, I would habitually daydream when the teacher spoke, and would have to go back and teach myself the material. I have to believe that in the *majority* of my classes throughout grammar school and high school, I paid attention a small fraction of the time. In spite of this, I was still able to get A's in most classes, as I had to learn early on how to teach myself, in my own way.

If someone is talking and I don't find it particularly interesting, my mind goes somewhere else in as little as five to ten seconds. The typical scenario when I'm with a group of people conversing, part way into the conversation I'll say something like, 'What are we talking about?' 'Who said that?' I have never outgrown this; it could even happen in important business meetings later in my career. With a lot of focus and concentration I can generally keep this under control, but it's not easy.

It's not a deliberate or even conscious thing for me to fade out, just my nature. I remember my junior varsity basketball coach getting annoyed at me a number of times because I didn't look at him when he spoke to me. I thought I was looking at him, and I probably looked when he first spoke, but my attention often turned elsewhere within seconds. I also remember a teacher of mine, from around ninth grade, commenting that even though I was a very quiet, calm-looking person, he thought I had a great deal going on inside me that I couldn't let out. I was startled that he'd say something like this, and even more startled by how well he read me. It made me stop and think.

I'm not sure what grade it was, but fairly early in grammar school I started becoming captivated by pretty girls in my classes. It was more than a healthy attraction. I habitually stared at them, while attempting to cover or disguise my leering. There was always one favorite girl who commanded my attention, and I would imagine being with her. This happened during class, after class, almost any time. Being bashful, I rarely did anything about my infatuation, beyond the occasional flirting. This near-obsessive thinking carried well into adulthood.

There were any number of things I'd daydream about. I was a big Yankee fan, mainly because of my boyhood idol, Mickey Mantle. Not content with just imagining how well he might do in an upcoming season, I actually recorded detailed statistics about the kind of season I hoped for. I had The Mick hitting something like 70 home runs, batting .380, driving in 160 runs, and performing numerous other heroic feats. Sometimes I did that for the whole Yankees team, and sometimes I did it for the Knicks when I grew a little older and became a fan. I also came up with fictitious super stars in baseball and basketball who could shatter all known records and lead my teams to championships. I created my own little world in my head, where I was happy and safe.

Being easily distracted, fantasizing, having thoughts jump in and out of my mind, feeling a disturbing inner turmoil—I've felt things like this my whole life, but wasn't necessarily conscious of them most of the time. You seem to get used to the things you do, and don't necessarily realize that you're different from others. It's natural that I became more conscious of these characteristics when I started exploring the roots of my illness. I was coming across information in books and on websites, including short tests you can take to assess your mood and personality, that suggested I had some unusual tendencies.

This made me think back to my college days. I didn't have a clear idea what I wanted to major in as an undergraduate, but since my father wanted me to be an accountant, presumably so I could help his business minimize taxes and expenses, I decided to try that route. It was crystal clear after two courses that I had absolutely no interest in accounting, but it was too late to switch from an economics / business major. So I just took as many courses as I could in social science, which interested me much more. I later decided to go to graduate school in sociology, with the idea in the back of my head that I could teach in college, or get a position doing research.

About a year into the PhD program at Brown, I started becoming disinterested and disillusioned. The subject matter just ceased to be engaging for me; somehow, leading sociologists had managed to essentially remove human beings from the study of society. There were incredibly intricate, complex theories and models about every excruciating detail of modern society, but there seemed to be little or no relation to real people and what they actually believe and do. I thought that perhaps the study of society had been dehumanized as much as society itself. I contemplated leaving the program.

Curiously, the other factor that led me to leave was the prospect of reading the thousands of pages of books, articles and studies required for the PhD program. Even though I was always a top student, I recognized that, for whatever reason, I generally had trouble reading and absorbing large volumes of material. Because I was so easily distracted by other things swirling around my mind, my limited attention span and ability to concentrate would have made it extremely difficult to read and master all the material. I could have done it, but it would have taken extra effort and time, and for a subject that no longer excited me. My grades were fine, but I eventually decided to leave the program with a master's degree. Life as an 'intellectual' just wasn't for me.

When I told my psychiatrist about my history of being easily distracted and disconnected, he wasn't at all concerned, saying that the symptoms of ADD and depression are often very similar. This was something I didn't know and wouldn't have guessed.

I also thought that I might be manic-depressive since I've often had large mood swings. My down days were pretty bad, but my up times were not as up as in most cases of bipolar, although I did have more energy and enthusiasm. My psychiatrist couldn't say definitively if I was bipolar, so he put me on yet another medication, a mood stabilizer, and we'd see if it led to any change. As it turned out, a minor improvement and stability in my moods did occur, but since my mood was improving overall anyway as a result of other aspects of treatment including psychotherapy, this trial of the drug was inconclusive. It now appears very doubtful that I was ever bipolar, but this kind of trial and error approach to one's health can be very disconcerting. The whole approach to medication for depression and anxiety is uncertain and troubling—it's all trial and error. The simple fact that medical science doesn't even understand the mechanics by which antidepressants alleviate depression is enough to completely undermine your confidence.

Apparently it's not at all unusual for a person to have two or more mood or anxiety disorders simultaneously. In fact, this 'co-morbidity' is the norm for anyone with a mood disorder. Depression rarely exists alone. Many depressed people also have PTSD, generalized anxiety, and other disorders. Although it is by no means a pretty picture of myself that I've uncovered, I find it very therapeutic and satisfying to at last begin to understand the complex web of factors that led to my condition. In *The Truth about Depression,* Charles Whitfield describes the key factors that produce and exacerbate these disorders:

The co-morbidity was more common and with a higher number of disorders according to the *degree* of trauma *severity*, perpetuated at a *younger age*, that is *repeated*, and finally *unaddressed*.

This knowledge has helped me immensely to understand the reasons behind my condition—not just why I became depressed, but why it was particularly severe and long-lasting. Beginning in *early childhood*, I had witnessed my father's *uncontrolled rages* and verbal abuse of my mother *countless times* over the better part of a *decade*. The impact on me was *never recognized* or addressed, and I *never even spoke* to anyone about it until well into adulthood. In my case it wasn't just the trauma; *all* the elements were present during the lengthy period of trauma and in the aftermath to produce very serious disorder. As Whitfield argues, when childhood trauma is *unrecognized, unaddressed and untreated,* the likelihood of subsequent mental disorder increases substantially.

As unsettling as all this might seem, in a way I felt kind of liberated by virtue of gaining this knowledge, finally. I certainly don't claim to understand everything about these mysterious and complex illnesses, but I now understood enough about the roots of my own condition to feel release of a terrible burden — of guilt and shame — it wasn't my fault.

At first I thought this essentially closed the book on the mystery of how my depression came to be, at least the analytical aspect of the story. Of course, I knew much more needed to be done about tapping into my emotions. But I figured this was all I was going to learn about the origin of my illness. However, in the coming months I was to learn there were still more pieces to the puzzle.

As I thought about my experiences, what struck me as terribly unfortunate is that the many different terms for the disorders we're talking about — depression, post traumatic stress disorder, generalized anxiety, etc. — suggest that these are different, separate ailments, when in fact they appear to be slightly different manifestations of the *same underlying condition* — a severely traumatized, paralyzed inner being. Perhaps depression and PTSD are really just different aspects of the same disorder. In the diagnostic manual, PTSD is currently classified as a different diagnosis than depression and it's considered an anxiety disorder. But what's curious is that not only are many of the symptoms the same, many of the same drugs are used to effectively treat both disorders. Furthermore, the psychotherapeutic treatments are very similar for both conditions, strongly suggesting common elements in the disorders (Flach, 2002). We'll have to let the experts figure this out, but one would hope there will be clarification of these closely related illnesses, and increased public awareness.

While I was out on disability, and since it was winter, it seemed to be a good time to get away to Florida to see two cousins, Skip and Mart, who were practically best friends of mine growing up. I hadn't seen Skip in three years since he moved to Florida, which was his lifelong dream. While I miss Skip, I respect and admire the way he took charge of his life and made such a big move, which made him much happier. Skip's situation with regard to his father was revealing in many ways—his parents were separated when he was young and he only saw his dad a few times a year. The visits became less and less frequent, and eventually stopped. Skip is an only child and lived with his mom, my Aunt Loretta. As I look at how he was affected by the distant relationship with his father, it clearly was not pleasant or supportive. However, I feel I can detect when someone I know well is very poorly adjusted or pathological in some way, and I haven't seen that in Skip. He is definitely eccentric and noncon-formist in many ways, and tends to be a loner. But in his own way he has become fairly well-adjusted, maybe because his mother was so devoted to raising him with enough love and attention to compensate for what his father didn't give.

Of course, I can't help but compare this to my relationship with my father, and it looks like an example of how no relationship with a parent may be better than a poisoned relationship. I feel terrible saying this, because there was a great deal of love between my father and me, and the way our relationship improved in his later years makes me feel guilty talking this way. Nonetheless, I know that the damage done in the early years was severe, to the extent that 'well-adjusted' would never describe me.

After three days with Skip in Naples, I drove a half day to Marty's home near Orlando, where I spent another three days. Marty and I spent the better part of an evening discussing our family's mental health history over a few beers. You can say I was doing some 'research' for this book, which included consulting the de facto family historian, my cousin Karen, who had also moved to Florida. Marty's father, like most of my uncles, had a habit of stopping by the local 'gin mill' for a few drinks. And he seemed to be a stern parent who scared me sometimes when I was young, so I kind of expected that he might be an angry or dangerous drinker. But that wasn't the case. He didn't seem to be a harmful person when he drank, and I could see that he and Marty had a very good relationship. I sometimes noticed that as a teenager, Marty would disagree about something with his dad and would state his beliefs very strongly. This is something I couldn't do with my father—I just didn't feel I had the right, or I was just plain afraid.

I also remember Marty and his two brothers, Lenny and Jimmy, joking about how their dad threatened to beat them with his belt when they misbehaved. Who knows how often they actually were beaten, but I was shaken up just hearing about it. Since I was pretty young at the time, it's odd that I remember something like this. Maybe it's because I was surprised they could joke about being afraid of their father, which tells me they weren't very afraid. I could never joke about being afraid of my father. It wasn't a threat of physical punishment, but it was chilling just the same. As youngsters, my cousins served as allies to each other, 'helping witnesses', to temper the impact of their father's threats. A child alone with his fear trapped inside creates an extremely dangerous and unhealthy situation.

It was very important for me to maintain a bond with Skip and Mart and I left feeling glad I made the trip down to Florida. We've been friends our whole lives, and not just because we're cousins. I had a great time on my visit and felt relaxed and rejuvenated upon returning home. Since it was late winter, I was also happy to just get away from the dreary, cold weather for a week of sun and warmth, not to mention a welcome break from my problems.

Even after three months on disability, I wasn't ready to return to work. Since it was now more than a year and a half into this episode, my psychiatrist and therapist felt it was critical that I fully recover before trying to return to work. However, a problem arose with my job at the market research firm once the 12 week Family Medical Leave expired and I didn't go back to work. I received a call at home one day from the HR director, the same person who had told me prior to my disability leave that the company would try its best to put me in a different position when I returned to work, offering me a fresh start away from the simmering, mutual bitterness that existed over my situation. From her ominous tone and the way she seemed to be carefully leading to a very serious issue, I knew something was wrong.

She began, 'The company has had to lay off several people due to the loss of our biggest client and the resulting loss of a big chunk of revenue.' I started expecting the worst.

'We plan to offer you a severance package,' she said softly but firmly.

'What?' I said as I struggled to digest this news. 'You're giving me a *severance* package?'

That's a nice way of saying 'you're fired.' I didn't know what to say. Being so abrupt, I was naturally shocked by this sudden course of events. I had been promised some sort of accommodation for my situation. What's more, in my first five years with the company I was never once considered for layoff when revenue dipped. In fact, on a couple of occasions when I asked about transferring—because I was starting to stagnate—I was told they wanted me to stay. I was needed there, and was rewarded with good raises in the following couple of years. Throughout this time I had been receiving important assignments and often dealt with some of the company's biggest clients. All indications were that I was a highly regarded and valued employee, until my condition became disabling and I was forced to go on medical leave. Then it was like I had the plague. They wanted no part of me after that. But I knew that it would do no good to protest my termination to the HR director. The decision had been made.

It all seemed so unreal to me, and so grossly unfair—being terminated while recovering from a serious illness. It's contrary to the purpose of the leave, since I was officially permitted to take another three months beyond the Family Leave to recover during the disability leave that could be as long as six months if needed. But apparently you can be terminated in this kind of situation. It's done all the time. It all depends on the reasons given for the termination. As in my case, there are many ways that a company can manufacture a legitimate-sounding reason. In the end, having been through this situation before, I was sufficiently jaded and wasn't really all that surprised at being terminated.

What complicates the situation is the way that depression can affect a person's attitude and actions on the job even before it becomes so severe that medical leave is required. A depressed person does not and cannot approach a job with the same enthusiasm and motivation as others. An employee with a continual negative mood is in all likelihood going to be viewed as one who does not care enough to work hard and perform well, especially in these times of intense competition and heightened expectations. This is why I felt I had to tell my superiors about my depression—so they'd understand my lack of energy and enthusiasm in the weeks leading up to my disability leave.

But they made absolutely no attempt to understand. What's worse, the minute they heard I suffered from depression, they perceived this as a fatal flaw in me as an employee, and they began to view everything I did as flawed. Things I had been doing effectively for years were now questioned and challenged. If someone looks hard enough for a problem, and with eyes colored with prejudice, they will be able to see the problem they want to see. As in the first episode at my prior employer, I tried my absolute best to work through the condition, but wasn't able to overcome the devastating affects of depression on my ability to work effectively. The company's HR director actually had suggested it was best for everyone for me to take leave.

I could only conclude from the circumstances that my temporary disability led directly to my termination, which would be unlawful discrimination. I was fired because I was depressed. It's extremely difficult to prove something like this, but I was angry and determined enough to do something about it. So I contacted a number of lawyers who specialize in employment law, discrimination and wrongful termination. The lawyer whom I selected based on his knowledge and confident demeanor felt this was a very strong case. His approach was forceful and assertive—a letter was sent to the CEO outlining the facts, stating the critical issues, and demanding a significantly greater severance to compensate for the illegal discrimination and lack of accommodation for my disability. The company had offered two months severance, which is not much for someone my age who is looking for a job. It was a costly gamble to challenge the company, but Joanne and I felt it was worth it. And I wanted to get back at them and kick some ass!

This was now the second job I lost due to depression. In both cases I was a well-regarded employee with a better than satis-factory performance record prior to the bout of depression. But once I became ill and unable to work effectively, there was no patience, no willingness to stay with me through the necessary steps toward recovery. I was just pushed out the door. This probably would not have happened 10 years ago or 20 years ago when most companies showed care for employees, and I don't know if it would happen today with a 'physical' illness. Depression is different.

Despite the anxiety about not having a job or adequate means of financial support, I was beginning to feel a greater level of relaxation. With the ample time I had while on disability leave, I was able to slow down my pace—spend some time looking for a job, do a few chores, read, take walks, etc. And I could take the time necessary to treat my various ailments, which ended up taking a great deal of time over several months. When an orthopedic doctor said operating might be the only way to address my back and neck problems, I elected go the chiropractic route, despite my long-standing skepticism about the practice. The treatment included trying a new technique for 'spinal decompression', along with acupuncture and the typical chiropractic adjustments, all of which required a few dozen visits for treatment over a period of more than three months. Each visit consumed up to two hours. I was willing to try just about anything to get better, so I also tried acupuncture for the depression, with little apparent benefit.

After investing all this time in treatment, I definitely felt an improvement in mobility in my neck and shoulders, along with a big reduction in pain. But having neglected the problems for so many years, complete elimination of the problems is too much to expect. The damage from my herniated, degenerating, arthritic disks couldn't be completely undone. I continue to have frequent tightness and discomfort in my neck—no longer what I'd call 'pain', but enough to bother me several times a day and distract me from whatever I'm doing. It can take me a half hour or more just to get my neck in a position comfortable enough to go to sleep. This is the price I'm paying for having long ignored my body's warning signs.

When my six-month disability leave expired, I felt well enough to go back to work, if only I had a job. I continued looking for work and managed to get a few interviews. I was generating some good prospects for jobs and began to feel optimistic. But when nothing materialized, I had to go on unemployment benefits, for hopefully just a short time. Based on the four interviews I had, it appeared that employers felt I was overqualified for some jobs, and positions at the next level up were few and far between. And I wasn't at all sure that I was up for a position with more responsibility, time pressure, and stress. I was again giving serious thought to a career change, but had a lot of trouble trying to decide what I wanted to do and *could do* at my age. Almost anything decent would require substantial training, and I didn't have the time or money to do this. We had a decent amount set aside for Steve's college, retirement and whatever emergency might arise. But I didn't want to deplete that.

With my immersion into a mission to understand the causes of depression, the plight of children of alcoholics, and the pros and cons of treatment techniques, I actually considered *becoming a mental health counselor*. I thought that this would be fulfilling and I could be a particularly effective counselor, in large part because I could understand and empathize with the many difficulties faced by victims. More than that, my new found passion for these issues has at times tempted me to dedicate my remaining career to alleviating the suffering from depression. I did a lot of research on distance and online educational programs and on certification requirements for counselors. For a period of several weeks, I felt a motivation and excitement that hadn't existed in some time. I recall taking a preference test at work a number of years ago, and my scores pointed out a strong preference for a career involving counseling of some type. This was another thing I ignored while remaining in a work environment that I was beginning to realize was a poor fit for me.

Unfortunately, my enthusiasm about getting into counseling was quickly squelched upon learning about the substantial time and money required to complete both the training and the considerable internship hours required. Being in my mid-fifties, it struck me as too late to start something like this. This may sound like just another negative thought colored by depression, but I think it's perfectly realistic—I simply didn't expect to live long enough to get much out of a new career that couldn't begin until maybe age 60. Depression can take a decade off your life, and my many deteriorating health issues indicated that I would be no different. Plus, I didn't have the energy to pursue another degree, not to mention the money. While I turned away from the counseling path, I continued learning as much as I could about the causes of depression.

Looking back now it seems odd that not until I read about meditation and mindfulness, and attended the retreat at the Omega Institute, did I realize how little time I was spending *in the present*. I hadn't even thought about this previously. Only then did I realize that I was spending most of my time ruminating about the *past*, second-guessing myself, or worrying about the *future*. Too often, I wasn't in the present, focused on the moment, where we need to be in order to remain well adjusted and healthy. With the increased distractions of modern society, it is likely that failing to focus on the present and live in the moment is another hallmark of our age. While I may tend to be less in the present than others, I am certainly not alone in this.

My therapist has helped me to obsess less about the past and the future. While you want to minimize *ruminating* about the past and second-guessing yourself, sometimes you have to recall and relive early events that may have brought you harm, so you can understand and resolve the issues, enabling healing to begin. Having been through two lengthy, taxing episodes of depression, I can't emphasize enough how essential it is to step back, face your demons, understand your wounds, and get help. Otherwise you may be doomed to be a victim of your demons over and over and never escape your past. I've always been one to hate asking others for help, but I learned the hard way how critical it can be.

It was quite evident that continuing a market research career on the business side would in time lead to another relapse. That just wasn't the job or the environment for me. In fact, I was to the point where the ethos of business in general no longer fit me at all. I'm not sure it ever fit me, but by now it was crystal clear that I needed a different environment. I seemed to have a basic philosophical opposition to the phony, constrained world of business, preferring a more open, honest and collegial environment. So, while I still looked for traditional market research jobs just to be able to help pay the bills, I sent resumes to several colleges in the hope that I could land at least a part-time job teaching market research, marketing or related courses. My 25 years of hands-on experience in the field had to be an asset, even though colleges tend to look for extensive teaching experience, and a PhD. I wasn't having much luck in this effort until out of nowhere I received a frantic, last minute call from a professor in Rutgers Business School.

'Can you teach a marketing research course at the Newark campus?' he asked.

Though I was in pleasant disbelief that such an opportunity would suddenly arise, I immediately replied, 'Yes, absolutely.'

'The only problem,' he cautioned, 'is that class is *tomorrow*.' He explained that the original professor had suddenly become seriously ill. Despite the short notice, I was of course excited to oblige. After all, I had time on my hands, and part-time teaching would give me a taste for the profession as I sought to make some type of career change. I was beginning to feel I had value, something to contribute again. I was back in the game.

This opportunity delighted Joanne and the children, who have been very supportive in a low key sort of way. I didn't want the children to know about my condition, but Joanne felt it was necessary so they'd understand the unusual behavior they would sometimes witness. I still have misgivings about telling them, feeling that it may create more problems than it solves. Rob, my oldest, was very upset when he learned of my depression, which concerned me a great deal. I just don't believe most people can understand what depression really is; hell, I didn't understand it until my second episode. Joanne said that I could educate them, but that's much easier said than done and it's not something I want to try. The last thing I want is for my children to even think about or sense the pain and despair associated with depression. Possibly the major motivation for my fight to recover was to keep depression from in any way *infecting my children*. The fact that it can be 'contagious' has always been my greatest fear. Not physically contagious of course, but contagious in the sense that a father's depressed bahavior can affect his children.

The legal challenge to my termination while out on disability took quite a while to resolve, making me anxious about where it would lead. I didn't want to settle for too little, but didn't want to risk a lengthy and unpredictable lawsuit either. I needed the money, and soon. The lawyer representing the company 'tested the waters' with a comment to my lawyer about increasing the severance from two months to four, which was clearly unsatisfactory, but that's an inevitable part of the negotiation. We were looking for a year's severance, which seems justifiable in view of my age and condition at the time, and my lawyer remained optimistic that we'd get a lot more than the original offer of two months. It's extremely difficult to get a comparable job at my age and with my recent medical history. The company seemed to be stonewalling and testing our patience, as the negotiations dragged along over a period of six months.

I got an unexpected call one day from my lawyer's assistant saying they needed to know my exact salary so they could calculate what eight months severance would amount to. This was an unusual way to learn the outcome, but I wasn't complaining. Eight months was just fine with me. I was relieved. Even after the lawyer takes his cut, that leaves me with about six months pay, which can hold the family another year when added to our part-time incomes. I felt a sense of vindication about receiving compensation for being terminated while on disability leave for treatment, which is a shameful and inexcusable injustice. To me the company's agreement to increase the severance that much is an admission of guilt in discriminating. That kind of thing happens all too often and I'd like to see employers pay through the nose for their uncaring and unlawful actions.

The money also made me feel better about all the time I was spending writing this book, which wasn't bringing in a dime and might never bring in a dime for all I knew.

Though I had but a part-time teaching position, by this time I was beginning to feel renewed hope and enthusiasm. Teaching allows the freedom and autonomy that I seem to need. In contrast to the trapped, subservient feeling I often had in my business positions, I have been feeling liberated, empowered and alive. I work at home primarily and enjoy the ability to manage my time and my activities, no longer having the stress of the numerous, changing rules and regulations, the tight deadlines, the crazy workloads. The marketing department head asked me to teach two courses the next semester, and there was a chance it could lead to a full-time position. I was also able to join the adjunct faculty at a small college, to teach sociology, which I had wanted to get back to despite some of my earlier reservations about the discipline. Not being a big fan of business or our commercialized culture, I prefer to be able to take the sort of critical perspective that sociology allows, with balance of course. I was interested in taking part-time teaching positions in order to build experience and credentials for a future full-time position.

Just as importantly, by adding courses to my teaching load I was able to gradually transition myself back to a full, active schedule, enabling me to feel productive and worthwhile again. Another of the destructive catch-22s of depression is that you're not well enough to work a heavy schedule, and you can lose a job that provides self-esteem and a sense of security, compounding the despair. While in recovery, you need to somehow stay reasonably active and productive, otherwise you can wallow in your misery. You need to get away from it and move your thoughts to other things, and teaching was doing that for me. Eventually I was able to piece together 4-5 courses per semester at four different colleges, which kept me reasonably busy, though with enough time to work on this book.

When I reflect on the more open, empowered nature of a teaching position, I realize that the remarkable recoveries I've read about by people who are artists, authors, professors and the like probably would not have been possible in the constrained, rigid, political world of big business. I know now that I need to stay in a position where autonomy and individuality are encouraged or allowed, if I am to fend off depression. In spite of the disappointingly low pay of part-time college teaching, I'm very happy to have the independence and flexibility at a time when I need to focus on my well-being.

I'm reminded of the day when I was released from my college infirmary where I had been quarantined for three days with a nasty strain of flu. I had felt so miserable that it was the greatest feeling to get well and be able to go out and enjoy a beautiful spring day by playing basketball with my friends. Maybe you can't fully appreciate the good times unless you experience some bad.

No one should go away thinking that my life has been all down, or primarily gloomy. Not at all. Another time my mind sometimes fondly returns to is eighth grade. It was such a great year—adventurous, full of fun, almost carefree. It was my first year in junior high and I made a number of new friends, many of them real characters that I would know for years. What was odd is that I was in the class ranked highest scholastically—at least in terms of aptitude, because some of the kids were not serious students by any means. There were a lot of shenanigans. We always tried to come up with a creative new angle on our antics to keep the teachers off guard, like when someone threw something in class and the teacher asked who did it.

We always did the opposite of what the teachers expected.

One of us would quietly admit that he did it, then someone else would say, 'Don't cover for me, I did it.'

And another would protest, 'No, *I* did it.' And so on. The teachers were totally at a loss, which caused us to keep doing it. We really liked confusing and outsmarting the teachers.

I also had a good year playing Pop Warner football. Determined to show that a top student can also be a strong athlete, I was understandably proud of a season where I played every down on offense, defense and special teams, and scored three touchdowns. But it was tough—as a running back and safety, I was involved in a violent collision on nearly every play, and I remember hurting so much afterwards that it typically took three or four days before I began to feel remotely capable of playing the next game.

Then there was that first steady girlfriend, which also happened that year. Perhaps for me the year was filled with enough fun and levity to carry me above the reach of the blue moods, tension, and disturbing distractions that would often visit me. Many times I've enjoyed that kind of lift, though less often no doubt than most people, and perhaps not quite enough to sustain a healthy mental outlook.

I know there are countless things that I've been blessed with, and I'm truly thankful. In addition to having a wonderful, loving family, I've experienced enormous gratification and enduring companionship from a number of great people. And I have developed some very meaningful and enjoyable activities and interests. The things that bring me meaning and enjoyment have changed and diminished in number following my episodes of depression. But the people that I cherished and the activities that I enjoyed became that much more essential as I healed and grew.

More than ever I get a feeling approaching spirituality when walking through a scenic forest, along a flowing river, or in view of a majestic mountain. And I'm continually enchanted watching wildlife gracefully go about their business. I am in awe of nature.

It's been a long time since I've believed in a deity—I see no need for it when we are blessed with the unsurpassed riches and power of the Earth, which gives us sustenance and beauty and the wonder of life. God can be no greater or magnificent than the Earth or the Sun and the life they give. When I walk out in the sunshine now, I can feel that it does shine for *me* as well.

After enduring an ordeal as overwhelming as depression, this is a time when you revisit your values and come to truly appreciate what's most vital to you— starting with family. For me, family has been a source of tremendous strength and ongoing fulfillment. My family has played an indispensable role in my journey to recovery. Despite the early dysfunctional, traumatic years that threatened to shatter the family and do irreparable harm to everyone, my original family—my mother and two sisters Donna and Diane—has endured to sustain and even strengthen the ties that bind us in a devoted, generous, resilient and loving relationship. And without my loving wife Joanne and our beautiful children, Rob, Lauren and Steve, I could never have found the will or the strength to pick myself back up.

Dr. Frederick Flach entitled his recent book *The Secret Strength of Depression* because the condition can be a great opportunity or even catalyst for positive change. Depression can be an opportunity for insight, for reordering of priorities and lifestyles, and for release from damaging habits and emotions.

There are countless examples, role-models if you will, of heroic ascent from the quicksand of depression. It's difficult to imagine any person having a more tragic and trying personal life than Abraham Lincoln. Coming from a very poor family, he had little education, and lived a lonely, isolated childhood. His mother passed away when he was nine, and he also lost a young brother. The woman who was his first romantic interest died young, and another relationship led to a broken engagement, leaving him in despair and anguish. He had a troubled marriage, and although it produced four children, two of them died in childhood. His early career brought failure and disappointment, as he was largely unsuccessful in business, and lost more elections than he won.

Of course, our lasting memory of Lincoln is as the president who held the union together during its greatest crisis, a bloody civil war, and who freed the slaves. He is often called the 'second father of his country'. But even as president, he was not popular or widely respected. In view of this unending litany of tragedies, it's not at all surprising that Lincoln suffered chronic depression all his life. He was a melancholy man with a sad, troubled face, who once said, 'I am now the most miserable man living...To remain as I am is impossible; I must die or be better.' (McCain, 2005).

It is incomprehensible to me how and where a person who suffered so many horrendous tragedies and ordeals could ever find the strength, the resilience, the faith to endure and become the Abe Lincoln who is one of the greatest heroes in American history, a man who saved a nation and fulfilled the promise of our founding fathers when they envisioned all men being equal.

Such an inspiring story has to be a source of strength and determination. It surely is for me. Increasingly, I have been feeling an inner strength like never before, as if a great burden has been taken off my shoulders. And without a doubt, I find myself appreciating things much more now than I had previously.

But, perhaps inevitably, there are lingering fears. Having been through two episodes of depression, it scares the hell out of me to think even for a moment that a loved one of mine could ever experience this horror. In particular, when it comes to my three children, I hesitate in pain to even acknowledge a remote possibility that depression could hit them sometime in their lives. I think that's why, subconsciously, I instinctively wall off my depression from my children. They are two separate worlds that I want to keep separate as long as possible. I want to insulate my children from this terrible illness, preferring that they not even conceive of depression as a possibility in their lives.

My anxiety on this issue has even influenced my writing of this book, and I'm not sure I've said enough about the central place of my three children in my life. My extreme walling off of my depression from my children is irrational I know, and something that Joanne and my therapist don't understand or agree with, but it would be extremely uncomfortable for me to do otherwise. In the presence of my children, I try very hard not to be a depressed person. In my mind, I am *not* depressed when I'm with them.

I'm also trying to shield my mother from knowing about the damage done to me in childhood by my father's drinking. Between the profound sorrow she'd feel for me, and the likely sense of guilt that she wasn't able to stop those incidents, this could devastate her. Why do this at her age (mid-80s) when she went her whole life not knowing this? What would this accomplish? Some feel it would help me to open up more and be better able to heal. I'm not sure about that, but I know it would devastate her. I love my mother much too much to take that chance.

Although I would describe my current state as somewhat 'mixed', I'm happy to report that I'm continuing to make good progress on the road to recovery. I don't know if anyone really 'recovers' from depression. 'Stabilize' is probably a more apropos term, because depression is something that may never completely disappear, but rather lurk in hiding ready to be reactivated if and when sufficient stress occurs. Since people with a predisposition to depression due to early trauma are more vulnerable to stress, it's absolutely critical to minimize stress in order to avert future episodes. Stress is harmful to everyone, often in invisible ways, but it's especially damaging to those of us with demons planted within, threatening to re-emerge if given the opportunity. I have to remind myself that people in a situation such as mine don't just *feel* stress like most people, we are condemned to *relive* the torturous emotions of the original traumas. It's like coming up to home plate with two strikes on you already.

While I continue with my various prescribed medications, the welcomed process of reducing dosages has begun, and I hope to be off all medication eventually, in consultation with my psychiatrist. I've learned the hard way that you shouldn't stop taking medication abruptly on your own. The times when I forgot to take my little pills in the morning, or thought I had taken them already but was mistakenly thinking of the day before, there was an immediate effect that lasted throughout the day and sometimes into the next day. It was pretty bad—even more 'physical' than the symptoms of depression I had experienced pre-medication. There was extreme fatigue, dizziness, headache and insomnia. The combination of fatigue and insomnia is a real double-whammy since you don't have the energy to do anything, but you can't sleep off the unpleasant effects. I had read warnings that an abrupt stop to taking Cymbalta could produce the symptoms I felt, but I had no idea they could begin almost immediately. These terrible 'withdrawal symptoms' have made me afraid to try the advice of many experts today and get off antidepressants entirely. Some feel they do more harm than good, as your body tries to adjust to the shifting brain chemistry.

Increasingly there are situations now when I surprise myself with my renewed mental powers—the ability to grasp things quickly, to perceive what had seemed hidden the prior few years, to analyze and understand what had been too much of a burden for my compromised mind. At times I feel like I must be watching someone else, because I haven't felt this sharp in so long. Of course, I tend to feel like I'm watching someone else a lot of the time anyway.

Today, as I complete writing this book, I feel well enough overall to do just about anything I did previously. Moving forward in the college teaching position, I've found what I had seen starting to happen in my reading and research about depression—my mind seems to have come back to essentially full strength! It still requires some effort to focus on something like reading a book, but it's coming easier now and I can absorb information much better. The sudden loss of mental capabilities is such a traumatic event that their return is an incredible relief. After years being in a mental fog, I feel sharp and alert once again, my mood is consistently better, and I enjoy a more settled temperament—most of the time at least. And I'm sleeping much better, no longer awakening at 3:00 or 4:00 AM every night for an hour or two, which can make you drag the next day. I occasionally still feel a lingering restlessness and unease, but it's far better than before.

One pleasant surprise that snuck up on me but is quite remarkable is my new-found ability to withstand bad news or rejection, things I couldn't handle during depression. A perfect example is the many rejections I've received from literary agents and small publishers as I try to publish this book. It's common to get a lot of rejections, especially for a book on such a dismal subject, but initially this was really bothering me. I was frustrated and often felt like giving up. Nearly a year now into this process, there has been some interest shown by a few agents and publishers, but I continue to receive quite a few rejections. Not only do I not feel that bad about them, many times I become yet more determined to publish the book despite the rejections. Rejection now seems to actually increase my resolve. This is a dramatic change for me. I have to believe it represents genuine hope for anyone suffering depression.

Often I am amazed that I don't feel worse given what depression has cost me— my marriage has been tumultuous and arduous; I lost two good jobs (well, decent jobs maybe); my family's financial security is evaporating; my prospects for full-time work given my age and condition are a question mark; my children have become bewildered about me and may have lost some respect for me; my health is poor in many ways and requires constant care and medication; and of course, the pain, despair, dread, turbulence, and numbness of depression itself, not to mention the loss of the ability to experience joy as others do. In spite of all this, having stabilized now from a second episode of depression, I don't feel especially bad about what depression has cost me. Maybe I'm learning serenity.

Perhaps the horrors of depression can be alleviated by a sense of achievement in conquering such a formidable enemy as you progress toward recovery. Yet I know full well that recovery, as wonderful as it is, is but partial and possibly temporary. Maybe the tempering of depression is like the joy of that first spring day following a long, cold winter. I think it's that, and much more. It's reaching down inside to find the strength and will to defeat a life-threatening disease, thereby discovering a depth of humanity not seen by most people.

Throughout my life I have sought to find an ever-elusive peace of mind, no doubt in reaction to the haunting inner turbulence, the 'unquiet' state of mind. Peace has always been frustratingly difficult for me to find for more than a few fleeting moments, but I remain determined to realize it, and I might say I'm even becoming *optimistic* that it can be done despite the demons and the ordeals. Just feeling occasional optimism is an achievement in itself for me given my history.

My improved outlook, however, is tempered by my innate realism that while I may be making significant progress healing, I suspect that some wounds will continue to exist, probably forever, because that's just who I am. I'm resigned to the need to seek out peace and solitude, and not because I don't enjoy people, but because I need to counterbalance the inner wounds and turmoil with healthy doses of tranquility. Excessive noise, activity and chaos bother me. I used to feel guilty withdrawing early from social gatherings, but no more. I am who I am, and that's OK. We cannot completely change who we are, nor do we necessarily want to. You become adjusted and even bound to who you are and to the life that you've lived, in spite of the ordeals. At best, change at this age is gradual and incremental, and there will always be setbacks. I'm resigned to this, and I've come to be basically OK with it.

Actually, I don't think I'd trade places with anyone.

9 The Journey Continues

He who knows others is clever;
He who knows himself has discernment.
He who overcomes others has force;
He who overcomes himself is strong.
He who knows contentment is rich;
He who perseveres is a man of purpose;
He who does not lose his station will endure;
He who lives out his days has had a long life.
Lao Tzu, Tao Te Ching

I gave an early draft of this book to my therapist for his review, feeling it might give him a better idea of what I was about and thereby contribute to the effectiveness of my therapy. I also thought his reactions could be helpful to me in ensuring that the book was telling the story I wanted to tell, and in a clear, coherent way. He reacted favorably, calling it a well-written statement of my personal experiences, constructively applying principles of psychotherapy to explain my experiences, while taking some unusual viewpoints and adding interesting philosophical commentary.

However, my therapist added that the early draft of the book showed I was still living 'in my head' primarily. 'You need to write from the heart also,' he said. 'I don't get a clear sense of how you *feel* about these issues.'

Confused and frustrated, I replied, 'I thought I was doing that.'

As I tend to do, I was analyzing and intellectualizing about my experiences and not truly feeling them and conveying the full depth of my feelings. Although somewhat surprised at these comments, which is telling in itself, I found this feedback both interesting and helpful, indicating that I had significantly more work to do on my openness to emotions. I'm still working on this, finding it more difficult than I could have imagined.

It's likely I was so totally cut-off from my emotions in childhood that an immense chasm has been created in me that I must continue to work at bridging. Quite a few times my therapist has asked me what something has felt like, and when I struggled to answer, he would reply, 'That's not a feeling, it's a thought. You're still analyzing, not feeling.'

Much of the time I've been unable to make that shift from analyzing to feeling, which bewilders and frustrates me. I wondered, is it possible that you can be so cut off from your emotions that it's a Herculean effort to reconnect? Apparently it was for me, which struck me as kind of odd and ironic because I've certainly *felt* emotions inside me, sometimes too much so. They can be overwhelming, no doubt more so when they're stifled by guilt and shame, forced to remain festering and hemorrhaging inside. The problem wasn't emotions per se, which I can in fact feel, though positive ones like joy don't last very long. No, the problem was mainly *expression* of emotion.

Numerous times over more than a year's time I went back over this book trying to get better in touch with my emotions and add more feeling, depth and personal experience to the story. As best I could I've poured my soul into this book, although it may not always appear that way. Some of these words I have wanted to say my whole life; others have come slowly as I painstakingly sought to articulate a nebulous thought. The quotations I've added from poetry, music and literature have served to express compelling ideas better than I could with my own words. But I can definitely express *this feeling* now—it has been immensely gratifying and fulfilling for me to tell my story and connect it, which in many ways is the story of millions of wounded people, with the critical, timeless issues of our era. I believe that people fighting depression are truly connected to a struggle with the most critical challenges of our era.

In this journey I have come to feel like the character Siddhartha who learned in his long search for wisdom that as people we need to work to shed our blinders and preconceptions in order to see the manifest reality that we are intimately connected to all people and all things. We need to unlearn the follies of our time before we can again see how we are but one part of the spectacular, singular natural world. We need to awaken and live with the recognition that we are vital, needful organic creatures, not mere tools in the never-ending production of yet more devices that steer us from our true nature. This is not to say that I know better than others; I say this as one of the many who veered off the path to his true nature.

I look forward enthusiastically to continuing my journey, knowing that I have been as culpable as anyone in forgetting myself and succumbing to a false life of working for the sake of things. When I was in college, this was called 'selling out'. My generation believed we were different, but eventually we were all beaten into selling out by our crushing civilization. One of my favorite songs, Jackson Browne's 'The Pretender', could be the theme song, epitaph actually, of my generation, who 'started out so young and strong, only to surrender.' Although I tell myself that I sought primarily to provide for my family, I am perhaps more culpable than others since I went astray even while suspecting that my life was becoming false, that I was trading my physical and mental health for a paycheck. It's bad enough to 'sell your soul', but if you're going to do it, at least get a good price. I should have known better. But it's not too late to see the light— and follow it. I saw it alright, I just didn't trust myself enough to follow it.

As upset and angry as I was about the treatment I received from my employer while fighting depression, I truly felt sadness and pity for many of the people there for falling blindly into the trap so common in today's insanely driven business environment. As an example, it was apparent in my last six months that my less-than-lovable team leader's health was sinking to a dangerous point, but she wouldn't give it the time or attention necessary for treatment. She was having a number of diagnostic tests, but didn't seem to be taking the time needed from her busy schedule for care and treatment.

One day as she was arguing with another woman in the company in an increasingly familiar display of tension, she shouted out, 'Don't give me a hard time today. I may have had a heart attack yesterday and I can't handle it now.'

Hearing this strange decree, I could only think to myself, what is she doing at work? Shouldn't she be with a doctor? How sad is it when a person has such blind loyalty to a job that she'd take that type of risk? How much risk or sacrifice does she think her employer would take for her? Someone like this working 60 or more hours a week will almost surely die before her time. I can imagine her funeral, attended by the obligatory handful of company executives, and no more than a few co-workers since this was a person who stepped on others in the course of her work as much as she stepped on herself. There no doubt would be a collection for a nice flower arrangement or whatever, and for several days people would say how shocked they are. Then it would be back to the rat race. And a family of five will have lost a mother and a wife. I've seen all too many people sacrifice their health for jobs that place no value on them as individuals.

In my ongoing therapy I'm learning a great deal about myself and about the reasons behind some of my peculiarities. For one, I learned why I tend to feel awkward and withdrawn in large groups. In my relationship with my father as a young child, I continually wondered if I had his approval, so I naturally sought out his acceptance at every opportunity. The excessive need for acceptance is typically accompanied by anxiety and unease around a lot of people, especially new people. After being established in your relationship with a parent, these traits can become a part of you as you mature, and it is common among children of alcoholics to seek approval in their interactions. Hyper-vigilance is also common because you're looking to read people to see if you have their approval, as opposed to a healthier attitude of, 'This is who I am, like it or don't like it.' But when facing a large group, it's almost impossible to read all the various people. You can become overwhelmed, and withdrawal is an easy solution. So, you're more likely to be silent, because in this large group of people with different personalities and values, it's impossible to know if you're saying the 'right' thing.

When my therapist interpreted this during one of our sessions, it gave me a profound sense of self-discovery. This explained some things I had observed numerous times but never really understood. I also felt a disturbing sorrow for myself that this kind of flaw or handicap could exist in me for fifty years as a result of repeated pathological interactions I had as a child with my father. That's very sad. And almost immediately after feeling this sorrow, I realized it's a good thing that I'm able to *feel empathy for myself*. Perhaps this is a sign of progress.

My therapist recommended that I continue to reflect upon my childhood, my father, and my feelings during critical moments of my past. I still need to get more fully in touch with those feelings. One exercise that he suggested was to compare what my father expected of me with my own ideals of a man.

Fundamentally, my father wanted me to be just like him. As I went through adolescence, I began to feel that I really wanted to be the exact opposite in many respects. However, not surprisingly, as his son I was torn between his expectations of me and my own ideals. I loved my father, and I know that he loved me much, much more than he could ever show. At times I felt like some kind of split personality, feeling I was eerily like him sometimes, and other times I was becoming my own man. It was because of my father that I often felt a push and a temptation to become the kind of tough, thick-skinned person that he was. This was a major factor leading to the disastrous inability to recognize and deal with my inner wounds and subsequent depression until decades had passed. Whenever I felt a strange inner weakness that suggested I may have suffered some kind of pathological damage, a part of me was always saying that a man just keeps moving on and doesn't let this kind of softness disrupt his life.

What a terrible shame I didn't address the issues sooner and stop the pain. The particular configuration of wounds inflicted upon me not only produced depression, but served to prolong its existence by inhibiting me from dealing properly with the problems. This, unfortunately, must be very common. I think part of the inability to recognize and deal with depression is the adoption in oneself of society's views of the illness, erroneous though they may be. They are internalized. Even today, after all I've learned and all I've experienced, I'm still hounded by a conviction that since most people view depression as weak, unduly fragile and self-involved, or just plain weird, I continue to be reluctant to reveal my condition. It's likely that, until a person can completely throw off that burden, that shackle, he will not be able to conquer the illness. I'm making progress here, but clearly I have much more fighting to do.

This problem is especially acute for men, who typically are raised as boys to be quietly strong and unemotional, and to conceal any pain they might feel. Psychotherapist Terrence Real, who has studied gender roles extensively, calls this socialization process 'masculinization' and argues that our 'rigid notions about masculinity' create disconnected, poorly adjusted men who cannot express or deal with emotions. This opens them up to a host of disorders including addictions, alcoholism, depression, and much more. In my situation, I suspect that part of the fear and emotional numbness deep inside me since childhood did not just stem from my father's repeated drunken rages, but also from the years of being afraid to reveal any fear or pain to him, since he had such an extreme sense of masculinity. When I did begin to reveal any such 'weakness', there was immediate, stern disapproval from him, which caused me to stifle any emotion and shamefully cease expressing anything. This repeated response can become a permanent part of your personality.

To say that my father's was a 'masculine' legacy is a gross understatement. Bear in mind that in my father, we have the sort of hard-nosed, thick-skinned, fiercely independent man who for decades refused to do as much as get a check-up or consult a doctor despite accumulating health problems, which included a painful ulcer, the loss of most of his teeth in a work accident, and finally, the lung cancer that ended his life some 15 years after he quit smoking. Who knows how long that cancer was inside him? He just went on with his business. We're talking about the son of a tyrant, who was also his boss for 35 years; about a man who quit high school to work during the Depression; who served as an Army medic in a bloody world war; and who worked six long days a week for 50 years while seldom taking a vacation of more than a couple of days. You can see how a person would have to be tough as nails to get through all this. And I guess he'd want that in his son too. I sometimes wondered if my father thought that subjecting his children to those drunken rages was his way of toughening them up. That at least may have been his rationalization for behavior he couldn't control.

I do feel that I'm making gradual progress in expressing emotions, evidenced by the fact that I actually spoke to my daughter Lauren recently about my condition, in an attempt to help her understand what an alcoholic father and depression have done to me. I expressed my profound sorrow for any problems it may have caused her or the family. For some reason, I find it less difficult to talk to a woman about these issues than to a man, perhaps because any discussion requires me to acknowledge deep feelings and 'weakness', which I've been programmed to feel that men don't discuss, at least not with other men.

The chart that follows is the comparison that I did between my father's traits and my ideals, which are typically the direct opposite. I should add that since my father was a product of his difficult environment, the traits he exhibited were no doubt needed to survive then.

Contrasting Traits and Ideals

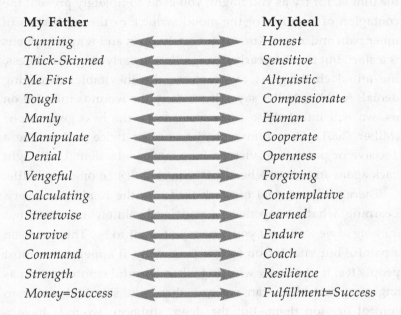

My Father		My Ideal
Cunning		Honest
Thick-Skinned		Sensitive
Me First		Altruistic
Tough		Compassionate
Manly		Human
Manipulate		Cooperate
Denial		Openness
Vengeful		Forgiving
Calculating		Contemplative
Streetwise		Learned
Survive		Endure
Command		Coach
Strength		Resilience
Money=Success		Fulfillment=Success

Some of my ideal traits have come naturally to me, while others have required continual effort. The task of changing, of improving oneself, is especially challenging for a person fighting depression. On the other hand, when you emerge from depression, you suddenly see what's truly important and meaningful, and you gravitate toward these things. That which previously was important may now disappear from view. This is a great opportunity for change.

Thus far I've had mixed results here, and moving forward I don't know how successful I'll be in reaching these ideals, but I believe they are instrumental to having a fulfilling, peaceful life. I would want my children to emulate these ideals. I've tried to be a good role model to them, but too often the inner wounds prevented me from being the kind of warm, open, nurturing parent I wanted to be. I think a critical part of recovery is finding *redemption*, atoning for the injury caused to others, most importantly loved ones. This is the most regrettable and tragic aspect of the illness, for try as you might, you can't completely prevent the contagion of anguish, or the mood swings, or the explosions of inner pain and anger. Knowing it can happen and why it happens is a start, but it's not nearly enough. In the early stages of illness, the initial challenge is to overcome the inevitable, damaging denial. As Alice Miller says, 'If we deny the wounds inflicted on us, we will inflict those same wounds on the next generation.' (Miller, 2001). Overcoming denial once or twice will not be a decisive or permanent victory. Like insurgents, denial will fight back again and again when least expected. It's an ongoing battle.

There's a great deal of work to do on the road to recovery. Learning what's happened to you is absolutely essential, but *learning alone* won't get you where you want to be. This has been a painful but vital lesson for me personally. It appears that most people feel if you know why and when harmful emotions such as anger or irritability can emerge, then you should be able to control or stop them. But the deep, stubborn wounds have a powerful hold on you that is extremely difficult to overcome. Again, Alice Miller:

...new experiences and information have no impact on fears deposited and stored in the child's body at an early age, and no impact on the barriers in the mind resulting from them. In certain cases the blows children receive will prevent them from achieving genuine adulthood...they remain emotionally crippled throughout their lives, tormented children unable to recognize evil for what it is, let alone to do anything about it.

You might think that many years of new experience and information would displace the old, crippled emotions, but sadly, that's not the case. However, Dr. Miller is not at all fatalistic about this, but rather has found that facing the truth about emotional damage can enable a person to restore sensibility and eliminate emotional blindness—with the right help. I'm still learning how all this works, but clearly, we victims need a lot of 'enlightened' professional help. Unfortunately, few professionals seem to be sufficiently enlightened with regard to effective healing for depression, and one must carefully screen and select a caregiver. Even the so-called experts on mental health routinely fail to recognize the severity and power of unhealed wounds. Psychologist Bruce Levine (2007) argues:

> If your wounds are unhealed, then you are alienated from parts of yourself and thus lack the strength of wholeness. So even with morale and knowledge of what constitutes constructive behavior, you may feel unable to act on that knowledge.

Knowledge about your wounds appears to be a necessary condition to healing, but not a sufficient one. Conditions that are conducive to healing are necessary, and this might require drastic changes to lifestyle that are difficult to make. The fact that knowledge alone is insufficient to avert the symptoms and traps of depression is lost on the majority of people, who cannot be expected to understand the intricacies of this mysterious disorder. I've encountered this mistaken notion from others including my wife Joanne, who assumed that my finally knowing the roots of my depression and the effects on behavior would be enough for me to fully drive out the demons. If only it was that simple.

Bruce Levine is but one among the many mental health professionals who argue that psychiatry today has lost sight of the significance of healing deep wounds, opting instead to peddle the quick fixes pushed by the pharmaceutical and insurance companies looking to simply minimize costs and maximize profits. The psychiatric profession has a profound vested interest in maintaining the mindset of a biological theory of mental illness since that is what supports their bread-and-butter product, psychiatric drugs. There is a large and growing community of 'critical' mental health professionals, including Levine, Charles Whitfield, Peter Breggin and others who oppose the mainstream, drug-oriented treatment programs. These critics often note that the psychiatric profession is unique in that it treats illnesses that have essentially no real, objective markers demonstrating their existence, employing means (drugs) for extended periods of time despite the lack of consistent evidence of their effectiveness. Antidepressants perform little better than placebos in many tests, can have many harmful side effects, and encourage dependency.

In this confusing state of affairs one doesn't know who or what to believe. While I put more credence in the drug critics, having experienced the terrible withdrawal effects of coming off the drugs, I've been scared into staying on them, like millions of others. But I'm still working on it.

At the same time I try to be a better person and maintain stronger relationships, I feel a need to follow my heart more religiously and stop making the compromises and concessions that can lead one astray. I need to march to my own beat. For too many years I followed someone else's prescription for living, a legacy of our seductive, toxic culture, and it failed me. I am throwing off the shackles of conformity and convention to lead the life I want to lead. If there's one thing I learned from these ordeals it's that I need to take better care of myself than I had been. Good health and sanity may dictate that you 'dare to be different'. If that means that I don't live what others consider a normal life, so be it. Depressed men need, first and foremost, to take proper care of themselves, argues Terrence Real, and only then will they be able to value and care for others.

And speaking of 'normal', there's one stunning fact I'll never forget that's worth noting here. In *The Politics of Experience*, psychiatrist R.D. Laing puts normalcy into a new light when he points out that in the 50 years leading up to his writing of the book in 1967, *normal men had killed about 100 million of their fellow normal men!* Maybe it's normalcy that's the problem. When those of you with mental disorders are called abnormal, you shouldn't feel offended; this can't possibly be worse than being normal.

In spite of the progress I've made in therapy, there often comes a point where you plateau and stop seeing improvement. That happened to me after about a year and half of 'talk' therapy in this second episode of depression. I still felt some lingering, internal disturbance and continuing the same old therapy didn't seem to be the best way to address it. The down, disturbed mood comes and goes, for what reasons I'm not sure. I'd like to be able to say something more specific than it simply comes in times of stress, but I can't. The downturn brings a kind of mini-relapse. Unfortunately, it's not just that I feel down when it occurs, but I'm also more prone to irritability and anger, which of course creates a whole set of problems, with family in particular.

For these reasons I decided it was time to try something new. I had read about the successful use of something called 'eye movement desensitization and reprocessing' (EMDR) for treating emotional trauma and related disorders, and decided to try this fairly new technique. Understandably, I was suspicious at first, wondering how on earth eye movement could address trauma wounds from decades ago. The critical function in this technique is reprocessing by the mind; the eyes are but one means by which the mind obtains information and then processes memories and perceptions. The reprocessing and rewiring in the brain relieves the harmful memories attached to perceptions. This technique is starting to be widely used for cases of abuse and trauma, and since my depression was essentially trauma-based, I figured this made sense for me. As with many treatments and medications for mood disorders, medical science does not appear to know exactly how EMDR works, but the technique reportedly has been effective in many cases, and that was good enough for me under the circumstances.

I looked at profiles of local therapists on the Psychology Today website and selected one who practiced this technique and who sounded knowledgeable and caring on the phone. Incidentally, after only a few sessions, she confirmed that my depression was trauma-based, essentially a type of PTSD, which my prior therapists largely ignored.

You need to do some homework in preparation for the EMDR by identifying your most positive and most negative life memories and the emotions they evoke. You then focus on the most disturbing memory during the EMDR treatment, and allow your mind to go wherever it goes from there. The idea is to gradually become fully empathetic, and forgiving I guess you'd say, and thereby desensitized about the pain, fear or other negative emotion of your memory. It's logical that when you look at that isolated negative memory in relation to the bigger picture of what's important in your life, you see where the pain or discomfort of that memory is dwarfed by the larger issues.

The treatment can actually be done with any of the senses, not just the eyes. The device used by my new therapist, Mary, worked through hearing—a series of short, beeping sounds in both ears—and through touch—vibrations transmitted by small devices held in the hands. As I write this, I'm in the sixth weekly EMDR treatment and I feel this is getting me much deeper into the issues and still closer to the roots of my illness. I'm also feeling a greater depth of sympathy for myself as that young, wounded child, much more so than before. It's like the emotional walls are coming down and the burden of guilt and shame is lifting.

The EMDR confirmed some things about my illness that I had

suspected or wondered about for some time. One was that I apparently decided at an early age that I couldn't trust my father as an authority about what's right and wrong, since he had lost my trust with his habitual rages. As my father, he had been the ultimate authority to me, but that was soon gone, and I had to rely first on foremost on myself. This seems to have produced in me a kind of mindset that questions and distrusts authority, leading to a very individualistic, almost stubborn set of my own principles. I resent orders and boundaries. I detest power and arrogance. Many times I've felt like an eccentric artist, having the artistic temperament, though not necessarily the talent.

More importantly, during the EMDR treatments, I kept coming back to a vision of my father frowning at me in disapproval. He didn't even have to say anything, the look on his face had such a chilling effect on me. My new therapist asked how often my father showed approval or warmth toward me when I was young. She was surprised to hear I couldn't remember anything like that until I was maybe in my teens. As a child I had so little interaction with my father, and when I did see him, I was set on trying to win his approval. I never knew what he thought of me. I was painfully afraid of him, no doubt from the drunken rages, and I must have felt the need for his acceptance and approval in the few times we were together.

Thinking back about this, I felt like I was being tested or auditioned whenever I saw my father, and I now wonder if this became a part of who I was and if the mindset of being auditioned carried with me throughout life. I've felt that way many times, and there's a tension and uncertainty that's terribly crippling. It appears that the trauma from the drunken rages was compounded by my constant search for approval from my father, which was not to be until it was essentially too late. This longing for my father's approval probably contributed to my unhealthy concern for what people think of me. I don't mind so much if people don't agree with me, as long as they hear my views and understand my situation. I feel an intense need to be understood, or it may be more accurate to say, a fear and loathing of being misunderstood.

Another vision my mind kept returning to in the EMDR treatments was viewing myself in a mirror as an adult and being surprised at the person I saw. It didn't seem like me, didn't seem real. This has happened a number of times over the years. The face I saw was serious and beleaguered looking, but beyond that, it appeared horribly pained and in despair. I didn't know I appeared this way. It sometimes made me think that I might actually be *two people*. One was the person I presented in public—inscrutable, a kind of false front. And the other was the real me—anxious, emotionally crippled, and just trying to cope the best I could. Many times I've felt pushed in two different directions by opposing 'conversations' within telling me what to do. I was torn and conflicted by this. There was an ever-present 'inner critic' scrutinizing and challenging everything I did. This inner critic has been part of me, and yet felt separate somehow. He's very tough on me, and I can do little without having to defend myself to his continual challenges. This is a tough way to live.

It's as if I've been leading a second life. The enormous guilt and shame I carried prevented me from sharing this side of myself with people. What's more, the conflicting internal conversations tore me so that *I wasn't even sure who I was*. I pursued a more or less conventional life and tried to appear normal, when in fact I felt very different from others and had a much different set of values. I wasn't true to myself, and until I am, I'm not sure if I'll be OK. Only when I'm able to fully accept who I am can I merge my private and public selves and be whole.

But I was to learn that there was yet more to my condition; mood disorders and mental illnesses seldom travel alone. Another significant aspect to my illness surfaces during the EMDR treatment, to my surprise and frustration considering all the time I've devoted to treatment over the past seven years.

Thinking about these opposing forces within made me recall what I had once read about a condition called 'dissociative disorder'. According to Mental Health America, 'Dissociation is a mental process that causes a lack of connection in a person's thoughts, memory and sense of identity.' Dissociation varies widely in severity. Mild forms involve such things as frequent daydreaming or forgetting where you've been or where you're going when you're driving. Severe cases involve amnesia, loss of identity, or multiple personality.

I told my therapist who was doing the EMDR that I've felt many of these symptoms over the years—being easily distracted, difficulty concentrating, inability to follow simple instructions, quickly losing focus while driving or reading, excessive daydreaming and fantasizing, feeling unreal and separate from real life. Everyone has these experiences from time to time, but mine were continual and pervasive. They defined me. There were those times I thought I might have ADD, then I thought it might be bipolar. I knew something was terribly wrong. My mind was too often bombarded by a collage of images completely unrelated to whatever I was doing or thinking at the time.

A few weeks into my sessions with the new therapist, number five I believe, I asked if my symptoms could indicate dissociative disorder. This therapist, who I like a lot and feel confident in, agreed to give me an assessment based on the symptoms I was reporting to her and on her observations of me in the half dozen sessions since I switched to her. She had also noticed my dissociative tendencies.

In spite of my suspicions, it seemed unlikely to me that another aspect of my illness would be uncovered this late in the game. It's reasonable for a patient to expect that complete diagnosis would take place within the first few months of care, by a therapist, psychiatrist, someone. But, as it turned out, I did in fact have a moderate degree of dissociation, enough to present serious challenges. My therapist seemed to suspect that I had an element of dissociation, but she appeared surprised by the degree when she scored the assessment. Apparently I've become fairly effective at covering my abnormal traits, which is a kind of automatic, built-in characteristic of mine rather than anything deliberate. Although my therapist felt that my dissociation was not severe, I've taken some self-administered tests where my score was quite high.

From what I understand, dissociation too can result from severe emotional trauma. At some point, often in childhood, a person can disconnect from reality as a defense mechanism, because it's so painful and unbearable. The disconnection, if severe and if repeated again and again over a number of years, can become a permanent part of personality.

Another significant piece to the puzzle was falling into place. I learned that an aspect of my variety of dissociation is something known as 'depersonalization', which is alienation or disconnection from one's body or one's life. This can create an 'out of body' kind of experience. How eerie it felt to learn that this explained my bizarre 'man in the mirror' — the sensation of sometimes seeing another person when I look in the mirror, or the feeling that I'm a spectator or commentator watching my life transpire. It's that other person in me, who's part me but somehow different, distantly observing and analyzing my life. Having had no idea that this was a 'disorder', I was understandably surprised and confused. At the same time I'm somewhat relieved to be learning the reasons behind my condition and my idiosyncrasies.

A related aspect of dissociation for many people is something called 'derealization', which explains that feeling I often had that life is unreal or distanced. This is but another sign of the disconnection from life that seems to come from the tendency of the inner child to hide during times of danger and fear. It's not difficult to see how this repeated hiding can produce unreal and depersonalized tendencies when occurring in the impressionable, formative years of youth.

In the extreme, dissociation and depersonalization can take the form of what was previously known as multiple personality disorder. Fortunately, my condition is much less severe than this, not quite qualifying officially as 'dissociative disorder'. Still, I suffer many of these disruptive symptoms. When my therapist happily reported to me that my dissociation was not severe and wasn't a serious problem, I asked, 'Well then, why does it bother me so much?'

Although you get used to it, I've almost always felt distracted, disconnected and unreal, and it can certainly create problems. It appears that dissociation, depersonalization and derealization are conditions I've had nearly my whole life, since early childhood, and I now know that they have been the major reasons behind my disturbing tendency to 'space out' and lose focus so easily and so often.

A big part of the distractions that continually hit me have been the challenges of my severe 'inner critic', who may have fed on the ample guilt and shame that I've carried for years. The instant I have even a thought that I might have done something wrong, or incomplete, or in any way questionable, I hear my inner critic begin to attack, and I start to prepare a defense. My immediate thought is, 'Am I guilty?' Then I have to explain to myself why I'm not.

But my perpetual inner critic has been by no means the only type of distraction I've had, as I could be easily pulled away from what I'm doing in a matter of seconds by any number of things, from the sight of a pretty woman, to ruminating about an argument with my wife, to thinking about a past or upcoming baseball game of my son's. This is often described as 'intrusive thoughts' and 'racing thoughts'. I know it all too well.

My head is spinning by now, struggling to grasp all this new information about my condition. It's like learning you were adopted 50 years after the fact. I'm 55 when I learn about my dissociation, roughly two and a half years into psychotherapy over two separate episodes. I feel a sense of satisfaction hearing this because it explains a lot of things, like *who I am*. But I'm understandably upset and frustrated that it wasn't found much earlier. For one, an implication is that I'll probably require yet another type of treatment.

I spent the next few days trying to comprehend the news about dissociation. A person forms a solid sense of self identity over the years, and for me this needed to be revised. I couldn't get my mind off my condition and what I was going to do about it. I had work to do for the courses I was teaching, but as I tried to read or prepare a lesson plan, my mind returned seemingly every few seconds to my 'new' condition. I had trouble concentrating long enough to read a single sentence and absorb its meaning. Of course, this isn't at all unusual for me, given the nature of disso-ciation, but it was especially disruptive now.

Perhaps one reason depression is so devastating is because it has so many allies in its battles; it seems to rarely strike alone. It's not at all unusual for a person to have a complex of conditions including PTSD, depression, some degree of dissociation or depersonalization, or possibly a bit of anxiety and OCD (obsessive-compulsive disorder) thrown in. These are actually common symptom profiles of adults who suffered severe trauma in childhood. The symptoms that often accompany these condi-tions are all too familiar— low self-esteem, shame, anger, intrusive thoughts, a sense of unreality, and intimacy difficulties, to name a few. I'm personally familiar with all of these. But in some ways I consider myself fortunate that I haven't been visited by the other, often more devastating allies of depression, which include addictions, personality disorder, eating disorders, psychoses, and schizophrenia.

What I think is most significant is that the evidence is increas-ingly revealing *trauma* at the root of many of these disorders. As described by Charles Whitfield (2003), the multitude of damages resulting from childhood trauma presents a chilling picture:

Chronic childhood trauma also fragments overall brain functioning, causing significant difficulty focusing, learning and relating to others...Chronic stress also damages the body's immune system...All of these injurious effects on the brain and the body leave the person at a distinct disadvantage in surviving and coping with life.

Whitfield (2004) goes on to point out that 'childhood trauma is common, destructive and has an effect that lasts a lifetime,' and it may be the 'most important determinant' of health and well-being. Numerous *physical* as well as mental disorders, both acute and chronic, often result from chronic trauma, and *underlying most of the mental disorders is PTSD*. Among the many physical aliments that Whitfield reports are significantly higher among those experiencing childhood trauma are chronic fatigue, chronic pain including headache and back pain, and gyneco-logical as well as gastrointestinal problems.

But in view of the latest news about my depersonalization and dissociation, what most caught my eye were Whitfield's comments that trauma survivors often have 'difficulty focusing' and are 'easily distracted'. They experience a 'constriction of feelings' and a 'persistent sense of being cut off from their surroundings' (Whitfield, 1987). How well these described me. Whitfield's work shows that dissociation is a common result of PTSD.

Unearthing the deep roots of my disorders was critical if for no other reason than it relieved the devastating guilt I've felt that I was somehow inferior, weak, and responsible for my own inability to be 'normal'. I shouldn't worry anymore about being normal because it's not possible to lead anything approaching a normal life with these conditions. I have no idea how I managed to lead the kind of life I led with all these disruptions and handicaps. These are sometimes only mild but annoying interferences—I think back to the countless times Joanne has asked me why I turn away looking bored or distracted while someone is talking to me. Or they can be life-altering disturbances, like continual inability to concentrate and perform work responsibilities, or to express any deep feelings, or to find a peace of mind away from the tension and turmoil.

My mood seemed to change a bit since I learned the latest news about my condition. Mood is always a kind of vague and fluid thing that's difficult to describe. I found mine becoming more uneasy and disturbed about my condition, characterized by a nagging impatience for relief. I look back at my life and see that dissociation has been yet another kind of disruption of mind and mood. It creates an unsettled and uneasy state. Thoughts and emotions and doubts are always intruding, constantly coming and going, rarely staying long enough for me to figure out what they're about or arrive at some understanding or resolution. I might be halfway toward understanding one question or doubt seizing my mind, when another darts in and commands my attention, and then another. No wonder I don't seem able to stay in the moment. Too often life is surreal to me, and not in the sense of an escape or respite. Distraction and disconnection present yet another obstacle, another burden to carry along the journey. Impeding so many routine functions and activities, they add layers of tension and stress on top of the already formidable layers that are the pollution of our hollow and harried lives. They require extra effort to overcome, and I'm getting so very tired of having to overcome things. All I want is some peace; understanding and acceptance would be nice, but I really need peace.

We temporarily suspended the weekly EMDR treatments to discuss the new development, dissociation. I had to try to get comfortable with what this is and how I'm affected by it. A few weeks later we returned to the EMDR treatments, which are challenging and taxing. They can be so exhausting that I feel it's impossible to do anything for several hours afterwards. But I'm definitely seeing progress from the EMDR and I remain hopeful and resolute. I'm proving to be a difficult case, what with my particular combination of stubborn conditions, in particular, my mind's tendency to drift away and lose focus. I do wish I had tried this treatment earlier—it's so much more productive than traditional talk therapy. It's enabled me to see things previously shrouded in mystery. Before you can fully heal, you need to bring all the wounds into the light, which I'm surprised to have to say I'm still doing even after all this time.

Guilt appears to be 'the final frontier' for me. In sessions with Mary, who's proving to be my most caring and effective therapist, it's become apparent that my biggest problem and one that stubbornly continues to linger is extreme, entrenched *guilt*. This seems to have developed out of a sense of weakness and failure that I wasn't the man my father would have wanted because I allowed myself to fall into a condition like depression. I don't actually believe that I'm weak, at least not anymore. But I used to feel weak; I seem to have been programmed to *feel* that way. You might say that sadness and fatigue and anger and distraction have been serious problems as well, and they certainly were. But guilt strikes me as the core of the problem because it causes many of the other destructive emotions. Guilt leads to things like sadness and frustration and anger, not the other way around. This has been a critical lesson for me in this long journey. If I had it to do over, and I surely wouldn't wish that now, I'd work on the guilt from day one. Mary and I are now targeting the lingering guilt in my therapy and EMDR. It's proving to be incredibly stubborn and resilient—I can *feel* guilty even when I don't *believe* that I am. It seems to be ingrained in me.

Further complicating the problem is the fact that when I can manage to forgive myself, for whatever, and relieve much of the overpowering guilt, I find a conviction that's replaced the guilt—that I've been terribly cheated—cheated in the sense that, OK so it wasn't my fault, but I've still lost out on the normal peace and pleasures that others seem to feel. I'm screwed in either case. Maybe this is the kind of automatic negative thinking that is part of baggage of depression. But it strikes me as valid, though I don't let it preoccupy me.

After one of my last EMDR treatments, I came home anxious to add an update to this book, or more accurately, this 'manuscript' since there is no certainty yet it will be published. Both Mary and I felt that the latest EMDR session brought me to perhaps the core issues in my troubles, as close to a 'conclusion' to my story as I had any right to expect. We tend to hope for a 'eureka' kind of moment when we can finally see all the pieces to the puzzle fall neatly together. In reality it rarely happens that way. Instead, you may see gradual progress over a period of time, interspersed with occasions of mixed results, and maybe even some movement backwards. But today we saw the hard work pay off as we were able to drill still deeper into the core issues.

I had been thinking for awhile that my sense of guilt seemed connected to feelings of being *defective* or damaged or inadequate in some way. And the connection makes sense, because these things can make you unable to be the kind of person you want to be and possibly should be, leading to feelings of guilt over that failure. Through a series of incidents I recalled from long ago, the EMDR treatment took me to the roots of that connection. The incidents I thought about started with a recent disagreement with my wife Joanne, ironically over my health and whether I was opening up and confiding with her. In these kinds of arguments Joanne made me feel markedly different from others, even odd or strange; she actually said that a number of times. In the EMDR I traced this feeling of being so different as to be defective back to other incidents, wherever my mind would take me. In a short time, it took me all the way back, not surprisingly, to my first memories of my father.

I had a lot of trouble trying to recall things about my father from my early childhood, but I did think of a few incidents. There was always that distancing and disapproval from him, and fear and confusion in me. But it was the nature and strength of the disapproval that was significant. Perhaps because I feared my father so much from the drunken rages, or because I felt I needed his approval that much more, I was very sensitive to his reactions, always seeking his blessing and respect, but often coming away with more self doubt. Not even for my biggest achievement, being a top student, did my father ever show any recognition or approval. In fact, I came to think he actually felt I was wasting time on schoolwork, because for one thing, it didn't bring in immediate dollars, which was his bottom line. My mother definitely approved, and with great pride, which was good, but I think the vastly differing reactions confused me so much that I was terribly torn and conflicted. This only added to the doubts and tension within me.

I also recalled things about the early times with my father that I hadn't thought about for years. He felt I wasn't tough enough. At times he called me a momma's boy. Again, there seemed to be some kind of jealousy or resentment from my father about my relationship with my mother. One especially disturbing memory I have was from one of the ugly drunken episodes. At the time I think I was defending my mother against my father.

'Do you want to suck your mommy's breast?' he asked me in mocking, taunting tone.

I was deeply embarrassed for my mother at this comment. And I was ashamed at the depth to which my family had sunk. I came away utterly hurt and confused. Isn't a boy supposed to love his mother? What was he trying to say to me? Was this my fault?

As best I can remember my father made these kinds of comments a number of times from the time I was maybe eight years old to my early teens. In time I came to get his point; for him a true man was as hard and cold as steel. He didn't cry or show weakness or have doubts. These things were never tolerated from me, not even as a young boy. So I was afraid to show emotion, I was afraid to open up in any way. What I did was try to be *tough enough*, to appear tough enough, even though I didn't generally feel it inside. I was ashamed of myself for not being the kind of man my father made me believe I should be, even though part of me was coming to learn that he was the one who should be ashamed.

I don't know how much of my problem stems back to this radical, macho disapproval from my father or how much was due to the drunken rages. The two no doubt worked together, but it didn't matter so much to me. The point is that I could understand what happened and that it *wasn't* my fault. Guilt was at the core of my problem, guilt over feeling *defective*. This feeling was put in me by my father. I didn't do it, and I didn't deserve it. I've believed that in my head for some time, but now I was starting to *feel* it in my heart. This is what I need to do.

The reason I needed to surface all this pain from the past is to reach some *forgiveness* of myself. If you can understand what happened to you when you were too young to do anything about it, you can start to forgive yourself. Only then can you relieve the crippling guilt and shame.

All in all, I would recommend trying EMDR as a treatment to anyone who may have emotional trauma at the root of their mood disorder, which might well include most sufferers since we've seen that trauma can often be a major but unrecognized component. In addition to its effectiveness, EMDR is very fast and easy, and consequently, much cheaper than the other techniques being used, which require months and months—of mostly talk.

At this stage of my discovery and recovery I feel that I have a fairly solid handle on the evolution of my illness that cuts through the fog and clouds of my life. I've sufficiently *deconstructed* my condition to understand what's happened. If I can use a simple analogy—my father's vicious, drunken rages directed at my mother planted the seeds of the poisonous, invasive weed that was to later become my depression. The fear, numbness, and constant tension resulting from the repeated childhood trauma watered and nourished the seedlings. A strained, distant relationship with my father, devoid of warmth and acceptance, served as the fertile soil in which the weed of depression could grow. The personality I took out of a trying and conflicted childhood—wounded, withdrawn, and weakened by inner doubt, turmoil and guilt—prevented healthy growth, opening the way for the weeds of depression and the related disorders to flourish. And the assaults of life's stresses so taxed an already weakened body and spirit that the weeds could not be easily pulled from their stronghold deep within me.

As a mental health 'consumer' (sufferer), you of course lack much of the information needed to make an intelligent decision regarding treatment, and your reasoning may well be poisoned in some way by your disorder. So, it's hard to make the right decision when it comes to changing therapists or types of treatment. In my case, I think that once again my determination to be patient and have confidence in the therapist as the professional to make the key calls caused me to stay too long with 'talk' therapy. This is a situation where patience can do you a lot of harm.

It's impossible to know exactly, but there's ample reason to believe that with all the different types of therapies, and the many therapists out there with varying competencies practicing on victims with varying and uncertain or even unknown diagnoses, it's likely that *millions of victims are being mistreated.* A recent survey reveals that only a very small minority of people with depression are receiving the 'dual therapy' that is considered optimal—prescription medication plus psychotherapy. And although most depression sufferers have symptoms of other disorders such as generalized anxiety, PTSD or bipolar, for only a small minority are these disorders diagnosed (NAMI, 2006).

As a consequence of the widespread misdiagnosis and mistreatment, millions of victims are seeing their recoveries prolonged or thwarted entirely. Many or perhaps most victims cannot effectively manage their own treatment programs, and it's unwise to put it in the hands of a single therapist or psychiatrist whose competence you cannot evaluate and who has a vested interest in you as a customer. The current seat-of-the-pants, trial and error approach to treatment is nothing short of inhumane and shameful. People are suffering unnecessarily. In my case, the origin of depression in childhood trauma *was not discovered by any of my caregivers,* and even after I suspected it based on my reading, it was largely *ignored.* And the dissociative condition took still longer to diagnose. So my illness was prolonged, until I took it upon myself to learn about the true causes of depression and finally find a therapist who could address them, and in a caring, effective manner.

Perhaps victims need an objective advocate who can monitor treatment, ensure progress, and steer victims to therapists and techniques most appropriate and promising for their particular conditions. I hesitate to say that a victim's health insurer is one party with the interest and the ability to do this. The idea of an *insurer* doing this would no doubt generate more apprehension than hope.

Some people have told me that I'm too critical of mental health caregivers such as therapists and psychiatrists, too impatient, and not appreciative of the progress being made and the help being given to sufferers. What do I mean by inadequate care? To begin, I've had therapists repeatedly yawn during sessions. That by itself would be OK with me (especially since I yawn a lot too) if it didn't conform to a pattern I was seeing—forgetting crucial information I had given previously; being unaware of the latest techniques; being unfamiliar with the most recent books on depression; failing to diagnose fairly obvious conditions even after dozens of sessions; trying techniques or medications for long periods of time without sufficiently evaluating the results. And so on.

I'm not saying these caregivers are uncaring or unprofessional. My experience seems to be pretty typical today. There needs to be more accountability to patients as well as more continuing education in order to ensure that caregivers are up to date on new developments in the field. There has been very slow progress in researching causes and effective treatments for depression, but even this limited knowledge isn't making it down to the bulk of caregivers. And how about if caregivers actually review your records periodically and re-evaluate the treatment and the progress? Why do you have to keep repeating things to them? I'm not just talking about my experience, but also about the many people I've spoken with, for example, in support groups.

I have to believe that the single greatest omission in the treatment of depression and other mood disorders is the failure to recognize the presence and the power of childhood trauma, 'the sleeping giant' as Whitfield calls it. It seems incomprehensible that thousands of bright, trained, well-meaning mental health caregivers could overlook or minimize a factor that we now see appears in the overwhelming majority of mood disorders, and mental disorders overall. But it happens, aided in part by the prevailing fixation on biological causes, not to mention the financial clout of the pharmaceutical companies looking to dispense their multi-million dollar drugs. Social scientists examining the scientific community have shown in numerous studies that even scientists typically share a common set of beliefs, values and perspectives that can produce a conformity in thought and a coloring of their interpretation of evidence. (A notable work in this area is *The Structure of Scientific Revolutions* by Thomas S. Kuhn.) The mental healthcare profession seems to be addicted to an outdated, ineffective model for diagnosis and treatment, unable to see the growing evidence that change is needed.

We indeed seem to be on the threshold of a radical change in the conception and treatment of depression and other mental disorders. It is striking that in his review of hundreds of studies, Whitfield (2004) found not one that proves 'the reigning biogenetic theory of mental illness.' Even such esteemed organizations as the American Psychiatric Association and the Surgeon General's Office have been unable to provide firm evidence of a biological or genetic cause of common psychiatric illnesses. For years a common conception has been that since mental illness runs in families, it must be genetic. But the research reviewed by Whitfield overwhelmingly shows that the tendency for mental illness to 'run in families' is due to continued patterns of harmful *parenting* that perpetuates dysfunction, abuse and trauma, not to genetics. It is the unhealthy parenting practices that run in families, the legacy of trauma that compromises the ability to be a protective, nurturing parent and that is passed down through the generations.

We need to completely re-think our conception of depression. We've been misinformed and misled. Depression is not genetic. It's not simply biochemical imbalance. It is a learned pattern of behavior, a legacy of victimization. Contrary to what we've been told for years, Whitfield's analysis of the research done by leading psychiatrists and scientists reveals that depression and most mental illnesses are *not genetically transmitted disorders of brain chemistry*. For one, the often cited theory of a deficiency of serotonin and norepinephrine has never been scientifically tested or demonstrated. There isn't even a way to *measure* serotonin levels in living people!

Medicine evidently has needed to come up with something

that resembles a cause for these widespread disorders. That's what we expect and that's why we listen and pay for all the costly healthcare. Medicine and psychiatry came up with the reigning biogenetic theory of mental illness. I don't know how much was the result of bad science, or indifference, or the temptation of billions in drug dollars. Medications of course would only be embraced by millions of sufferers if they thought drugs would address the supposed chemically-based causes of disorders. The easiest—and most profitable—thing to do with mental health sufferers is to medicate them and make them go away, until the next monthly, $150 dollar appointment. But we're beginning to learn that brain chemistry is not the primary cause, and drugs are not the answer.

Today one hears about more and more mental healthcare professionals who've been strong advocates for medications, including clinical practitioners, authors, and professors, but who failed to disclose funding from the pharmaceutical industry. Do you think $1.4 million in income from a drug company might influence a person's likelihood to endorse a drug? That was one Harvard psychiatrist's undisclosed income from the drug industry discovered by Congressional investigators (MindFreedom website www.mindfreedom.org). Does failure to disclose income as required by universities and many organizations suggest anything we should worry about?

Insofar as the latest evidence suggests it is primarily a *symptom* of other disorders such as PTSD, rather than a separate, clearly identifiable *disorder*, the term 'depression' itself seems to have outlived its usefulness, hopelessly laden as it is with confusion, ignorance, and prejudice. Although I was never one to place much importance on names, I think it's time to put the term to rest and come up with new language based on what we now know about the true causes and effects of mental disorders. 'Depression' is no longer a meaningful term, and its misuse is not just among the public, but also in the mental health community.

For one thing, the means of diagnosing depression are completely arbitrary, subjective and unverifiable, lacking the basic elements of science. There is no objective test for identifying depression. Diagnosis is based on highly subjective tests or self-reported symptoms that are compared to criteria in a psychiatric manual (the *Diagnostic and Statistical Manual of Mental Disorders* or *DSM*) that, according to Whitfield, has changed little in the five decades since its inception. On this archaic and dubious medical foundation is built the treatment that affects the lives and well-being of millions.

To this point, in *The Truth about Mental Illness*, Whitfield proposes a complete revision of the classification of mental disorders and of the DSM. Recognizing the full, pervasive impact of trauma and PTSD, Whitfield recommends a broad heading called 'trauma spectrum disorders', which would encompass the many disorders resulting from trauma. This would include depression, anxiety disorders, dissociative disorders, alcohol/chemical dependence, eating disorders, and more, since these are all *trauma-based* according to Whitfield's compelling findings. It's difficult for the layman to assess the current medical debate, but I think we're seeing the onset of nothing short of a revolution in the medical conception of mental disorders, which will hopefully lead to better treatments focusing on the true causes.

Admittedly, identifying childhood trauma in patients is not always easy for caregivers. As Whitfield (2004) points out, as many as a third of patients experience 'traumatic amnesia' where they are unable to recall the incidents, and many others are reluctant to report events such as abuse or neglect because of intense shame or due to privacy concerns, fear of disclosure, etc. Nevertheless, we're seeing more and more therapists and researchers finding patterns of destructive childhood trauma lying behind most cases of depression and other mental disorders, and this has clear implications for treatment. If trauma often causes depression, then it is essentially a form of PTSD and needs to be treated as such.

Author and psychotherapist Bob Murray is among those who've seen the trauma-depression link again and again, and he offers this comment about appropriate treatment (Murray, 2008):

> In my treatment of PTSD sufferers I have achieved most success when I examined and treated the earlier childhood traumas and resulting depression first rather than the more obvious secondary trigger. The original trauma can induce a rather rigid, fearful personality, one less able to cope flexibly with stressful events in later life.

Unfortunately, most therapists do not seem to be following this logic, and many of the countless trauma-based depression sufferers are not being effectively treated. There is widespread failure to deal with the underlying causes. Apparently turning its back on Freud and a host of others who have demonstrated the importance of resolving unconscious issues through psycho-analysis, mental healthcare today is preoccupied with symptoms. The question is, can a depression sufferer recover fully, and in a timely way, if the causes are ignored? Murray comments that childhood trauma 'lodges in the body' as inhibited development and malfunctioning of the amygdala, which is in the brain and part of the limbic system, the system that governs the body's response to stress and danger. The trauma and its effects often show up later in the form of depression. You cannot defeat depression simply by changing your thinking because the problem is not all in your head. But you can undo substantial damage through new experiences, including psychotherapy, which helps rewire neural networks. According to Dr. Louis Cozolino, author of *The Neuroscience of Psychotherapy*, neuroscience is just beginning to reveal the intricate inner workings of the brain and how it continually 'rebuilds' itself through new experiences.

The current state of affairs leads to me to believe that the lack of progress in the diagnosis and treatment of depression reflects not only a bias toward the highly profitable brain chemistry / medication mindset, but also a widespread lack of concerted effort in the mental healthcare community and the health insurance companies. It also indicates a very low priority as a public policy issue. Again, one has to suspect that behind this reluctance to take more action is the widespread belief that people with depression and similar disorders don't have 'real' or serious illnesses. The stigma and the ignorance are pervasive.

It seems to me that in view of the ample new evidence of the underlying *physiological and neurological aspects of mental illness*, the inescapable conclusion is that *there is no such thing as 'mental illness'*. Yes, symptoms may appear to be primarily 'mental' or emotional, but there are physical symptoms as well, and more importantly, there are defining physical conditions and neuro- logical factors driving those symptoms. So, how different is that really from a typical 'physical' illness? Perhaps we ought to simply stop using the term 'mental illness' since it is so loaded with misinformation and ignorance that it does little more than perpetuate a destructive stigma. There are countless illnesses with mental or emotional symptoms. What useful purpose does the term 'mental illness' now serve?

This is the point in my diagnosis and treatment where I currently find myself. While I've healed a great deal and no longer feel the full, terrible burden of depression, I still suffer crippled emotions. I continue to feel anger and guilt and sadness much more than I feel peace or joy. Though not as often as earlier, there remains a disturbing and unsettled color to my mood much of the time. So I'll continue to move forward and strive to learn and to heal. I don't imagine the journey will ever end. I need to keep chipping away at the terrible guilt that has been at the center of my troubles.

Depression is something that impacted me primarily in the two episodes that lasted a combined four years, although I've felt some of the less severe symptoms at other times. And depression is often the most visible and most widely known type of mood disorder. But the damage from childhood trauma has been with me my whole life and has been essentially invisible despite its terrible destructiveness. Whether we call it PTSD or dissociation or some other term that the 'experts' come up with to explain away the latest evidence of the role of trauma, it's part of my personality and it's affected every aspect of my life. For me, this is by far a larger issue than the occasional bouts of depression, as horrible as they are. I find myself in the strange position of saying that not only is depression but a *part* of my illness, I'm not even sure it's been the biggest part, my greatest problem if you will.

It's really good that I'm now well along the road to recovery because thinking about all the disorders that have apparently struck me sometimes makes me feel totally screwed up. But if this seems like a lot of disorders, we have to remember that these things are more like symptoms than separate disorders, and I'm convinced that they stem from the same underlying cause. What really frustrates and saddens me immensely is that while I was dealing with these powerfully destructive conditions, which have caused untold problems in my life, no one could comprehend or appreciate the extent of the condition. The often unbearable burdens I carried were largely invisible to others, which, ironically, was largely my own doing since I habitually hide any sign of weakness

They say that every depression is a bit different. My personality emerged from childhood trauma with this particular mix of traits and wounds that conspired to create the flavor of depression that struck me. It doesn't appear that anyone can pinpoint exact causes, but I have to believe that my depression would not have happened without the dissociation, the crippling emotional inhibition, the terrible guilt and shame, and the ever-present inner critic, all of which compounded the underlying vulnerability to illness and made diagnosis and treatment that much more difficult. My inner wounds went unresolved far too long.

A number of times I've actually found myself wishing I had a 'physical' illness instead, which is tragically telling. I've experienced so many of the problems associated with a misunderstood and stigmatized illness such as depression. My condition has been misdiagnosed several times. I was given a number of treatments that were ineffective. I was prescribed medications that were ineffective or produced side effects as bad as depression itself. I tried ten different medications. My recovery was delayed and my illness prolonged. I had to go on disability leave twice. I exhausted my disability benefits. I lost two good jobs as a result of depression, essentially destroying my career. I had difficulty finding a job and changed careers. I had to see five different therapists and four psychiatrists before achieving substantial recovery. I faced limitations on my healthcare due to having an emotional rather than physical illness. I couldn't afford the type of treatment that would have most expeditiously treated my illness. I couldn't afford to maintain my family's lifestyle. My marriage was severely strained by the prolonged duration of my illness.

And, what's perhaps most surprising but also most significant, my situation is not unlike that of *millions* of others. I absolutely feel for these other sufferers, but right now it's little consolation to know I'm not alone. I'm still too disillusioned and angry to feel that way. I've been knocked down so many times I can't count anymore. And when I'm down, I don't always get up right away. But I do get up, I'll always get up, and I fight back.

I encourage everyone to fight back in whatever way possible, although my humbling experience allows me to empathize with those who cannot fight due to the terrible devastation they suffered. When I hear of a depressed person committing suicide, which happens with shocking frequency, I now say to myself that *they* didn't really do the killing. Rather, a big piece of them may have been killed years earlier, what we sometimes call the 'spirit', and they no doubt did their best to hang on desperately for years, less than half alive. Childhood trauma can destroy the ability to live and to enjoy life. This comes to mind sometimes when I have trouble mustering a smile.

Very often I am indeed bitter and resentful about my plight, sometimes downright hostile. Rather than be remorseful about my reactions, I'm *glad* I feel this way—because I want and need to *feel something*. It's significant progress for me. I've seen that a strong reaction such as resentment can be a source of energy and even strength. We tend to view many emotions as being drastically different from one another, even opposites. But I see that they're actually very similar to each other, the most important element being that they're all emotions, and when you're able to enter that domain and truly feel, you can begin to move freely from one emotion to another. I have to be open to them and allow them to live and flourish.

One of the many ways that victims can fight back is to play an advocacy role and contact elected representatives encouraging them to support legislation to improve mental healthcare and achieve insurance parity with the so-called physical illnesses. Organizations such as the Depression and Bipolar Support Alliance (DBSA), Mental Health America and MindFreedom International will email alerts to interested parties regarding pending legislation and current issues in mental healthcare, and provide information on how to contact representatives. I would urge all sufferers of mood and mental disorders who've encountered inadequate healthcare or unfairly restricted insurance coverage to become active in supporting reform efforts. Do not tolerate prejudice or discrimination.

But first and foremost, a person carrying the wounds of

severe trauma must protect himself by managing stress and practicing the principles of wellness. If it's indeed true that early trauma creates a physiological vulnerability to later stress in life, a clear implication is that someone who's experienced severe trauma needs to carefully manage stress in order to avert a disorder like depression. Something as serious as damage to the brain and neurological system cannot be ignored. For one, it can produce a predisposition to what we call mental disorder along with a host of other potential illnesses. Major stress is bound to occur at some point in life and this could overtax an already weakened system, leading to a breakdown of sorts. This is an instance where an ounce of prevention is worth a pound of cure.

In concluding this book, and particularly since I've been so critical of my father at times, I would be remiss if I didn't reiterate my deep love and respect for him and emphasize that by no means are my feelings for him largely unfavorable. That's not at all the case. He was, after all, my father and I always knew that he loved me with all his heart, and I loved him, in spite of it all. That's just part of the contradiction, the mystery, which I don't claim to understand. My father is part of me, and I see him in me, for better or worse. Many times I've actually felt he's been a source of *strength* for me. Though it happens less frequently than years ago, I still feel a profound love and mourning for him, like when I hear the late singer / songwriter Dan Fogelberg's touching ballad that he dedicated to his father, 'The Leader of the Band'. I too feel my father's spirit within me.

I've always felt a confused mix of love, respect, shame and contempt over my father, which I may never reconcile. It has ripped me apart over the years, in ways I may never fully understand. I'm trying now to concentrate on moving forward.

Although I can't say I ever would have wished for it, my depressive disorder and its accompanying conditions have taught me so many invaluable lessons about myself and the infinite depth of character and strength of will for fighting and enduring such ordeals. These lessons from my bouts with depression suggest some overarching guidelines about how to lead your life that would be helpful to maintaining a healthy mental outlook and a balanced life. I'm trying to follow these simple guidelines myself and would recommend them to anyone who is seeking not just to recover from something like a mood disorder, but also to maintain or maximize your wellness:

- Be alert for any issues that repeatedly disturb you
- Talk to someone about this; be open
- Get professional help if an issue continues to affect your mood or your activities; better to see a specialist rather than general practitioner
- Don't run from your feelings—embrace them
- Try to resolve painful issues; grieve as necessary; forgive whenever possible
- Learn the origin of any unhappiness, despair or fear; recognize what you can control and what you can't
- Make your health, both mental and physical, priority one
- Ensure that your work brings fulfillment, pride & peace
- Don't let the need for money make you stay in a job you don't like—better to do without some things than to 'sell your soul'
- Take steps to minimize daily stress
- Simplify your life; cut back on non-essential activities you don't enjoy
- Do something for yourself every day; allow time for things you enjoy
- Spend time with the people you enjoy and love
- Contemplate the things that you most value & cherish
- Spend time enjoying nature—take a walk in a park, hike up a mountain, camp by a beautiful lake, listen quietly to a waterfall, observe birds or squirrels engaged in their daily rituals right in your backyard

- Do 'random acts of kindness'
- Celebrate your life!

For each of us there is so much to celebrate, in spite of the many terrible ordeals you may have had to endure. If you do not feel there is, give yourself something to celebrate. Today. You owe it to yourself.

I've given myself this book, which is a sort of emancipation proclamation for me. Writing this has truly been a labor of love. I only hope that others can find something worthwhile here. I wrote this book in the hope that by passing along the lessons I learned about mood disorders, it will help others to better understand their own conditions and experiences.

To anyone who as much as suspects he might be burdened with wounds or destructive issues from the past—I urge you too to tell your story; tell it in any way you can, to anyone who will listen with understanding and empathy. Telling your story will little by little release any pain, guilt or shame, and enable you to reconnect—to yourself and to your life. It can be trying and painful, but it works, and it's absolutely worth the effort, Herculean though it may be.

I am determined to never again suffer, or cause a loved one to suffer.

I celebrate myself, and sing myself,
And what I assume you shall assume,
For every atom belonging to me as good belongs to you.
I loafe and invite my soul,
I lean and loafe at my ease observing a spear of summer grass...
Walt Whitman, Song of Myself

Epilogue

Observing without evaluating is the highest form of human intelligence.

J. Krishnamurti

As I write this epilogue, it's almost three years since I started writing this book, and a year since I completed it, save for some editing here and there. Over the past year I've been doing part-time teaching—it's actually more like facilitating—for groups of mental health patients on principles of wellness and recovery. The program is conducted by Collaborative Support Programs of New Jersey, a trailblazing, peer run agency that performs training and various support services for mental health consumers, mostly low-income people lacking private health insurance, which encompasses a disproportionate number of the mentally ill.

I find this work more meaningful and fulfilling in many ways than teaching college students, which I'm still doing. The people in the groups, most of which are with outpatients, come in with serious, committed and sincere attitudes, and I feel at home with them, although many have pretty severe, often disabling conditions that I can't readily relate to. Unlike most college classes today, with all too many casual students looking for an easy route to a diploma, there is something truly vital at stake in these wellness and recovery groups, and I feel like I'm making a difference.

As with my observations throughout the book, the information I'm about to pass along admittedly is not 'evidence'. Rather, it's 'anecdotal', but I think it's worth mentioning. Many times in our group discussions the subject comes up of how the patient became mentally ill (I really hate this term, but don't know how else to communicate it). That is, the possible causes of the illness come up. *In every single instance where patients have discussed causes, there was abuse, violence or other severe trauma during their childhood.* What's more, most of them don't see the trauma as the likely origin of their illness. They cite heredity, chemical imbalance, and the other stories pushed down their throats by the drug companies, psychiatrists, and others in the mental health community, despite the lack of evidence for the contentions.

Don't these patients deserve to know the truth about what's happened to them?

I should add here my impression is that the mental healthcare workers in the trenches are doing a most admirable job, although there does seem to be a bit of resistance to the use of 'peer' educators such as myself, creating a counterproductive turf war of sorts. But the social workers who serve the underprivileged strike me as wonderfully giving people, whose trying jobs are made more difficult by heavy caseloads and lack of strong direction on causes of mental illness and on the latest, most effective treatments. Many of these patients can't get regular one-one-one counseling in public programs, and they can't afford to pay for it outside. And you won't see the latest techniques and treatments used here—they tend to be expensive and time-consuming. But I'm told the situation is much better than years ago.

Although some of these out-patients work part-time, most simply cannot work, certainly not while they're in the program, which requires a time commitment like a full-time job. But their symptoms are the bigger issue. Contrary to prevailing opinion, they would love to work and have tried many times, but their illnesses have compromised their capabilities and performance, or created hostility from the many employers who stigmatize mental illness. So they come to their group therapy and talk about the same issues over and over, sometimes for years. And while many are able to recover enough to go back into the community, too many don't get any better. I'm told there isn't nearly enough public funding for more intensive treatments that might enable many to leave these programs in months rather than years. But wouldn't it be less costly for taxpayers in the long run to provide expedited, intensive treatment where possible and enable some to recover enough to leave the program much faster? And ideally, become able to work? The ones who leave now tend to rely on public assistance. In comparison, I feel very fortunate that I had private health insurance to pay for decent treatment. Yes, my treatment could have been better, but it also could have been a lot worse.

All in all, there is dire need for more research and better science on mental illness—unbiased by the billions of drug dollars out there looking to support those willing to sing their song. And the knowledge gained needs to find its way to all practitioners, many of whom are now using outdated information and obsolete techniques. I have to believe that the large initial cost of improving treatment would pay for itself in the long run through speedier recovery and lower demand for publicly supported programs.

One result of this situation is that countless patients aren't being informed about the critical role that trauma may have played in their illness. Again, don't these patients deserve to know the truth about what happened to them? And wouldn't that knowledge enhance their treatment and recovery? For one, if some of them are anything like me, and I have reason to believe many are, this knowledge could be crucial in relieving the guilt and shame they carry for an illness that is essentially blamed on them by the general public and often by the patient's own family. The most serious problems that patients bring into our groups are that they cannot get jobs due to their illness, and their families become impatient, frustrated and often angry with them when they exhibit even mild symptoms of mental illness— fatigue, forgetfulness, inability to focus, etc. One woman was beaten whenever symptoms of depression appeared, first by her father, and later by her husband. How can such ignorance and inhumanity exist in this day and age?

These people are second class citizens in our society, simply because they had the misfortune of suffering serious trauma as children, which will taint what they do the rest of their lives. But then the rest of their lives may not be very long since people with severe mental illness die 25 years earlier than the general population (National Association of State Mental Health Program Directors, 2006). While most of the patients I see may not qualify as 'severely' mentally ill, you get the idea.

We have a long, long way to go in providing the care these people need and deserve. Further progress on this front depends largely on the public's ability to understand depression and mental illness in general. Admittedly, it's extremely difficult for a non-sufferer or layman to begin to comprehend these illnesses. The question is, has there been sufficient attempt? It's ironic that there has been substantial progress of late in public under-standing of a disorder similarly connected to brain development and functioning—autism. But a disorder like depression, which is acquired rather than inborn and manifests as 'soft' symptoms such as fatigue, sadness, and erratic mental functioning, seems to be viewed as less valid or excusable than one that limits certain learning and communication abilities among children. But are these conditions really very different?

Prevailing public opinion on depression has no factual basis, no connection to reality. To the many people who stigmatize and distort the illness, I have to say, 'it's all in *your* head'.

Acknowledgements

Special thanks go to three people who graciously took the time to read earlier versions of this book and provide invaluable feedback and suggestions: Bruce E. Levine, PhD, a clinical psychologist and author of several books and articles on mental illness; David A. Karp, PhD, professor of sociology at Boston College and author of numerous scholarly articles and books; and Charles L. Whitfield, M.D., a physician, psychotherapist and author of a number of well-known books on mental illness and recovery.

I'd also like to acknowledge several others who were essential in bringing this book to fruition. My agent Krista Goering of The Krista Goering Literary Agency has patiently guided this novice author through the daunting process of getting published. John Hunt of O-Books was also indispensable in answering my many questions and helping me through the nuts and bolts of bringing a book to market. I also want to express my gratitude to Mary Quirk, M.A., L.P.C., N.C.C., a counselor who showed me extraordinary empathy, a rare willingness to listen to my problems, and the know-how to find solutions.

In particular, I have to extend my deepest appreciation to my wife Joanne for her patience and support in the two-plus years when I often hid in the basement office to work on this book. Writing a book seems to require that you hurriedly get fleeting ideas down on paper before you can share them with anyone, lest you forget a key point. So, I was especially isolated and unavailable during this time.

Finally, grateful acknowledgement is given to the following for permission to reprint passages:

Charles Whitfield's passages from his book *Healing the Child Within*, 1987 Charles Whitfield, Health Communications, Deerfield Beach, FL.

Charles Whitfield's passages from his book *The Truth About Depression*, 2003 Charles Whitfield, Health Communications, Deerfield Beach, FL.

Bruce Levine's passages from his book *Surviving America's Depression Epidemic*, 2007 Bruce Levine, Chelsea Green, White River Junction, Vermont.

David Karp's passages from his book *Speaking of Sadness*, 1996 David Karp, by permission of Oxford University Press, Inc., New York.

Alice Miller's passages from her book *The Truth Will Set You Free*, 2001 Alice Miller, Anchor Books, New York.

Wayne Kritsberg's passage from his book *The Adult Children of Alcoholics Syndrome*, 1988 Wayne Kritsberg, Bantam Books, New York.

Erich Fromm's passages from his book *Man for Himself*, 1947 Erich Fromm, Fawcett Premier Books, New York. By permission of The Fromm Estate.

References

American Psychiatric Association. 1994. *Diagnostic and Statistical Manual of Mental Disorders (DSM-IV)*. Washington, DC.

Anda RF, Whitfield CL, Felitti VJ, Chapman, Edwards VJ, Cube SR, Williamson DF. 2002. *Adverse Childhood Experiences, Alcoholic Parents, and Later Risk of Alcoholism and Depression*. Psychiatric Services 53: 1001-9.

Beck, Martha. 2001. *Finding Your Own North Star: Claiming the Life You Were Meant to Live*. New York: Three Rivers Press.

Burns, David B. 1980. *Feeling Good: The New Mood Therapy*. New York: Harper Collins.

Cozolino, Louis. 2002. *The Neuroscience of Psychotherapy: Building and Rebuilding the Human Brain*. New York: W.W.Norton & Co.

Depression and Bipolar Support Alliance. 2006. *The State of Depression in America*. Chicago.

Flach, Frederic. 2002. *The Secret Strength of Depression*. Long Island City, NY: Hatherleigh Press.

Fromm, Erich. 1947. *Man For Himself: An Inquiry into the Psychology of Ethics*. New York: Fawcett Premier Books.

Goffman, Erving. 1963. *Stigma: Notes on the Management of Spoiled Identity*. Englewood Cliffs, NJ. Prentice Hall.

Hesse, Herman. 1951. *Siddhartha*. New York: Bantam Books.

Johnson, Steven. 2004. *Mind Wide Open: Your Brain and the Neuroscience of Everyday Life*. New York: Scribner.

Karp, David. 1996. *Speaking of Sadness: Depression, Disconnection and the Meanings of Illness*. New York: Oxford University Press.

Kritsberg, Wayne. 1988. *The Adult Children of Alcoholics Syndrome*. New York: Bantam Books.

Kuhn, Thomas S. 1996. *The Structure of Scientific Revolutions*. Chicago: University of Chicago Press.

Laing, R.D. 1967. *The Politics of Experience*. New York: Ballantine Books.

Lao Tzu. 1963. *Tao Te Ching*. Middlesex, England: Penguin Books.

Levine, Bruce E. 2007. *Surviving America's Depression Epidemic: How to Find Morale, Energy and Community in a World Gone Crazy*. White River Junction, VT: Chelsea Green Publishing.

McCain, John, and Salter, Marshall. 2005. *Character is Destiny*. New York: Random House.

Middlebrooks JS, Audage NC. *The Effects of Childhood Stress on Health Across the Lifespan*. Atlanta (GA): Centers for Disease Control and Prevention, National Center for Injury Prevention and Control; 2008.

Miller, Alice. 2001. *The Truth Will Set You Free: Overcoming Emotional Blindness and Finding Your True Adult Self*. New York: Basic Books.

Miller, Alice. 1990. *The Untouched Key: Tracing Childhood Trauma in Creativity and Destructiveness*. New York: Anchor Books.

Moore, Thomas. 1992. *Care of the Soul: A Guide for Cultivating Depth and Sacredness in Everyday Life*. New York: Harper Collins.

Murray, Bob. 2008. *PTSD and Childhood Trauma*. Uplift Program website *www.upliftprogram.com*.

National Alliance on Mental Illness (NAMI). 2006. National Survey on the Treatment of Depression.

National Association of State Mental Health Program Directors (NASMHPD). 2006. Morbidity and Mortality in People with Serious Mental Illness.

National Center for Health Statistics, U.S. Dept. of Health & Human Services, 2005.

National Institute on Alcohol Abuse and Alcoholism website www.niaaa.nih.gov.

National Institute of Mental Health website www.nimh.nih.gov.

National Mental Health Association (now known as Mental Health America). 2001. *Labor Day 2001 Report*.

Paterson, Randy J. 2002. *Your Depression Map: Find the Source of Your Depression and Chart Your Own Recovery.* Oakland, CA: New Harbinger.

Plath, Sylvia. 1996. *The Bell Jar.* New York: HarperCollins.

Putnam, Robert D. 2000. *Bowling Alone: The Collapse and Revival of American Community.* New York: Touchstone.

Real, Terrence. 1998. *I Don't Want to Talk About It: Overcoming the Secret Legacy of Male Depression.* New York: Fireside.

Reinhold, Barbara Bailey. 1996. *Toxic Work: How to Overcome Stress, Overload, and Burnout and Revitalize Your Career.* New York: Penguin Books.

Solomon, Andrew. 2001. *The Noonday Demon: An Atlas of Depression.* New York: Scribner.

Styron, William. 1990. *Darkness Visible: A Memoir of Madness.* New York: Vintage Books.

Swarbrick, Margaret. 2006. *A Wellness Approach.* Psychiatric Rehabilitation Journal. Spring 2006 — Volume 29 Number 4.

Teicher, Martin H. 2000. *Wounds That Time Won't Heal: The Neurobiology of Child Abuse.* Cerebrum: The Dana Forum on Brain Science, 2(4), 50-67.

Thoreau, Henry David. 1967. *Walden.* In *The American Tradition in Literature.* New York: W.W.Norton.

van der Kolk, Bessel. 1987. *Psychological Trauma.* Washington, D.C.: Psychiatric Press.

Whitfield, Charles. 1987. *Healing the Child Within: Discovery and Recovery for Adult Children of Dysfunctional Families.* Deerfield Beach, FL: Health Communications.

Whitfield, Charles. 2003. *The Truth about Depression: Choices for Healing.* Deerfield Beach, FL: Health Communications.

Whitfield, Charles. 2004. *The Truth about Mental Illness: Choices for Healing.* Deerfield Beach, FL: Health Communications.

Woititz, Janet. 1983. *Adult Children of Alcoholics.* Deerfield Beach, FL: Health Communications.

Recommended Reading

Flach, Frederic. 2002. *The Secret Strength of Depression*. Long Island City, NY: Hatherleigh Press.

A distinctive feature is the emphasis on the positive aspects of the illness in generating insight and learning, releasing damaging emotions, and producing healthy changes in lifestyle.

Fromm, Erich. 1947. *Man For Himself: An Inquiry into the Psychology of Ethics*. New York: Fawcett Premier Books.

In his timeless commentary on the human condition, psycho-analyst and humanist Erich Fromm presents a piercing analysis of modern society and man's contemporary predicament.

Hesse, Herman. 1951. *Siddhartha*. New York: Bantam Books.

The classic novel about a young man's epic journey in search of wisdom, meaning and fulfillment. The book's statement on the need for connection is especially recommended for those who've become disconnected, e.g. as a result of depression.

Kritsberg, Wayne. 1988. *The Adult Children of Alcoholics Syndrome*. New York: Bantam Books.

Therapist and author Wayne Kritsberg shares the many learnings from his extensive clinical experience with children of alcoholics and victims of childhood abuse.

Laing, R.D. 1967. *The Politics of Experience*. New York: Ballantine Books.

A book that will jolt you out of your normalcy and conformity, just as Laing intended. Though somewhat dated, it's as relevant as ever.

Lao Tzu. 1963. *Tao Te Ching*. Middlesex, England: Penguin Books.

Ancient, timeless wisdom compiled by a contemporary of Confucius, this must-read book that flows like poetry will broaden your perspective and call to question your fundamental values and beliefs.

Levine, Bruce E. 2007. *Surviving America's Depression Epidemic: How to Find Morale, Energy and Community in a World Gone Crazy.* White River Junction, VT: Chelsea Green Publishing.

A clinical psychologist, Levine links the epidemic-like growth of depression to our increasingly materialistic and meaningless consumer-based lifestyle.

Miller, Alice. 2001. *The Truth Will Set You Free: Overcoming Emotional Blindness and Finding Your True Adult Self.* New York: Basic Books.

One of several powerful, eye-opening books by the renowned psychotherapist and best-selling author. While the focus here is largely on corporal punishment, this is merely one example of childhood trauma that creates severe emotional damage in need of repair.

National Mental Health Association (now known as Mental Health America). 2001. *Labor Day 2001 Report.*

An informative and useful report that looks in particular at the economic costs of depression in the workplace.

Real, Terrence. 1998. *I Don't Want to Talk About It: Overcoming the Secret Legacy of Male Depression.* New York: Scribner.

The therapist and author effectively intersperses his personal story and those of his clients with penetrating analysis of the causes and effects of male depression. Insightful and informative in the linking of depression to childhood traumas.

Reinhold, Barbara Bailey. 1996. *Toxic Work: How to Overcome Stress, Overload, and Burnout and Revitalize Your Career.* New York: penguin Books.

Anyone who even suspects that work may be compromising his or her health would benefit by learning more about the relevant issues and the steps that can be taken to address problems.

Solomon, Andrew. 2001. *The Noonday Demon: An Atlas of Depression.* New York: Scribner.

A blend of personal memoir and virtual encyclopedia of knowledge about depression, this is a very engaging and informative book.

Styron, William. 1990. *Darkness Visible: A Memoir of Madness*. New York: Vintage Books.

A beautifully written, intimate chronicle of the best-selling author's fall into severe depression.

Thoreau, Henry David. *Walden*.

Slow down, take a deep breath, and let the champion of the simple, authentic life take you on a journey to get back in touch with nature and with yourself.

Whitfield, Charles. 1987. *Healing the Child Within: Discovery and Recovery for Adult Children of Dysfunctional Families*. Deerfield Beach, FL: Health Communications.

In this classic in the field of recovery and inner growth, physician and psychotherapist Charles Whitfield offers a concise but compelling analysis of childhood emotional injury, along with steps for recovery.

Whitfield, Charles. 2003. *The Truth about Depression: Choices for Healing*. Deerfield Beach, FL: Health Communications.

Whitfield reviews hundreds of studies of depression, unearthing overwhelming evidence of its trauma-based roots and its physiological implications. Nothing short of shocking and revolutionary in refuting the prevailing biogenetic model. A must-read for anyone suffering from or interested in depression.

Whitfield, Charles. 2004. *The Truth about Mental Illness: Choices for Healing*. Deerfield Beach, FL: Health Communications.

Continuing in the vein of *The Truth about Depression*, Whitfield chronicles numerous studies linking early trauma to a host of disorders including generalized anxiety, substance abuse / chemical dependency, eating disorders, dissociative disorders, and schizophrenia.

Woititz, Janet. 1983. *Adult Children of Alcoholics*. Deerfield Beach,

FL: Health Communications.
The path-blazing, best-selling book that brought needed attention to the damaging effects of growing up in an alcoholic household.

Helpful Websites

Adult Children of Alcoholics: http://adultchildren.org/

Anchor Magazine—Conquering Depression:
http://www.anchormag.com/

Anxiety Disorders Association of America:
http://www.adaa.org/aboutadaa/Introduction.asp

The Bright Side: http://www.the-bright-side.org/site/thebrightside/

Collaborative Support Programs of New Jersey, Inc. (CSP-NJ):
http://www.cspnj.org/index.html

Depression and Bipolar Support Alliance:
http://www.dbsalliance.org/site/PageServer?pagename=home

Depression and Related Affective Disorders Association
(DRADA): http://www.drada.org/index.html

Depression Is Real Coalition:
http://www.depressionisreal.com/depression-about-coalition.html

Gift From Within— An International Nonprofit Organization for
Survivors of Trauma and Victimization:
http://www.giftfromwithin.org/index.html

International Foundation for Research and Education on
Depression (iFred): http://www.ifred.org/about.html

International Society for the Study of Trauma and Dissociation:
http://www.isst-d.org/

BOOKS

O is a symbol of the world, of oneness and unity. In different cultures it also means the "eye," symbolizing knowledge and insight. We aim to publish books that are accessible, constructive and that challenge accepted opinion, both that of academia and the "moral majority."

Our books are available in all good English language bookstores worldwide. If you don't see the book on the shelves ask the bookstore to order it for you, quoting the ISBN number and title. Alternatively you can order online (all major online retail sites carry our titles) or contact the distributor in the relevant country, listed on the copyright page.

See our website **www.o-books.net** for a full list of over 500 titles, growing by 100 a year.

And tune in to myspiritradio.com for our book review radio show, hosted by June-Elleni Laine, where you can listen to the authors discussing their books.

MySpiritRadio

Many Voices— Words of Hope for People Recovering from Trauma and Dissociation:
http://www.manyvoicespress.com/index.html

Mental Health World:
http://www.mentalhealthworld.org/index.html

MindFreedom International: http://www.mindfreedom.org/

Mosaic Minds: http://www.mosaicminds.org/rroom/nindex.shtml

National Alliance on Mental Illness (NAMI):
http://www.nami.org/Hometemplate.cfm

National Association for Children of Alcoholics:
http://www.nacoa.org/intromem.htm

National Mental Health Association (now known as Mental Health America):
http://www.mentalhealthamerica.net/go/about-us

Radical Psychology: http://www.radpsynet.org/index.html

Self Help: http://www.selfhelpmagazine.com/index.html

Sidran Institute—Traumatic Stress Education & Advocacy:
http://www.sidran.org/index.cfm

Whitfield's Recovery Resource:
http://www.barbarawhitfield.com/recovery.nsf/CharlesMainPag e!OpenPage

The World Federation for Mental Health (WFMH):
http://www.wfmh.org/index.html